W9-CCS-785

Saving Jesus

"Instead of entering into debate with the so-called 'Right' on the basis of their interpretations of Jesus, Carter Heyward calls forth rich and deeply compelling images of Jesus, of the Sacred Power, and of diverse ways of experiencing mutuality. By showing us the power of life as being-in-communion with all of creation, her book calls us away from comforting religiosity and challenges us to live boldly and passionately, as did Jesus. This passionate living will lead us to be totally present in our world, as we struggle for justice and equality for all."

—**Elias Farajajé-Jones**
Starr King School for the Ministry

About the Cover

"Guatemala: Procession" by artist Betty LaDuke reflects a vibrant "following" among common folk in relation to a simple, peasant JESUS who was one of them. People past, present, and (I imagine) future are joined by beast and birds, mountains and flowers, representing all creatures, in this procession that no doubt embodies celebration and grief, sorrow and gratitude, as does all honest worship. The colorful painting evokes, for me, the Spirit connecting us all—in each particular historical place and between and among our diverse places, cultures, and species in history. This cover is timely. As the book goes to press, the President of the United States has admitted that, in the 1980s, the U.S. backed the brutal, repressive regime of Guatemalan General Rios Montt, a self-proclaimed born-again Christian. I hope that *Saving Jesus from Those Who Are Right* will help lift up the strength and integrity of the indigenous Guatemalans, and those in solidarity with them, who have struggled for bread and justice in the face of reprehensible evil, too often waged by "those who are right."

De la Cubierta

"Guatemala: Procesión" por la artista Betty LaDuke refleja un emocionante "acompañamiento" de la gente común frente a un simple Jesús campesino que fue uno de ellos. La gente pasada, presente (e imagino) futura se une a las bestias, los pájaros, las montañas y las flores, para representar a todas las criaturas, en esta procesión que sin duda incorpora la celebración, el dolor, la pesadumbre y la gratitud, como lo hace toda adoración honesta. El emocionante cuadro evoca para mí el Espíritu que nos conecta a todos en cada lugar histórico particular, a diversos lugares y entre diversos lugares, culturas, y razas en la historia. Esta cubierta es apropiada al momento. Al imprimirse el libro, el Presidente de los Estados Unidos admitió que en los años ochenta, los Estados Unidos respaldó el brutal y represivo régimen del general guatemalteco Ríos Montt, que se proclama a sí mismo un nuevo cristiano. Espero que *Saving Jesus from Those Who Are Right* ayude a elevar la fuerza e integridad de los indígenas guatemaltecos, y aquellos en solidaridad con ellos, quienes han luchado por pan y justicia frente a la reprehensible maldad, demasiadas veces enarbolada por "those who are right."

Saving Jesus

From Those Who Are Right

Rethinking what it means to be Christian

Carter Heyward

Fortress Press
Minneapolis

SAVING JESUS
From Those Who Are Right
Copyright © 1999 Augsburg Fortress. All rights reserved. Except for brief quotations in criti-
cal articles or reviews, no part of this book may be reproduced in any manner without prior
written permission from the publisher. Write: Permissions, Augsburg Fortress, Box 1209,
Minneapolis, MN 55440.

Scripture quotations are from the New Revised Standard Version Bible, copyright © 1989 by the
Division of Christian Education of the National Council of the Churches of Christ in the USA
and used by permission.

Additional materials related to this book are available at fortresspress.com. Enter
"Saving Jesus" into the search box and follow the link to the book's webpage.

Cover art: *Guatemala: Procession* by Betty LaDuke. Used by permission of the artist.
Book design: Beth Wright
Author photo by Susan B. Sasser

The publisher gratefully acknowledges permission to reprint the following material:
Excerpt from "The Creation" in *God's Trombones: Seven Negro Sermons in Verse*, pp. 19–20, by James
Weldon Johnson, copyright © 1927 The Viking Press, renewed 1955 by Grace Nail Johnson.
Used by permission of Viking Penguin, a division of Penguin Putnam, Inc.
From "Opening" in Carter Heyward, *Touching Our Strength: The Erotic as Power and the Love of God*,
p. 157, copyright © 1989 Harper San Francisco. Used by permission.
"Blessing the Bread: Litany for Many Voices" (pp. 49–51) and "A Eucharistic Prayer" (pp.
148–50) from Carter Heyward, *Our Passion for Justice: Images of Power, Sexuality, and Liberation*,
copyright © 1984 Pilgrim Press. Used by permission.
"Blessing" by Carter Heyward, from Ward, Wiley, and Morely, eds., *Celebrating Women*, p. 39,
copyright © 1986 Holy Trinity House. Used by permission of the Society for the Promotion of
Christian Knowledge (SPCK).
"The Great Thanksgiving: A Rite Based on the Song of Mary" by Carter Heyward, from Kittridge Cherry and Zalmon Sherwood, eds., *Equal Rites: Lesbian and Gay Worship, Ceremonies, and
Celebrations*, pp. 113–15, copyright © 1995 Westminster John Knox Press. Used by permission.

Library of Congress Cataloging-in-Publication Data
Heyward, Carter.
    Saving Jesus from those who are right : rethinking what it means
to be Christian / Carter Heyward.
        p.   cm.
    Includes bibliographical references.
    ISBN 0-8006-2966-3 (pbk. : alk. paper)
    1. Christianity—Miscellanea.   2. Jesus Christ—Person and
offices.   3. Liberalism (Religion).   I. Title.
BR124.H49 1999
232—dc21   99-37663
                                                               CIP

The paper used in this publication meets the minimum requirements of American National
Standard for Information Sciences—Permanence of Paper for Printed Library Materials, ANSI
Z329.48-1984.

Manufactured in the U.S.A.
07   06   05   04   4   5   6   7   8   9   10   11

For Dorothee Soelle
Because our hands are God's hands in the world

and

for Barbara Clementine Harris
La lucha continua

Contents

Preface

Why it matters

Plans for this book began to stir in me more than twenty years ago when I first taught a course in "Christology" (the study of the person and redemptive work of JESUS CHRIST) at the Episcopal Divinity School in Cambridge, Massachusetts. Years earlier, as a religion major at Randolph-Macon Woman's College in Lynchburg, Virginia, and then as a student at Union Theological Seminary in New York City, I had been fascinated by all the tensions and drama surrounding arguments among Christians over the centuries about who JESUS was and what this CHRIST has been about historically for Christians—and, as importantly, for persons who are not Christian. Throughout my growing interest in Christology—as a teacher, theologian, priest, and most of all a Christian person in the world—I have wanted to write about JESUS and/or CHRIST (how to put them together is a core question for many of us). In particular, I have wanted to write about why it matters so much what those of us who are Christian actually believe about JESUS CHRIST, since all along I have known that it *does* matter. It always has.

It matters because, for two millennia, many followers of JESUS have borne powerful witness to the presence of the Spirit of radical love-making in history, God of justice and compassion, Holy One of wisdom and hope. Despite the widespread institutionalization and cooptation of Christianity by dominant economic and political forces in the West (increasingly, throughout the world), many JESUS-people, or Christians, have struggled courageously to be a Body of Lovers of this earth and its human and other creatures. This root of Christian vocation—the call to love radically, passionately, and steadfastly—with our whole heart and soul, mind and body—is the foundation of JESUS' own faith and work and of his invitation to the rest of us to "go and do likewise." This is why it matters what we think and teach about

JESUS CHRIST. But there are other reasons too, many of them terrible, why it matters.

It mattered in the Crusades and in the witchcraze purges of strong women and other heretics in Europe and North America. It mattered on the mission fields in Africa, Asia, and Latin America. It mattered in the relentless drive to eliminate the Native American people, cultures, and religions; in the construction of slavery as an economic, cultural, and theological system in the South; in the Holocaust as "the final solution" to a "problem" in many ways created by the anti-Semitism which Rosemary Radford Ruether has named as "the left hand of Christology."[1]

It has always mattered what Christians believe and pass on to others about JESUS CHRIST. It has mattered to women and children of different races, classes, and Christian cultures, because as the centerpiece of one of the world's foremost patriarchal religions, "JESUS CHRIST" has been used consistently and naturally to put women and children under the authority of fathers and husbands who have learned to assume that they themselves reflect most fully the image of God the Father. Moreover, as a religious system in which "morality" has been reduced too often to *sexual* control, Christianity has continued for most of the past two millennia to be a movement of men's domination and women's submission "in the name of CHRIST," as Tom F. Driver has noted.[2] Christianity has been, in many of its manifestations, a movement to repress those uppity women and men who have dared to resist sexual and gender control.

But what we Christians believe about JESUS CHRIST matters not only to people of minority racial, tribal, cultural, and religious heritages and to women, children, and all queer people—by "queer," I mean gays, lesbians, bisexual, transgendered folk, *and everyone standing in public solidarity with us.* What we preach and teach and think about JESUS CHRIST matters in basic, life-or-death ways to all people, other creatures, and the earth itself.[3] It matters because, for the past several hundred years—and especially here as we turn toward the third millennium, C.E.—Christianity has been conspiring with capitalism to build a global system of economic, political, spiritual, and psychological control steeped in the material and psychospiritual assumption that the *self* matters more than anything—more than communities of any sort, more than others, more than making right relation with others, and certainly more than the earth and creatures that are other than human.

It is true that, as a global movement, Christianity has engendered a Western-style individualism that fosters an aspiration among men and women to become autonomous (albeit male-defined) beings who are entitled to certain possessions, rights, and freedoms of mind and movement. Certainly, this is not all bad—the right to education, to health care, and to one's own body and reproductive choices are spiritual blessings and should be universal political rights. And many Asian feminist Christians, such as Chung Hyun Kyung and Kwok Pui-lan, and African women like Mercy Amba Oduyoye and Elisabeth Amoah bear powerful witness to the *mixed* blessings and curses that have been delivered historically to their people by Christian missionaries.[4]

But Christianity's respect for the individual self does not and cannot bear the moral weight that is absolutely essential today for the salvation of the world from the greed and gluttony and self-absorption of the so-called First World. We First World Christians have had more than enough of what Beverly W. Harrison has aptly called "capitalist spirituality." Our self-preoccupation and self-absorption are the root of the moral rot that we in the Christian West—and especially in the United States—have been transporting globally in the name of freedom, democracy, private enterprise, and the good life.

Ironically, many feminists, other political progressives, and theological liberals and radicals of all faith traditions share this deeply moral concern with our sisters and brothers on the "Right," including many fundamentalists of different religions. But those "who are right," I will suggest in this book, propose a solution to the problem of Western self-absorption that is very different from what many feminists, womanists, liberation theologians, and other theological progressives are affirming. In fact, I am proposing in these pages that "those who are right" (of whatever religion or politic) tend to espouse authoritarian, moralistic, and adversarial relationships with those whom they believe to be "wrong" and, in so doing, tend to promote their own ideologies of self-absorption. It is my belief—and it is the basis of this book—that many of us who are caricatured by the Right as being heretical, or wrong, need to be evermore public and enthusiastic in *living* relational spiritualities that are mutual, passionate (fully embodied and present), forgiving, and nonviolent.

As we move into the twenty-first century, it may be that the only force in the world that comes close to being a serious threat to

Christianity's own global capitalist agenda is Islam. In any case, it will matter a great deal in years to come whether we Christians (and others) are genuinely open to learning with people of other faith traditions how to cultivate more truly mutual relation with those whose religious beliefs, tribal customs, racial heritages, sexual/gender identities, and even species may be very foreign to us and so alien as to frighten us.

It is in the Spirit of yearning for mutuality that this book of mine, I trust, has come to be. Over the years, the book has grown progressively smaller! What began as a thirteen-chapter proposal has been whittled down over the past few years into this compact volume. (Readers may find helpful the additional materials about this book available at http://www.augsburgfortress.org/fortresspress.) Perhaps, if it were not clear to me that it is time to bring this project to a close, this book would eventually be condensed further into a few pages! Indeed, if I had time and energy to shape it further, it might read something like this:

What the book is about[5]

Christians are called more than anything to be faithful, not "right." Faithful not to religious systems or creeds; faithful not to particular saviors or institutions; and faithful certainly not to any tradition or custom that requires us to cast out or punish those who seem to us heretical, or wrong, in their beliefs or in their nonviolent customs and behavior. Even when confronted, as we are constantly, with violence around us and among us, Christians are called—yes, beckoned by the Power of Love in history—to seek nonviolent ways of responding, so as to call forth the very best in even the very worst of our brothers and sisters. This "revolutionary patience"[6] with one another is in keeping with how much we ourselves yearn to be called forth by those who still believe in us—those who still believe that we are able to be loving, creative, and liberating persons, regardless of how far astray we may have gone.

Through his teaching, healing, and prophetic resistance to state-sponsored and religious-based legalism that disregarded human need, JESUS reflected the incarnate (embodied) Spirit of One who was not then, and is not ever, contained solely in one human life or religion or historical event or moment. God was JESUS' relational power, more

specifically his power for forging right (mutual) relation in which
JESUS himself and those around him were empowered to be more fully
who they were called to be. We today are also empowered by this same
mutual relation.

Each and every one of us—whatever our religious, non-religious,
or anti-religious identity today—lives *in God*. I mean by this that we
are all relatives, spiritual kin, bound by a power moving among us that
transcends any one time, place, or person and connects our lives and
generations and communities far beyond any of our capacities to see
many of these connections, much less to understand them. Still, living
as we do, in God, it is never too late for any of us, regardless of
whether we "believe" in God, to "go and sin no more"—that is, to
come out, whoever we are, and join in the ongoing struggle for right
relation with other humans, creatures, and the earth. Oregon artist
Betty LaDuke's vibrant painting on the cover of this book represents
to me the wonderfully colorful and active "procession" of creatures of
many kinds and cultures coming out into our shared power, with
JESUS, to god in the world.

In the historical place and moment in which I write, recovering
addicts may realize as well as anyone, and better than most, what it
means to join in the struggle for right, mutual relation. It means to
make amends for the harm we have done (and we are all involved in
doing harm) and to walk a spiritual path of recovery one day at a time,
never relying solely on ourselves, but rather always drawing strength
from our connectedness with sisters and brothers who walk the path
with us.

Despite the sexist language and assumptions of its founders and
many of its adherents, and despite the narrowly Christian framework
that some people continue to impose upon its meetings, Alcoholics
Anonymous and some of its Twelve-Step derivatives are filling up
church basements with Christians and atheists and Jews and pagans
and political conservatives and liberals and others, while the sanctuar-
ies of many mainstream white Protestant churches sit half full. The
reason for this seems to me quite simple. Alcoholics Anonymous
invites all people to come as we are and, through sharing our vulnerability, to touch our strength and share a Higher Power, however we
may experience "Him," or "Her," or "It"—even if our experience of

this Power is a void or a blur, an angry feeling or a painful spot somewhere inside. There is no heretic. No one is right or wrong about the
Higher Power. No one is even right or wrong about drinking alcohol
unless, in our drinking, our lives have become unmanageable and our
behavior irresponsible.

So too with Christian belief. No one is right or wrong about God
or JESUS or the Trinity or any other doctrine of faith. No one is even
right or wrong in our living unless our lives are becoming unmanageable—that is, violent—and our behavior irresponsible, which is what
happens whenever we live primarily for our selves and our own, indifferent to others' well-being and often hostile to those whose ways of
speaking, dressing, thinking, believing, making culture, or making
love may frighten us.

To whom am I writing?

I have written this book as a theological resource for spiritual transformation and social change to those who have had it with churches
that make "right thinking" a criterion for membership and usually also
for entry into what JESUS called "the kingdom of God." Sisters and
brothers, we can be Christians without having to pass any such litmus
tests—and indeed many of us *are* Christian.

I offer these pages to those who are disturbed not only by the Religious Right but by all self-righteousness that comes dressed in religious garb. There are many ways to live as fully human beings in God.
Religious self-righteousness is not one of them.

I write to Jews, Moslems, Buddhists, pagans, and people of other
faith traditions and spiritualities who must wonder if a "Christian" is,
by definition, a narrow-minded, self-righteous, and often mean-spir-
ited bigot. The short answer is "no." A longer answer is in this book.

I offer the book to Christian liberals, radicals, and others who love
JESUS and have no desire to be "right." Keep the faith, good friends.
Hold it gently, with an openness to all you cannot know.

I offer this book to feminists, womanists, *mujeristas,* and other
strong, women-loving and men-loving women whose strength and
passion are a source of bafflement to most Christian prelates, pastors,
and theologians of all colors and cultures. Sisters, may you keep your
courage (and humor!).

I offer this as a resource to folks of various faith traditions who share a passion for justice with compassion and good humor. You are the hope of the world!

I write to those who are in recovery from addictions of many kinds—and those in recovery from "church abuse" and from what Dorothee Soelle once called "Christofascism" (violence done by Christians to people of other faith traditions as well as to those Christians have judged to be "wrong"). Yours truly is the realm of God.

I write to those who will not make peace with Christian anti-Semitism, Christian imperialism, the white racism of the Western church, or the class elitism of much Christianity around the world. You are the saviors of God, of JESUS, and of the rest of us.

I offer these pages also to those who (blessed be) will not make peace with the trivialization of, and contempt for, pagans, goddesses, and earth-based spiritualities. Your Wisdom is nourishment for all creatures on this planet and for whomever or whatever else there may be in time and space beyond us.

I offer this book to those academics who are not afraid of simple books, activists who are not afraid of complex ones, and all folks who are too smart to be "right thinking" Christians. Trust your intelligence.

I am also addressing "relational" consultants, organizers, therapists, ministers, and other healers and pastors who are weighted down these days by "professionally correct" ethics and expectations. You and we deserve a more morally honest struggle.

I offer this as a resource to mothers and fathers, aunts and uncles, neighbors and friends, teachers and preachers, priests and religious leaders who want to help raise children "in faith" but who cannot, in faith, raise them up to be "right thinking" Christians. Don't lose heart! It is too important—for the children and for us all.

I write for queer Christians. There are more of us than you may realize. Come on out—there's plenty of work to do, and plenty to celebrate.

I write also on behalf of (if not to) other earth creatures like the maple and moss, nuthatch and hawk, our animal companions both "tame" and wild, as well as the stones and mud and water that meet us in ways sometimes welcoming and life-giving, sometimes terrifying and death-dealing, as in the hurricane which, even as I write, has devastated Honduras and Nicaragua. I do not pretend to understand how it is that we are all connected as members of creation, all of us in God—especially how we are connected with all that is so terrible and terrifying and deadly. But I believe that, somehow, we are all part of a whole—and that there are more faces of JESUS on earth, throughout history and all of nature, than we can begin even to imagine—wherever there is a spark of hope for the sparrow or the child, the sea turtle or the prisoner.

Finally, I offer this resource in and to the Christic Spirit of Life in which we can learn and grow together, and only together, sisters and brothers. My hunch is that the best way to read it may be, for most of you, the way it was written—slowly. I hope you will take the time you need.

1. Origins

. . . . .

In this introductory chapter, I begin to explore the origins of this christological adventure. "JESUS"—what does this name mean to me? What am I inviting you, the reader, to assume with me? I suggest that, consciously or not, we begin *in God* and in prayer. In this study, I am especially attentive to the theological claims of "those who are right" and to presenting an alternative way of thinking about what it means to be Christian.

"Those who are right" refers not only to the Religious Right in the United States and elsewhere today, but moreover—and more importantly, probably— to all of us whenever we assume that we know it all or that our way is the only way to think or act. Those who are right tend to be impatient, I suggest, with God, themselves, and others. They do not accept the incompleteness of God's creation. Their response to the soul's yearning is to block it with easy answers rather than more graciously to hold the unfinishedness and mysteries of God and God's creation.

Trying to be clear and firm, Christians who are right often imagine that JESUS is an authoritarian Lord, a righteous moralist, an embattled adversary, and an obedient Son to a righteous Father. In this book, I offer alternative images to the authoritarian, moralistic, adversarial, and obedient JESUS of the right. I suggest that mutuality, passion (or real presence), compassion, and forgiveness are more genuinely moral relational possibilities for our life together.

As the chapter ends, I cite origins of this book in my own life-journey.

. . . . .

> What is the kingdom of God like? And to what should I compare it?
> It is like a mustard seed that someone took and sowed in the gar-
> den; it grew and became a tree, and the birds of the air made nests
> in its branches.
>
>   JESUS, according to Luke

Speaking of JESUS

"JESUS." What does this name mean to me? Of whom or what do I
believe I am speaking here? And what am I asking you, the reader, to
assume with me?[1]

I assume that JESUS actually lived; that he was a man about whom
we know little, probably less than we think we do, certainly less than
a literal reading of the biblical record would suggest. At the same
time, I recognize that JESUS is a figure of mythic (symbolic) propor-
tions about whom we may know a great deal more than we often
imagine we can, more than the Bible actually can tell us.

We know that the stories surrounding JESUS' life were told and
passed on and are interpreted to this day by people whose lives have
been transformed by them. These stories, derived mainly from the
Christian Bible, are mixtures of history, legend, and myth. Biblical
scholars have shown over the past century how little biographical
information we have about JESUS. Secular historians show, for example, that we know much more about the Caesars, and other rulers
such as Herod, than about the enigmatic figure JESUS who lived in
their midst. Yet, by leading us more fully into the historical, social, and
literary contexts of JESUS' life, biblical scholars often have helped
secure the faith of Christians in the God whom JESUS loved, indeed the
God whom we meet more fully through the stories about JESUS—perhaps even through JESUS himself as he lived and lives among us.

Still, who is this JESUS whom people like me and unlike me claim to
have met as a friend or brother, a lover or savior? Do I really think that
the Bible presents us with true, accurate pictures of a man named
JESUS? I do not believe that most of the images of JESUS, including
those I am exploring in these pages, can be taken "literally," as if they
are recounting biographical details of what JESUS actually said or did
when he was, say, having dinner with Mary and Martha. And yet I do

believe that something lively and spiritually empowering abounds through these images and stories and that through them we are invited by the Spirit to listen carefully, from one generation to another, for what may be revealed to us this time.

Every generation, on the basis of its own social and cultural history, tradition, education, and experiences, reads the Bible in ways that our ancestors would not recognize. This is because we always read the texts of our own lives in relation to the biblical text, and these resources of truth and inspiration mutually inform one another. Because of the Bible, we people grow and change. Because of us, the Bible also grows, through changing interpretations. Both the Bible and the people often grow in surprising ways, taking twists and turns we could not have anticipated. We ask questions and offer responses our ancestors could not have imagined—about capitalism, for example, and about class and race; gender, sexuality, and reproduction; space ships, nuclear power, and computer games; and the environment.

So too with JESUS. Because of him, we Christians are stretched beyond what we might have been without these stories and images of a radically faithful brother. And because of us, his sisters and brothers, the images of JESUS are stretched way beyond the horizons that we, or those who have gone before us, could have envisioned.

In this way, we and all who have preceded us, including authors of the Bible, have shaped JESUS, making him what he is today. Moreover, through the Bible and Christian history, we have shaped not one, but many, images of the same historical person. To name just a few, there is the empathic healer and the hot-tempered critic of religious hypocrisy; the enigmatic rabbi and the hometown son; the itinerant preacher and the adversary of corruption; the intimate friend and the political problem. This multiplicity of images is common to most humans. Just think of how many images of ourselves in different situations we can picture! Think also of how often these images confuse us, or others, especially when lifted out of context. So too with JESUS, whose stories, told countless times over two millennia, have generated multiple images.

We are drawn selectively to certain images and stories of JESUS (and of ourselves) on the basis of our cultures and communities, faith journeys, personal needs, and political commitments. The JESUS images in this book reflect such a selective process. Furthermore, I do not assume that the JESUS of whom I am speaking literally did or said, much less thought or felt, exactly what I attribute to him on the basis of my interpretation of the Bible as informed by my own religious communities, spiritual journey, politics and priorities, and other commitments.

You might say that the JESUS in this book does and says only those things that I myself can see or hear as I study the JESUS stories through particular lenses. Through these lenses, which I name in this text as the existential, political, and mystical moorings of my epistemology (how we know what we know), I have created the JESUS whom you will meet here.

But do I assume that "my" JESUS is the only true JESUS? I do not make such a claim. To the contrary, I would say that we need about as many images of JESUS as there are creatures on this earth. But is he perhaps the best possible JESUS whom you or I could know, the JESUS in these pages? I do not make this claim either. I can only tell you what I believe and am thinking about JESUS these days and invite you to think with me.

But is it, after all, "only" a story? Or was this JESUS real, and is he still? I believe we are met here, in this writing and reading as throughout our lives, with stories, images, and memories of someone who really lived, really died, and is really present still—through the power of relation working through community and faith. Because many Christians, however, are such literalists and most modern and postmodern Westerners are such empiricists, many may find it hard to believe that this JESUS of multiple images lives among us still. I like to think that this small book will help some of these folks begin to break out of theological literalism and out of the intellectual constrictions and spiritual conformity that fester in it—and in reaction against it.

Throughout the book, the name JESUS, as well as his messianic title CHRIST, is printed in small capital letters. This stylistic irregularity is meant to give the reader at least an occasional pause. I am hoping to remind you, along with myself, that the JESUS in these pages—and everywhere his name is spoken—is a deeply human, significant social construction and also a figure of stunning spiritual energy in the lives of countless communities great and small throughout the world. This

JESUS is not simply JESUS of Nazareth, whoever he may have been; nor does this JESUS often have much in common with "the Son of God" whom many Christians, believing themselves right, have lifted up above the rest of us and worshipped as if he and he alone were God.

I trust that the JESUS in this book does indeed originate in the life of the brother of Nazareth, mystical friend, and liberating spirit whom many Christians have called "CHRIST," a figure who here, as always, is being shaped by our need and *phantasy*—German feminist liberation theologian Dorothee Soelle's wonderful word for a blend of imagination, intuition, and freedom.[2] We ought probably to meet this JESUS much in the way we meet poetry or music—with all the heart and soul we can bring.

Meeting in God: Beyond self-absorption

We should be clear that this book is not primarily about JESUS, but about you and me, along with JESUS, in the context of a self-absorbed spirituality that perpetually distorts and will surely destroy our relation. By "self-absorbed," I mean one of the primary consequences of the individualism raging in the West and spreading like wildfire around the world. To be self-absorbed is to be turned in toward oneself and one's own (family, property, race, class, gender, religion, etc.) as the Alpha and Omega, the beginning and the end, of whatever really matters.

I am also not writing about "God" as if we could think about the source of all creation as we might an interesting film or rare plant. I am not much of a theist, but I believe in God. By this I mean that it is actually *inside* God that I believe; inside God we live, grow, die, and go on together through this power that connects us, each and all, to humans and other species of all generations.

I believe that this "power in relation"[3] is sacred because it holds us together far beyond our capacities to imagine and because we can draw upon this power, taking it in, embodying it, bringing it to life again and again in the world. This we can do, together.

I believe that this relational power is the same God that sparked the life and infuses the ongoing presence of our brother JESUS, just as it moves you and me into each new day.

It is through this power that we meet on a page and with this power that we can change the world in ways large and small. This should be the primary aim of theology—to help generate the passion and the intelligence, the commitment and the vision, to help us make history in just and compassionate ways.

In relation we meet near the heart of God. In our meeting, this book seeks to shed some light upon our common life, for even amid its fragments and particularities, it is a *common* life with roots in God. Of that I am sure. And several other things I know: that we humans are basically good and so too is the world; that we and the world, like our Sacred Source, are badly broken by evil; and that we need one another's help to heal. Socially and politically, spiritually and morally, this is our life's work—to be healers and liberators of and with one another. It is an ongoing life-project, one that is never fully accomplished, and it has as much to do with other creatures, with stars and snails, eucalyptus and elephants, as with you and me.

JESUS of Nazareth, whom early Christians designated "the CHRIST," was such an earth-creature, a healing and liberating brother through whose life the Spirit revealed—we might say, clarified—itself as the presence of love among us, the power of love in history. But we might also ask, "What is 'love'?" since we tend to cherish primarily our own definitions.[4] Certainly many voices preaching at us from the Right—the so-called religious and political Right—are clear that God Himself (and He most surely is a He) is clear about what is, and is not, loving from a Christian perspective. Moreover, we who would wish to distance ourselves politically and theologically from the Right are no less clear that these sisters and brothers on the Right are just plain Wrong about love and JESUS, about God and the world, and certainly about us.

I am trying to speak truthfully about love and about this JESUS, whose way of being in history—and, through the eyes of faith, eternity—clarifies what love does and does not mean. I am not speaking about "The" truth, for I do not suppose that there is only one truth to be spoken about JESUS. Nor is this book simply about "my" truth, as if my faith, theological explorations, and personal experiences belong simply to me, because they do not. This book is about truth borne, as Martin Buber would have it, "in the relation" between and among those who would live it, claim it, and speak it, those who have done so in the past, those who do so now.[5] Here as elsewhere in my work, I am attempting to articulate a relational theology of liberation that is shared and celebrated, cultivated and taught, wherever "two or three are gathered together" in the irrepressible Spirit of "justice-love."[6] We need to be clear that this is a Spirit and a commitment, not a state we reach perfectly or fully, ever.

In prayer

If we experience the relational fabric of our lives, we are likely to begin in prayer. Not necessarily as we often pray, speaking words out loud or even silently "to God," but with sighs and groans too deep for words. Prayer is an opening of ourselves to the presence of the Sacred, a spiritual yearning in which, to varying degrees, from moment to moment, we realize our intimate and immediate involvement with God.

It is right that a Christology begin with prayer, since this surely is how JESUS began and how the Spirit always begins, again, with us.

It is not simply that *we* start with prayer here and now, or that JESUS did during his lifetime or does with us now. The Creative Spirit begins with us, moving us to pray—giving us the feelings, intuitions, and sometimes thoughts and words we need, thereby speaking through us.

As the nineteenth-century liberal Anglican theologian Frederick Denison Maurice wrote, "We are dwelling in a Mystery deeper than any of our plummets can fathom, a Mystery of Love. Our prayers do not spring from us. [The One] who knows us, teaches us what we should pray for, and how to pray."[7]

The One who knows prays with us in this moment for this writing, this reading, this day, this time in our lives, the life of the world, and the life of God. She prays through us to herself, opening more fully to her own purposes, and ours when we go with her.

> "Glory be to our Mother, and Daughter
> And to the Holy of Holies,
> As it was in the beginning, is now and ever shall be,
> World, without end. Amen."[8]

Re-imaging JESUS, re-imaging ourselves

> JESUS went on with his disciples to the villages of Caesarea Philip-
> pi; and on the way he asked his disciples, "Who do people say that I
> am?" And they answered him, "John the Baptist; and others, Elijah;
> and still others, one of the prophets." He asked them, "But who do
> you say that I am?"
>
> —Mark 8:27-29a

> Image: They said, "You are the Christ."
> Re-image: I say, you are someone in whose way of being I see the
> power of justice, the power of right mutual relation. I say, you can
> help us see the power, love the power, claim the power, use the
> power.[9]

In *The Redemption of God: A Theology of Mutual Relation* (1982), I worked
toward "re-imaging" JESUS as one of us rather than as the Son of God
in and of himself. Rather than embodying, all by himself, the power of
God, he was someone through whose presence and with whom
friends and strangers began to notice the power of God stirring among
them, with them all, perhaps actually "in" them from moment to
moment. From this perspective, JESUS was not the exception, he was
the norm—the normal human being, what each of us is created to be.

God's power is not JESUS' power to bestow upon us, but rather is
ours to be called forth by one who sees us as we are meant to be, in
the fullness of our humanness. That was the essence of JESUS' ministry:
to see us as we are meant to be and to call us forth.

That is the essence of our lives as well: to see one another as we are
meant to be and to call one another forth.

That is why violence against one another—humans, creatures,
earth—is violence against the Spirit of God.

When we violate one another, we are assaulting not only our own
brothers and sisters but also tearing at the heart of the Sacred. This is
the case, regardless of what violence we are waging: systemic political
violence such as poverty, capital punishment, torture, and war; interpersonal abuse such as beatings, shootings, stabbings, and sexual
assault; or creature abuse such as the slaughter of animals, devastation
of the earth, and pollution of water.

Over the years it has become increasingly clear to me that as we
meet JESUS spiritually, politically, or intellectually, we encounter JESUS

through a variety of double images—simultaneous images of power as well as vulnerability, inseparably linked. We see two JESUSES at once— a powerful presence and a suffering brother, images that can appear to be contradictory but are not. These images correspond in many ways to the more traditional understanding of the "fully divine" and "fully human" character of JESUS, and to common Christian perceptions of him as the King of Kings, on the one hand, and a poor man from Nazareth on the other.

JESUS' power to heal and teach, to inspire and change people, was rooted in his vulnerability—that is to say, in his openness to those around him and to the Spirit of life connecting them. When we dwell on either of these images—JESUS' power or his openness, his strength or his vulnerability—apart from the other, we fail to see JESUS at all.[10]

Like ours, JESUS' world was fraught with oppression and violence, disease and poverty, indifference, cruelty, and collusion with evil by state and religious leaders. This was a world in which JESUS was a common person living and acting in solidarity with other common people—carpenters, fishermen, prostitutes, tax collectors, those less popular, those less socially prominent, those poorer members of the human family. Speaking and acting on behalf of these people in the context of a social order fastened in contempt for them, JESUS opened himself to the hostilities of state and religious leaders.

And he was no fool. JESUS knew the rules, just as you and I know what is likely to happen if we push hard against the tide, scrape abrasively against the protocol of the institutions, communities, and societies in which we live. JESUS is bound to have known the risk. Still, he lived a deeply human life, and he died violently not because either he or God "loved" death, "chose" it, or "willed" it but because he loved life and sisters and brothers and the God in whom he, and they, had their being.

We do not know JESUS at all, and we cannot know him, unless we see that the justice-loving brother who refused to collude with the injustices, corruption, and pettiness of both the state and parts of his religious tradition was one and the same rabbi who kept the Sabbath and practiced Judaism, who prayed, fasted, and healed the sick. JESUS the prophet and JESUS the teacher was both a social activist and a religious leader. If we experience this activist, spirited JESUS as real and present today, we will recognize both the JESUS who suffers with his companions because he is deeply human, and the JESUS who, for this reason, is alive in the Spirit, source of "living water" and "bread of life" then and now.

The more closely we look at JESUS, the liberator and the suffering one, the more clearly we will see ourselves and one another, for his story is a window into our own, which is why we tell it, share it, pass it on.

The more fully present we become to one another and ourselves, the more surely, like JESUS, we become lightning rods for the rage and indignation of principalities and powers in our own time.

The more open we are to one another in the Spirit of justice-love, the more fully human we are able to become together, committed to one another's well-being, mutually related as sisters and brothers.

And so we go, catching one view, finding another:

The more fully human we are, the more connected we are not only with other humans but with the rest of creation.

The more happily we assume our own relatively small places in the universe, the larger we become through right-relatedness with those who tug our lives and commitments beyond the boundaries of our own skins, tribes, creeds, and even species.

The better we see that in this expansive Spirit of justice-love we are connected with all tribes and creatures, the more confident we can be that God is with us and not just us—God is also with others, moving through and among "us" and "them," empowering each and all to take only what we need and to share what we have.

Meeting the Spirit in this way, we find ourselves as well.

This double imaging always keeps us a little off-balance. For just when we think we understand what JESUS was about, the image shifts—and we hear the voice not of a comforting friend who has seen us through a hard time but of an angry stranger challenging our attitude. Just when we think we've got the answer, we see we're no longer asking the right question. Looking for God, we discover something new about ourselves. Looking for serenity, we are found by people who care about us. Wanting acceptance from those who will not give it, something stirs in our soul and we know that, still, all is well.

So when we think we've got it right and want to keep it the way it is—JESUS or God, the Spirit or ourselves—we'd better think again, because the story is just beginning, our own as well as JESUS', as it was in the beginning, is now, and will be forever.

"Those who are right"

The immediate context of this writing project has been the emer gence of the so-called Religious Right as a major political force in the late twentieth/early twenty-first century Americas, North and South. In this situation, "Saving JESUS from Those Who Are Right" is a title that has grown on me. I do not mean to imply by it simply that pro-gressive Christians must somehow rescue Christian faith from right-wing[11] ideologues, though I do believe we must be politically savvy and active.

Although my concern about the Religious Right (particularly the Christian Right in the United States) was initially the spark for this project, my interest has broadened and deepened considerably since I began working on it several years ago. While I remain troubled by the theocratic aims of the most narrow-minded, politically reactionary religious forces in the Americas and throughout much of the world today,[12] my desire in this book is no longer to analyze or refute those right-wing Christologies to which Dorothee Soelle has referred as "Christofascist."[13]

"Those who are right" refers even more basically in these pages to all persons whose socio-political commitments are hardened fast and whose psychospiritual dispositions are tightly boundaried. By this I mean people who are so sure they're right that they don't seem to notice moral complexity and don't want to be bothered by those who do. "Those who are right" can be any of us, feminists and others (and this is most of us at least some of the time), so set in our ways or judgments that we assume we "have" it politically, intellectually, or spiritually.

The suggestion that JESUS must be "saved" reflects the perception of justice-minded Christians that what this brother lived and died for— his passionate commitment to justice-love, or mutual relation—is under fire in these times (as always) and that those who are right are now (as ever) its most formidable adversaries. I doubt, however, that we who hold progressive political perspectives often view ourselves as adversaries to justice and mutuality. We need to help one another understand that, whoever we are, we are enemies of the Spirit of Love and Justice whenever our minds are shut and our hearts hardened to the humanity of those who oppose us.

That the religion generated in JESUS' name *can* be saved from "those who are right" signals my faith not in JESUS himself but in the Spirit in which he lived and died, which is *our* power in mutual relation to challenge the structures of the self-absorbed spirituality that invariably accompanies being stuck in one's own sense of "rightness." From a traditional Christian perspective, this book is more a "Spirit-ology" (Pneumatology) than a "Christology." To me, as a Christian at the turn of the third millennium C.E., they are identical.

My aim in these pages is to present an alternative to those teachings about JESUS, God, ourselves, and the world that invariably shut out those whose religious, moral, or metaphysical understandings differ from those of "right-thinking" Christians. The book most surely means to refute right-wing christological images because I believe that they propagate evil. In these pages I attempt to show why. As important, I am attempting to challenge all assumptions about JESUS CHRIST that are secured in self-righteous moorings, whether they appear to be matters of more private or more public interest and whether they seem, on the surface, to be serving "right," "left," or "centrist" political agendas.

The difference between self-righteousness and right relation

In an engaging book on "chaos, crisis, and the emergence of community," justice activist and theologian Rhea Miller writes of JESUS, "He was not preoccupied with rules; he never asked people to be right. Instead, drawing on his own cultural heritage, he called people to be faithful, faithful to relationships and the Relationship."[14]

Miller is drawing a critical moral distinction between rules and right relation as the basis of authority. Not that rules are unimportant; without them our life together would be overwhelmed by chaos and fear. But rules and the self-righteousness that thrives on them cannot bear the weight of moral authority. Later in this book, we will consider moralism (rule-based ideology) as a serious spiritual problem. For now, I want to emphasize the significant theological and ethical, pastoral and political, difference between trying to "be right," on the one hand, and the struggle to generate more fully mutual, or right, relation on the other. In the former instance, our efforts to be right are wed to rules, abstractions, ideas about right and wrong that may or may not help create faithful, just, and loving relationships. Creating "right relation," or mutuality, by contrast, is a dynamic relational process that draws on a Sacred Power that is essentially ours only in the struggle for more fully mutual relation. This process spontaneously generates more of itself, more right relation, more mutuality, more "righteousness" or "justice." *Sedeq*, which refers in Hebrew Scriptures both to the right relation of humans to one another and to the relational covenant between God and the people of Israel, is not an abstract notion. *Sedeq* refers to a dynamic relational commitment and struggle "to do justice, and to love kindness, and to walk humbly with our God" (Mic. 6:8b). To be in right relation, according to the prophetic tradition of Israel in which JESUS himself stood, is to "let justice roll down like waters, and righteousness like an ever-flowing stream" (Amos 5:24).

Self-absorbed spirituality

During the last two centuries in the predominantly Christian West, the more self-absorbed impulses in Christian thought (such as the male of the ruling tribe having a "right" to his property, including his wife, chattel slaves, animals, house, etc.) have merged in significant ways with the aims of the dominant economic system, which reaches far beyond the wildest dreams of common folk who wish to be able to make a living and earn a decent wage. In the last few years, the merger of Christianity's and capitalism's focus upon the betterment of "the self" has spread beyond the West and is becoming increasingly global. This means that Christian spirituality and a profit-driven economy are fueling the same self-absorbed ideology at the turn of the twenty-first century.

It is important to note here that capitalism's historical roots in Euro-American cultures are racist and sexist to the core. This means that its primary beneficiaries have been, and continue to be, white males[15] who control immense wealth. It is also true, however, that as capitalism advances globally and becomes increasingly Christian, some few men and women of color (that is, people from non-European tribes, with indigenous roots in the Americas, Africa, and Asia) and some few white women are, as individuals, as self-absorbed as their white male models and mentors. That this often is heralded by civil rights and feminist leaders as an "achievement"—and even as "justice"—suggests how morally complex and distorted our justice-visions can be.

Enter the Religious Right in the United States—at its core, Christian. For more than thirty-five years, beginning with the failed 1964 presidential campaign of Barry Goldwater, the Christian Right has been organizing in the United States. Its fundamental spiritual motive is a completely and unambiguously self-absorbed reaction against any social justice movement that threatens to broaden and deepen our senses of ourselves and "ours" (our people, our interests, our nation, etc.) to include the well-being of "others."

The political platform of the Religious Right, which often includes like-minded Moslems, Jews, and others who are not Christian, is basically threefold: (1) *economic self-absorption,* which, as Pat Buchanan's 1996 campaign illustrated,[16] does not yet fit easily with the global movement of capital; (2) *national self-absorption,* whose foundation is militarism and an enthusiasm for war if it serves the interests of the United States; and (3) *patriarchal self-absorption,* which is the core of Christianity, the dominant religious tradition in the United States and Europe. Christian teachings about male headship of families, sanctity of heterosexual marriage, control of women's sexuality and reproductive options, contempt for homosexuals and others who engage in sexual acts outside the boundaries of a "compulsory heterosexuality,"[17] physical discipline of children, availability of a cheap labor force, and domination of the earth and all creatures are essential to the governance of a patriarchal society. These values serve also to strengthen nationalism and a capitalist political economy.

As these three foundations—capitalism, nationalism, and patriarchy—are brought together theologically and politically, which is the Religious Right's theo-political agenda, fascism comes knocking at the door. By "fascism" I mean here a theo-political commitment to and a systemic effort to secure the "self" as the one and only image of God, and the self's possessions, desires, and worldview as sacred. For the fascist, the self and only the self is right, and public policy is put in place to secure this self-righteousness. Fascist governments of the twentieth century have emphasized law and order and other policies to uphold the special rights and privileges of white people, males, Christians, and the dominant economic forces and its primary beneficiaries. A decade before the founding of the Christian Coalition by Pat Robertson and Ralph Reed in 1990, Dorothee Soelle, no stranger to what fascism can do to a people, named the "Christofascist" demon that she saw twisting its way into the mainstream churches and political economy of the United States.

How then in this context can we save either JESUS or ourselves from this evil growing among us, winding its way into our spiritual practices and daily lives?

Who is JESUS CHRIST to those who are right?

In college during the 1960s, I studied the work of Charles Williams, an Anglo-Catholic writer and literary companion of such luminaries as T. S. Eliot, C. S. Lewis, and Dorothy Sayers. Like these friends, Williams wrote out of a strong sense of Christian orthodoxy, or "right thinking." Throughout his novels,[18] though he seldom uses explicitly Christian language, Williams employs images of greed, fear, lust, darkness,[19] despair, and ultimately defeat and death to portray the visible forces of evil that contend here on earth against the often invisible and ultimately victorious power for good. Of course this mid-century Englishman was not connected with the "Christian Right" as a theocratic political movement. Nonetheless, as a practitioner of Anglicanism, which has evolved over four centuries as the official religion of Britain and its empire, Charles Williams was a theocrat. Like many Englishmen, he believed that the state ought to be governed by Anglo-Christian principles of good and evil. Thus, even without a connection to any explicitly theo-political movement, Charles Williams, like C. S. Lewis and T. S. Eliot, placed himself and other orthodox Christians among "those who are right."

I make this point about Williams for two reasons—first, to illustrate that "those who are right" are not by any means simply the most vocal Christian traditionalists in the United States today who are luring the Republican Party to the right; second, to suggest that it is not hard to imagine the slippage of good faithful people increasingly toward assent to what we assume to be a *benign* theocratic state.

I think of the strength of my own belief that there is a sacred power from which we draw hope and the capacity to make justice-love, whether we are heterosexual, lesbian, gay, or bisexual in our primary erotic yearnings. This passionate belief—and my wishing that somehow everyone could share it—is fine. But it would not be fine for me, or for others who share this belief, to make our faith a requirement for membership in civil society and its institutions.[20] Those who on the basis of their Christian faith censor stories of gay and lesbian families out of public libraries are doing exactly that—insisting that their faith-based values be shared by all who wish to participate fully in our society and its institutions.

And how do those on the Christian Right understand JESUS CHRIST as the impetus of their effort to keep materials that affirm gay and lesbian families out of the hands of school children?

It's important to note here that, for all Christians of whatever political moorings, the figure of JESUS is significant—biblical stories about him; images of JESUS as teacher, healer, prophet, etc; and the various ascribed theological and christological meanings that the church traditionally has given to these stories and images. In a very real sense, there are as many images of JESUS, and as many feelings and thoughts about him, as there are Christians. Just as one church or person can raise up an image of a JESUS CHRIST who requires that all homosexuals repent our sexuality and be born again in order to be saved, so too can another church or person celebrate a JESUS CHRIST who was himself a lover of men like John the Evangelist and who is calling us to "act up" on behalf of queer justice.[21] This tension bears witness to both the power of the multiplicity of JESUS-traditions to generate and regenerate images of JESUS and the power of the human imagination to construct whatever we think we need in order to make sense of our lives and world.

The *problem* posed by the Christian Right's "JESUS CHRIST" is *not* that he is a cultural artifact or a political construct. *All* JESUS-images are

culturally and politically derived. This is true even of those portraits of
JESUS embedded most securely in the Christian Bible—the more historical images of him as Mary's child, son of the carpenter Joseph,
Jewish teacher, healer, and friend, and the more theologically ascribed
images of JESUS as "Lord," "Messiah/ CHRIST," "Son of Man," "Son of
God," "shepherd," "vine," and "bread of life." All of these and many
more ways of looking at JESUS and discovering his connections with us
are laden with political meanings and cultural assumptions that derive
from both his own time and place in history and ours.

So the problem with the JESUS CHRIST of the Right is not that he is
a cultural creation. The problem with the Right's JESUS CHRIST is that
he is being spawned as a spiritual rationale for the authoritarian,
moralistic, and adversarial posturing of self-absorbed Christian politicians and leaders who teach fear of those different from them, a fear
that too often leads to hatred and violence. Where fear and hatred
thrive, violence will never be far behind—witness the bombings and
shootings at abortion clinics and the upsurgence in queer-bashing in
the past decade. Even as I have been preparing the final draft of this
book, two such killings have dominated the national news, the mur-
ders of Matthew Shepard, a college student in Wyoming, and of Bar-
nett Slepian, an obstetrician in Amherst, New York. The former was
killed because he was gay; the latter because he performed abortions.
In this context, we need to be clear that the problem with the Right's
JESUS CHRIST is not that he reflects a particular set of cultural values,
but that he is being used to stir fear and hatred and justify violence.

Frank Peretti, for example, is a Christian writer whose 1986 novel
This Present Darkness has sold millions of copies. Writing on this side of
the Atlantic, a half-century after Charles Williams, Peretti's literary
themes are similar to those of the more theologically sophisticated and
subtler Williams: Good Christians must be vigilant against the dark
forces of Satan that are constantly active among us. Presented as ugly,
black (note the racist imagery), gargoyle-like figures that are invisible
but ever-present to ensnare us, these demons can only be defeated by
the angels who also are with us, to guard us, if we turn to them in the
name of JESUS CHRIST. These angels, whom Peretti describes as white
male figures (with a few exceptions), often dressed in military
fatigues, are ever-ready for mortal combat with the demons who are
spreading their evil among us in the guise of feminists, abortionists,

secular humanists, homosexuals, and supporters of the United Nations and global monetary systems, which, Peretti contends, have more than a few Jews in charge.

It is easy for those who are more sophisticated theologically to dismiss Peretti, and most other producers of such "Christian" books and artifacts, as simple-minded and ridiculous. But we need to be aware that it is authors like Frank Peretti, not James Cone or Rosemary Radford Ruether and not even the currently very popular liberal theologians Marcus Borg or John Spong, whose books are reaching millions of adults and children today. Moreover, for each person who reads a book today—even a Peretti book—there are dozens who watch television and are reached by the 700 Club and other "Christian" programs designed to capture the imaginations and stir the fear of very large numbers of an increasingly multicultural population.

Interestingly, as I began reading materials and listening to voices of the Christian Right, I realized how seldom they mention JESUS CHRIST in their public political work. Such men as Pat Robertson, Jerry Falwell, Ralph Reed, and Gary Bauer have a great deal more to say about Bill Clinton's sex life and Tinky Winky's sexuality than about the man from Nazareth.

I suspect there are at least two reasons for this: First, it is hard not to read the biblical stories of JESUS as testimonies to the power of God's special love for the poor and outcasts among us. Since the struggle for economic, racial, and gender/sexual justice is seldom a commitment for the Christian Right, the less said about JESUS, the better. Second, if this is the case, it seems likely that JESUS of Nazareth must be kept in the background precisely so that JESUS CHRIST as Lord and King of All can be fashioned and adored by those who are right. This JESUS CHRIST becomes thereby an icon of human aspiration for economic, intellectual, gender, racial, and other forms of social, political, and psychological control.

While a reluctance to speak boldly of the poor man from Nazareth seems to characterize the Christian Right, it is also a strong feature today of most Protestant, Catholic, and Orthodox Christianity in the West. It is not accurate or fair, therefore, to blame the Christian Coalition or other constituents of the Religious Right for the christological manipulations performed over the years by leaders of mainstream churches. Indeed, the Christian Right's apparent indifference to the very human brother JESUS represents the Christologies of most right-thinking Christians, past and present.

In this book, I am suggesting that, among right-thinking Christians, at least four images of JESUS have been forged historically:

- JESUS CHRIST as authoritarian Lord
- JESUS CHRIST as moralist
- JESUS CHRIST as adversary against his enemies
- JESUS CHRIST as obedient son of his Father

These four theological portraits of JESUS no doubt have represented the real faith of countless Christians over the centuries and around the world. But they also reflect the efforts of bishops, pastors, priests, theologians, and rulers to consolidate, *in the name of* CHRIST, their hold over the people, their authority over the church, and not infrequently their control of the larger social order. In each case, the image of JESUS functions like a mirror—to reflect the image of how Christian leaders have experienced or aspired to the exercise of power as control.

In the first three of these images, JESUS is invested with the kind of social power as control that he emphatically repudiated early in his ministry when confronted by the devil (Luke 4:1-13). The fourth image—of JESUS CHRIST as obedient son of his Father—can be the most spiritually seductive of the four because, at a glance, it suggests a renunciation of control. Unlike the other three images, this one implies that the good Christian life, like JESUS', will be that of the passive servant who does what he or, more often in Christian life, she is told. The spiritual and political problem with the image of JESUS and the rest of us as obedient servants is contextual. In most real life contexts, the image of JESUS' willingness to obey, regardless of the consequences, is a bait to lure us into obeying those "fathers" who are exercising their power as control, not obedience. Thus, the image of the obedient son can be and has been used politically in conjunction with the other three images—authoritarian lord, moralist, and adversary—as an effective instrument to control slaves and workers, women and children, poor people and all those deemed subordinate to Christian leaders and rulers.

These four portraits of JESUS are deeply embedded in the faith systems and politics of most Christians who are right—and keep in mind that all of us who are Christian are, at times, among those who are right. Often, these christological images are revealed as much through our Christian life and practice as through our rhetoric.

This book is meant to offer alternatives to these particular images of JESUS. I am suggesting that authoritarian, moralistic (self-righteous), adversarial posturing that requires obedience does little to help create, redeem, or sustain the work of justice, the vitality of loving relationships, or the general well-being of God's people and creatures. As an alternative to authoritarian understandings of social/relational power, I propose *mutual relation* as a way *to god* (verb). I then discuss *evil* as the betrayal of mutuality and propose that it requires a more creative response than "obedience" to God or one another. As a more creative response to evil than self-righteous moralism can be, I suggest *passion* as real presence and also as a way of more fully embodying morality in right relation. Finally, I commend *forgiveness*—which involves stepping back from adversarial posturing—as an opening to the possibility of nonviolent struggle as the most moral, and probably most reliable, path we can take through fear, hatred, and violence.

The remainder of this present chapter is to further explore the origins of the Christology in this book.

Loneliness as a root of God, JESUS, and right relation

In the midst of the sufferings in our world, communities, and homes, *Christology* begins with our personal and, I believe, our common experiences of a loneliness at the heart of God and with our shared yearning for right relation with one another, the world, and that which is our sacred root. More than anything perhaps, this book is an attempt to help illuminate whatever may be true in this claim.

We begin here together, relative to one another, sisters and brothers in Spirit, in and beyond the universe as we know it. We are not alone. This is as true spiritually as it is physically. This relation—our spiritual connectedness with one another—is our *soul*, a dynamic, intimate meeting with one another and God. Be clear that our "souls" do not belong simply to us, but to our power in mutual relation, which is God. Soul is a relational movement through us. We are created to be a soulful people, all of us together, and each of us.

At the same time, we are lonely, sensing from time to time a "spot" deep inside that is ours and ours alone, a little part of us that no one else can reach and that even we ourselves cannot quite take hold of. This small, lonely spot is not our soul but rather like a tiny window into our soul.

Writing my doctoral dissertation twenty years ago, I spoke of our loneliness as a theological and ethical *problem*. It certainly can be and often is, especially as shaped in the modern world and exploited today by capitalism. As a socially constructed alienation from ourselves and one another, an alienation that is indispensable to the global political economy, our *experience* of loneliness becomes both "normal" (just the way it is) and often unbearable (without drugs, dependencies, or violence). There is nothing sacred or creative about this "capitalist spirituality"[22] in which loneliness is either a problem to be solved and removed, or a troubled state of being to which we sadly and resentfully resign ourselves.

But there is a dimension of loneliness in us that is not basically alienation, not at root a product of capitalist spirituality. I am referring to a loneliness that reflects an emptiness at the heart of God, a void that, try as we may, we cannot fill. In God's image, the most we can do is learn, with the help of our friends and God working through them, to accept this lonely spot as a sacred space, a fully divine and fully human/creaturely place of mystery and awe and fear and hope, and of a yearning for love that is beyond all love. It is a place in us of an insatiable desire that cannot be met except in "intimations and glimpses"[23] on the road we experience together as life.

The JESUS story was conceived and born in this desire. The story has been formed and re-formed countless times over the last two millennia. It has been passed on through the sacred relational power in our midst that yearns for friends. It is a lonely story—"My God, my God, why hast thou forsaken me?" And it is a story each of us lives to the extent that we, like JESUS, are alive in the yearning for justice and compassion, solidarity and friendship. This yearning is the Spirit of God.

Over the years I have been consumed by three theological passions: the struggle for justice as the work of the Spirit; the sacred character of "unalienated" erotic (creative, liberating) power,[24] which I have understood as a synonym for the love of God; and the JESUS story in its Christic[25]—liberating—dimensions. I have attempted to notice and study the relation between these three interests, which Christians often perceive as separate and disconnected and, especially in the case of erotic power, as oppositional to the other two. What I have suggested previously, and will again in this book, is that the connecting threads among justice-making, erotic power, and the JESUS story is the struggle toward "right" or "mutual" relation that meets us in each of these human experiences that can be powerful conduits of the divine. In this project, however, I go a step further in suggesting that our sacred power in mutual relation is so deeply the root of our yearning for right relation that we honestly can describe God *as* the yearning, God *as* the desire for justice and compassion, solidarity and friendship. Indeed, not only is God "in" the depths of our longing for mutuality and justice-love, God *is* the depths.

It was *in* this God, *in* this desire, that JESUS was born and lived and died and lives among us to this day. It is in this same Spirit, this yearning, that we and all creatures come into life on the earth and begin our journeys, all of us together, none of us alone. Yet each of us is always a lonely bearer of God, custodian of an empty spot, a hungry place, a small space that cannot be filled by anything *except* God's own yearning for justice-love and friendship with all of creation.

I believe that the Christian Right originates in a frantic effort to fill this small sacred space with answers and certainties rather than with the questions, mystery, and ambiguities that thrive at the heart of God.

Similarly, I believe that the assumption on the part of any of us (left, right, or mainstream; feminist or masculinist) that we know the right spiritual path for others (or even for ourselves in a fixed, static, and absolute way) is fraught with the same frenzy to satisfy a spiritual hunger that cannot be satisfied except through our experiencing the *unmet* hunger of God for justice-love in all creation. I am suggesting that the only way we can live fully in God in this world at this time is to embody God's own yearning for that which is not yet[26]—the completion, or fulfillment, of creation. In the meantime, to be faithful is to be spiritually hungry—for God and in God and with God and, in God's own image, unable to be satisfied.

Suffering, evil, and human impatience

Unsatisfied desire is a dimension of experience common to many, probably all, people. The overly consumptive character of the so-called "American Dream," which at the turn of the twenty-first century has been globalized, represents more than anything the extent of this unmet craving for more—but more of what? Surely not primarily for the latest in gourmet foods or fashion, cars or technological gimmicks, or even for dreams of fame or immortality. What do we long for with and in the Spirit?

We long for serenity, I believe. For confidence in the midst of confusion and chaos. For a "peace that passes understanding" in a world shattered by violence around, among, and within us. For some genuinely right relation with one another and the world itself. Do we not long to "know our place,"[27] and to know that it is a good place, in which we are, in the best sense, at home with ourselves and one another, connected in mutually empowering ways?

From the beginning, the most basic obstacle to our knowing this peace and confidence has been the experience of *suffering*, which, like our longing in God, is common to all humans, to all creatures, and indeed, to a "suffering God" as well.[28]

Suffering originates in two universal "places" that in real, everyday life are never mutually exclusive. Both are ancient, tenacious realms with roots that reinforce and strengthen each other.

In the first, there is the pain that we cannot in this world avoid, the suffering steeped in the *unfinishedness of creation*.[29] In this context, our common experiences of fear and anxiety, loss and sorrow, disease and death, reflect the incompleteness of the realm of God that is not yet finished. We are on our way home, but we are not yet there. This kind of suffering is often terrible—who can describe the anguish of bodies eaten by cancer or people washed away in floods? And, although we may realize that many so-called natural disasters and diseases are, at least, exacerbated by human greed and violence, most progressive Christians do not hold ourselves personally responsible for them. While such suffering may be experienced by many of us as a *spiritual* problem—why does God permit it?—we do not, perhaps often enough, treat it as a moral problem that we ourselves can resolve by changing how we relate to one another or to God.

The other realm of suffering, by contrast, consistently puts before us basic moral as well as spiritual and political issues—and it shapes and reinforces the suffering we incur through the incompleteness of creation. I refer here to the suffering resulting from the *brokenness of creation*. This is the context that liberal and mainstream Protestant and Catholic Christians, as well as feminist and other liberation theologians, associate most readily with "evil," which is *the* basis of all moral problems.

One of the primary themes in this book is that the suffering rooted in evil is greatly increased by our collective failure to accept the suffering that is rooted in the incompleteness of God's creation. We are impatient with one another, ourselves, and the Spirit. And our refusal to accept our common life—the human, creaturely, and creative condition of our life together in all its unfinishedness—gives rise to much evil: greed and envy; cutthroat competition to be first, do best, get most; and other ways of being that set us against one another rather than drawing us together.[30]

Christian anti-Semitism is such a case in point. The hatred of Jews by Christians reflects a massive failure among Christians to accept the unfinished, ongoing character of salvation, as a sacred process of healing and liberation that is both temporal and eternal. From the early days of Christianity—beginning no later than Paul, himself a Jewish convert to CHRIST—church leaders have sought to explain JESUS' specialness by presenting him as "the completion" of God's saving work in history rather than as a window into the ongoing processes of a creation that is unfinished, and as a partner in the saving work of healing and liberation.

Rather than helping one another live with greater serenity through the sufferings that are our common lot as earthcreatures, many Christian leaders and theologians have manipulated the figure of JESUS to place him, and ourselves in his spirit, *beyond* our common creatureliness. Rather than helping generate faith that the Spirit is not only with us but is working through us toward the completion of God's realm, we have created a "savior" to set ourselves *apart* from human and creaturely misery. We have invented "CHRIST" to raise us *above* others in the realm of suffering. Throughout the history of this theological fantasizing, our primary spiritual nemesis has been "the Jews," who are not only our religious ancestors but moreover those whose spirituality does not encourage such escapism from the real world.

Thus, from the very beginnings of the church, we Christians have had great difficulty living as participants in an unfinished, imperfect creation, embodying a "revolutionary patience"[31] with one another, ourselves, and God. Our difficulty with this participatory way of living in the Spirit has produced a number of terrible theological misunderstandings, including the misleading, only partially true, notion that *God became fully human in one person, JESUS, and him alone* (the basis of most doctrines of the incarnation) and an equally distorted assumption that *our salvation was accomplished through this brother's death on the cross* (in later theological developments, the basis of a doctrine of atonement).

In this book I suggest that these understandings of *incarnation* and *atonement* reflect our difficulties and impatience with an incomplete, unfulfilled creation. Rather than presenting our yearning for fulfillment as sacred, a dimension of God's own presence with us, the church has tried to complete the redemption story by suggesting that, in JESUS' death, God's desire for right relation with creation was finally completed or "satisfied." I believe that such a theology short-circuits the Spirit's movement in history, and, moreover, I believe that through JESUS' living and dying and through our lives as well—in our yearnings for a righteousness that is unfulfilled, a justice-love that has not been satisfied—God's longing is God's holiness, and so too is our own.

Christians who believe that God is beyond all such longing, vulnerability, and incompleteness are bound to reject the *sacredness* of this deeply human yearning and may even see it as a sign of spiritual weakness, confusion, or bad faith. Trying to combat the notion that such human vulnerability images God—an assumption that undermines traditional understandings of God's omnipotence—the Christian Right has no use for the sacralization of either human or divine vulnerability, longing, or incompleteness. For the Christian Right, as for most Christians, JESUS CHRIST is perfect, invulnerable, and complete. In this book, I suggest that such assumptions diminish, rather than strengthen, the power of God with us.

A white Southern Christian girlchild from the "muddled middle"

Every Christian has some knowledge of JESUS in which our understandings of God and ourselves, our communities and the world, our values, our faith, and our doubts take root.

JESUS has been on my mind for as long as I can remember. As a child raised in a moderately liberal white Christian home in North Carolina, I was drawn to JESUS much as I was to characters in other bedtime stories. They were real to me—JESUS, Black Beauty, Cinderella. The "good" characters—victims (who had to be saved from evil powers) and heroes (their saviors) attracted me, just as they were meant to. No question that good (or God) would triumph, anywhere and everywhere, if only JESUS and people like him, and people like the Prince and Princess in "Sleeping Beauty," and people like me were involved. And that was pretty much it. JESUS was a hero and I thought he was neat, and I wanted to be like him much as I wanted to be like Superman and the Lone Ranger as I began to watch television.

My spirituality at age four, six, ten, was simple because life, as I experienced it, seemed simple and uncluttered. Like other white kids, I lived mostly oblivious to the savaging effects of white racism, by which my whiteness was being shaped and secured every day—mine and JESUS' too, as I pictured him much in the image of a white, Euro-American man.

I was also largely unaware of poverty and, like many other children, was ignorant of how class was making me who I was becoming. My family was "middle class" by way of education, income, and standing within the local communities (towns, churches, businesses, schools, scout troops, etc.). Although I knew that JESUS was a poor man, I really didn't know what poor men were—unless they were "colored," "Indian," or the kind of white men I didn't want to get close to: "poor white trash," "drunkards," other sad, bad, or unfortunate men.[32] I hadn't an inkling that, along with white supremacy, a pernicious class-elitism was molding my consciousness, my sense of self, my goals and fantasies, and certainly my images of JESUS and God (that is, of what is best among us).

Nor did it cross my mind that being a girl made any difference at all to how I was appropriating, deep in my soul, the meanings of the JESUS story. I didn't question either his maleness or his Father. Of course the Son had a special place in God's family! And naturally, God was the Father of the family. He was the Head, wasn't He?[33] That's just the way it is and how it's supposed to be, on earth as in heaven.

These were christological assumptions, largely unconscious and wholly unarticulated, in my childhood: JESUS was *naturally* white and male and, despite being poor, had middle class sensibilities and manners and values. These assumptions were products of a relatively sheltered childhood spent romping through the woods and fields in the North Carolina mountains, often with my imaginary playmate, Sophie, who also liked JESUS a lot and was more alert than I to his free-spirited, boundary-breaking style. Sophie helped me see that, if we were going to be like JESUS, we couldn't just play it safe.

Adolescence was for me as turbulent as childhood had been serene. The period between about age twelve and my early twenties threatened to break my spirit and strip my voice, much as it silences so many girls becoming women.[34] During this confusing time, I came close to forgetting entirely my earlier images of JESUS as a human hero. In his place, I began to worship CHRIST, who wasn't really human at all, but was more of a "divine man," a God-man in heaven, "sitting at the right hand of the Father."

Back then I was a sacristy rat. I loved going to church and just hanging out around the priest and other "holy" things like vestments and chalices and communion wafers. With my two best friends, Fran and Jane, I went to church as often as we could either walk or get our parents to take us, preferably every day if we could find a service somewhere. By age 14, I had "given my life to CHRIST" at a Billy Graham rally in the Charlotte Coliseum. I was also becoming, in my daily spiritual practices, an Anglo-Catholic, although the Episcopal parish my family attended, like most in the South in those days, was thoroughly Protestant in style and substance. The Episcopal priest hardly knew what we meant when Fran, Jane, and I announced that we wanted to "make our confessions" and learn to "pray the rosary."

Readers familiar with my work may recall that I argue against the popular psychology in which just about every symptom of personal woundedness is interpreted as a sign of early childhood trauma and/or sexual abuse.[35] Over the last twenty or so years, I have learned

that being a white middle-class teenage girl in the United States South
in the 1950s and 1960s was itself a form of spiritual and sexual abuse.
In my life, as in the lives of many girls and women, I am certain,
bulimia was not a response to rape or molestation, but rather was the
most visceral response my body could make to becoming and being a
woman in a world-church that fears and loathes women's power. I was
vomiting up the tension between the woman I knew myself to be—
my fully human self—and the woman I had to pretend to be in order
to be "good."

The sweet heroic JESUS of my childhood was no help to me in this
situation. I wanted a mightier savior, one to take my pain and carry it
miraculously away. At this point in my life, as I sank into the pits of
body-loathing, the classical Christian doctrine of substitutionary
atonement provided an escape from the pain. JESUS CHRIST, I learned,
had died "to take away my sins"—especially, I trusted, the lustiness of
my erotically energized bisexual adolescent female body. As my faith
in this CHRIST increased, I split into two different and oppositional
selves—a spiritual self, learning to be a good Episcopalian, and a sexual self, learning to stuff the erotic power that, ironically, I would later
recognize as sacred power. CHRIST became for me, during my teen
years, a disembodied heavenly man to deliver me from my own body.

By the time I was in college, I was throwing up my sexual feelings
on a regular basis and, as a religion major, becoming intellectually
turned on to the Bible, "the historical JESUS," the work of German theologian Dietrich Bonhoeffer, and several contemporary U.S. writers
on "the death of God."[36] These academic explorations, bolstered by
splendid professors and my involvement in anti-racist activities and
opposition to the Vietnam War, weakened my atonement spirituality
and prompted a renewal of my interest in the very human JESUS as a
prophetic and liberating figure.

These interests led me from college to Union Theological Seminary
in New York City, to study theology in a progressive, justice-minded
community among students and teachers who were organizing serious
resistance to the War. My first year in seminary was a *kairotic*, sacred
moment, in which the Spirit of God came blowing through my life like
a hurricane. Through the anti-war movement, anti-racist work with
Professor C. Eric Lincoln, my first explicitly sexual experiences, the

assassinations of Martin Luther King Jr. and Robert Kennedy, meeting other Episcopal women seminarians and wondering together why we could not be priests, I was swept into the midst of personal and vocational crisis: Who was I, and what was I doing—as a white person? in my most intimate relationships? in seminary? in the church? in the world?

I took a leave of absence after the first year in seminary and returned to North Carolina to explore such questions. Interestingly, although I didn't have much sense of who *I* was at the time, I had come into a strong faith-awareness that JESUS was a fully human brother with a mind, heart, and soul set on a God who moves the struggle for justice, an understanding that has grown clearer and stronger with time.

During the past thirty years, my desire to join in struggles for liberation and, increasingly, my involvement in the work of healing (which I see as inextricable from justice-making) have intensified my interest in JESUS. Thus, CHRIST*ology*—studying in what ways the JESUS-story is one of salvation—has been foundational to all of my theological work.

Throughout, I've benefited from studying and sharing collegially with some of the finest theologians in the world, including those whose work on JESUS CHRIST has been stunning in its depth and implications: Dorothee Soelle, Tom F. Driver, Delores S. Williams, and Kwok Pui-lan are among those whose christological pursuits have sparked and sharpened my own.

At the same time, with these and other feminists, I have become ever more mindful of the horrendous extent to which the name of JESUS has been wielded as a weapon against women, children, racial/tribal minorities, poor people, Jews and participants in other faith-traditions, queer folk, people with disabilities, and the earth itself. In the context of this shameful, ongoing situation, I have thought often about leaving the church, breaking with at least the institutionalized "JESUS-tradition."

Even as I have headed for the door, however, someone or some world event has called me back—and somehow, each time, I have discovered JESUS anew. Through involvement with particular groups of people—Nicaraguan campesinos; African American women colleagues; South

African, Korean, Costa Rican, Ugandan, German students; lesbian, gay, bisexual, and transgendered friends; mental health workers hungry for justice and spirituality—I have discovered that the JESUS story is not only meaningful (in positive *and* negative ways) for countless people who struggle for justice. It is often critical to their survival. In order to be in right, mutual relation with these sisters and brothers, I have had to listen to their JESUS-stories and try to learn from them—even when, personally, I have had it with the church as I know it.

So, even as I have pulled against deeper involvement in Christianity, I frequently have been drawn into dialogue about JESUS, especially with Christian women from different cultures and many parts of the world. And what I hear myself saying echoes the voices of these women: that JESUS was a fully human brother with a mind, heart, and soul set on a God who "makes justice roll down like water, and righteousness like an everflowing stream." In various conferences and projects over the last several decades, women and marginalized men (men of color, men with HIV, radical white men, queer men), Christian liberation theologians and feminists have kept alive for me questions about JESUS. Continent to continent, we have affirmed our shared faith in the Spirit that energizes us and moves the struggle, the same Spirit that infused the life of JESUS and generated a "Christa/community,"[37] a "discipleship of equals,"[38] a historical movement of "justice-loving friends,"[39] a compelling "ministerial vision."[40]

I continue to learn and teach Christology, and, I must say, it never gets old, it's never done. Studying JESUS with seminarians, parishioners, and other spiritual sojourners and political activists is for me a fresh, energizing intellectual and political adventure. This book is offered as a testimony.

2. Speaking with Authority

. . . . .

Why do I speak here mainly of JESUS, less often of CHRIST or JESUS CHRIST? And who am I to speak at all, and who are you to speak of these matters? In this chapter, I explore what would be called, in more traditional theology or philosophy, the "epistemological" basis of this book. "Epistemology" refers to how we know what we know. Here I examine the existential, political, and mystical ways I have come to make the spiritual, intellectual, and political claims I make in this book. With sister theologians Kwok Pui-lan and Dorothee Soelle, I also lift up the role of theological *imagination* as a primary resource for knowing what we know about JESUS, about ourselves, about God and the world.

Finally, I look at the "postmodern" underpinnings of much theological work being done today, and I cite ways in which this study is, and is not, in my judgment, an addition to postmodern discourse.

. . . . .

> I tell you, if you have faith the size of a mustard seed, you will say
> to this mountain, "Move from here to there," and it will move; and
> nothing will be impossible for you.
>
> JESUS, according to Matthew

The language of this book

Why do I speak here mostly of "JESUS," less often of "CHRIST" or "JESUS CHRIST"?

For much of Christian history, "CHRIST" language has been the language of Christian imperialism, exclusivism, and domination. "CHRIST" has been shorthand for the raising up of JESUS as the firstborn Son of God who was and is eternally God himself—God the Son, the second person of the Trinity. When "CHRIST" is named, there seldom is room for anyone else to be the Daughter or the Son of God simply because we are members of human- and creature-kind.

I use the name "JESUS" more often than his Christic title because I believe that "CHRIST" language too often obscures the Christic—redemptive—meanings of the JESUS story: In making JESUS the sole proprietor of the title "CHRIST," we Christians not only have heaped violence upon those who are not Christians (Jews, Moslems, pagans, Buddhists, et al.), but also have disempowered ourselves as Daughters, Sons, People, and Friends of the Sacred, bearers together of the same sacred—Christic—power that JESUS experienced in relation to others in the Spirit that drew them together.

To speak of "CHRIST" surely can be, and sometimes has been, a creative way of trying to speak of a Holy Spirit that we share. This is historically what Christians at their best have tried to do. Nonetheless, given our Western minds, which have been shaped to think in "either/or" terms, it is hard for us not to get stuck in the faulty assumption that JESUS was, and is, *The* CHRIST in a unique and singular way that applies to him alone; to imagine that he—not anyone else with, before, or after him—was and is *The* Savior, who saves only those Christians who hold this "right" view of him. Others are condemned by faithlessness to float beyond the capacity of even God Himself (and it is almost always a "Him") to save them from the hellfires of eternal estrangement from God.

The problem with getting stuck in this traditional ("He, not we") Christology that turns JESUS alone into CHRIST, or God, and Christianity alone into The Religion of Those Who Are Right is that it weakens our spiritual ability to experience ourselves-in-relation to others—including non-Christians, non-humans, and everything radically "other" than ourselves—who also are God-bearing in the world.

If we are to speak of CHRIST at all as a healing and liberating Spirit, "CHRIST" must be a synonym for the risen, ongoing, spiritual presence of JESUS with us as a fully creaturely brother, or sister, seeking to be in right—mutually empowering—relation with other creatures. If we are committed to "CHRIST" in this sense, then we realize that we, like JESUS, are lured by the Spirit of justice-love into a shared commitment to be Christic—liberating, God-bearing—characters together in history.

No question JESUS walks with me, hand in hand, along the path I take today: dark prophetic brother from Nazareth; depressed sister from Chester, South Carolina, who tells me she hates being lesbian; nephew Robert turning twelve today; my friends Margaret Moshoeshoe Montjane from Soweto and Dorothee Soelle from Hamburg and Oh Dong Kyun from Seoul—you are JESUS, blessed be!

Claude Barton's cows, the dogwood and the holly, the copperhead keeping its distance as we step on by, water rushing down Dunn's Creek—step carefully with us, brother.

"He" who is also "she," "they" who are also "it"—you of multiple names and identities that reach always beyond the "self" and always beyond all notions of "other"—you sing and slither with us! you invite us to notice your presence!

You take shape in relation to us and all others being formed in relation to you, suffering sister, whoever you are for me today, wounded brother; I notice that by yourself, liberating advocate, you have no power to make justice roll down like water, and that neither do I, faithful lover, but that together, we are here to save the world—blessed be your holy names.

With you, I see that neither you nor I, nor any person or culture, nor any tribe or religion or species, nor past, present, or future holds the keys to heaven, and that only together can we save this earth and liberate one another from those who are right—thank you, JESUS, sweet sister!

We can envision ourselves in right relation: joined with JESUS of Nazareth, with Margaret Moshoeshoe Montjane, Dorothee Soelle,

Oh Dong Kyun and—in ways too mysterious to grasp—with cows, copperheads, waterfalls, and all creation in saving the world from those who are right, including ourselves when we are stuck in our fear.

Spiritual authority and knowledge of God

In order either to write such a book or to take it seriously as a reader, you and I must grant our experience considerable spiritual authority, and I do not mean by this simply our individually subjective experience. We must give authority to *our* experience as relational beings who share this planet as home. It is hard for most Christian readers to take human experience seriously as sacred source because our religious tradition has promulgated a strange notion that God and JESUS CHRIST are "above" or otherwise "outside" of human experience, life, history. We have learned that God and JESUS CHRIST have spiritual authority "over" us, as if they are Persons to whom we must look not only "outside" our bodyselves but over and against us in order to know what is right or wrong and even to know what or who we are. For us to be in right relation to such a God or His Son is to put our experience, our lives and history, under His rule and will, subject to His authority.

For this reason, "good Christians" in general and good Christian women in particular have not on the whole experienced our bodyselves as bearing our own spiritual truths. Yet we *do* bear our own spiritual truths to the extent that our spiritualities are truly of the God whom JESUS loved. This does not mean that we and *only* we bear these truths, but rather that they are, in Jeremiah's words, "written in our hearts"—yours, mine, ours, and theirs—if these truths really, truly, are of God.

But we must be careful here, especially if we are white Christians, because most Euro-American Christian theologians and churchpeople have assumed that theological truth can be "applied" universally, like a coat of paint, to all people in all places at all times.[1] Historically, such Christian theologians, priests, and pastors (mostly men of the ruling class and tribe) have attempted therefore to be "impersonal" in their teachings, trying not to be too personally revealing, experiential, or subjective, lest they draw attention to themselves rather than to that which is more applicable to "everyone," hence more fully "true." Against this effort to keep theology free of particular human experiences, Christian feminist, womanist, and liberation theologians in the West have insisted that, to the contrary, it is spiritually dishonest, politically irresponsible, and intellectually shabby to deny that our own daily lives play a major role in shaping theologies that bear any relation to reality.

At the same time, most feminists, womanists, and other liberation theologians would agree with the *claims* of Eurocentric men, past and present, that it *is* intellectually arrogant to give our own personal experiences of God, the world, others, or ourselves, an absolute spiritual authority that is over/against, or indifferent to, others' experiences of themselves and God, the world, and us. We would point out that all efforts to make sacred truth universally "applicable"—as if theology can be carried around and imposed on others, irrespective of their embodied cultures, experiences, lives, and histories—represent precisely such intellectual arrogance and theological stupidity. Yet, this is what most malestream theologies have assumed. Their protests against "experience" and "subjectivism" in theology notwithstanding, most ruling class and tribe churchmen have created "God," "CHRIST," and "church" in the image of their own privileged experience—and baptized it as universally true.

Still there *is* a truth revealed to us, not only through JESUS but moreover through living with hearts open to the world, and this is it: None of us—neither pope nor atheist, prince nor homeless mother—knows what is absolutely true about him or herself, much less about God, JESUS, or the rest of us. There *is* a way to know and love ourselves, the world, and God: *We can truly know only that which we are not afraid to love, and we can truly love only that which we are not afraid to see.*[2] Only in relation to one another can we know and love what is true. This we can do by looping backward and forward in time, crossing the boundaries of culture and religion, class and gender, ability and even species, generation to generation, person to person, now and forever. Does this mean that we must be highly educated, widely traveled, well read, or intellectually sophisticated people in order to know and love one another and our sacred source? To the contrary, the basis of the knowledge and love of God is simply a heart open to the world, to other creatures, and to the spiritual transformation that inevitably takes root in such openness or vulnerability.

What we know about God, any of us, is always being simultaneously shaped by communal forces and experienced by individual persons. Just as theological knowledge is being generated by individuals, it is also working its way into the re-creation of societies, movements, and institutions. Moreover, the more social forces and more personal dynamics are always mutually interactive, so fundamentally that it is usually impossible and pointless to ponder which comes first in either time or significance.

This dialectically dynamic interplay of social and personal is critical to this book on JESUS for two reasons: The first has to do with its origins, which are simultaneously social and personal. The book ought not to be read simply as one woman's personal statement nor primarily as a socio-political tract. The lens through which I explore the material in this project is neither simply my own life nor the life of the larger world-church. This Christology originates in the "meetings" of larger and smaller, the world of others' experiences and my own experiences of the world. If *Saving Jesus From Those Who Are Right* is read *solely* as a confessional statement or as a political manifesto for social change, it will be misread—because it is both, always both, never an "either/or," and always as much one as the other.

The second reason the dynamic of social and personal is critical to this particular project is that it carries us into the meanings of the JESUS story itself—which are simultaneously personal and social. It is simply not the case that Christian faith should be more a religion of personal salvation than a vehicle for the liberation of oppressed peoples and creatures from injustice, violence, and neglect. But it is also not true that Christianity ought to be primarily a social or political movement and only secondarily a spiritual home for persons yearning for redemption from despair, purposelessness, and loneliness. *Christianity is both and always both: a revolutionary political call and a spiritual home.* In the context of massive suffering and violence—which *is* the context of our common life—the JESUS movement is constantly generating the revolutionary and holy Spirit of freedom and liberation; in the same moment and place, it offers "a balm to heal the sin-sick soul" of each and every one of us, oppressor and oppressed, in whatever ways we ourselves are broken—in wrong relation, that is, with one another, ourselves, and the Spirit that connects us.

Hence, I use the terms "liberation" and "healing" to refer to the *same* process of salvation, a movement among us that is always simultaneously social and personal, spiritual and material. We cannot enjoy the spirituality that truly is of God unless we are enjoying the struggle for justice-love, compassion, nonviolence, and forgiveness in the world. And we cannot stay in the struggle unless we are drawing personal strength from the God whom JESUS loved, however we may experience and image this sacred power.

Liberating oppressed peoples and creatures—

Healing personal wounds, ours and others'—

Liberating us from fear, greed, and lack of confidence—

Healing peoples, nations, tribes, and earth—

It all goes together in God.

This christological project is an effort to help us come together as sisters and brothers, JESUS among us, one of us. It is an invitation to come wrestling fiercely with dynamics of good and evil that are structured tenaciously around, among, and within us. Only if we come together can we save JESUS, one another, or ourselves along this most amazing life-journey we share. My hope is that, through these pages, you will draw strength from me much as I do from you as we meet here and there. May we give to each other courage for the social, political, and spiritual tasks at hand. May the book help generate justice-love among us, ground us in compassion, teach us peace, and season our wisdom.

Like Frederick Denison Maurice, I too have no great interest in theological "systems"—and for much the same reason: they inhibit the Spirit. My aim in this book is not to produce a "systematic" Christology but rather, in the eclectic religious and theological traditions of Soelle, Buber, and Maurice, to draw from different sources in thinking about what the Sacred Spirit of all Creation is *doing* with us, through us, and by our hands.

But on what authority dare we speak of this? How do we make such claims as these—to "god," to stand *with* JESUS rather than beneath him, and to love rather than worship this brother?

Kwok Pui-lan and other Asian colleagues remind us that Eastern cultures historically have located the "self" in relation to society very differently from most Eurocentric philosophies. The distinctions between Eastern and Western ways of knowing and experiencing authority—including the authority to know anything—might be sketched as follows:

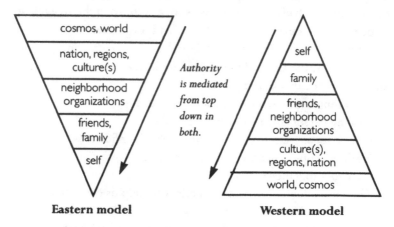

How authority is mediated. In both East and West, the normative "self" is male.

Moving from top down, we see through Eastern eyes that authority is mediated "down" to the self through larger communities, such as families, nation, religion, and even the earth and cosmos. The individual male, and especially the female, has little autonomous authority in relation to the community.

In the West, by contrast, the individual (historically, the white male) starts with himself at the top and works his way down into connection with communities of various sorts, including perhaps the earth (though, until recently, this has seemed optional). In this "enlightened" European schema, the self masters knowledge and holds authority in relation to everything, including himself. Thus, "autonomy" has become a chief psychological as well as spiritual virtue in Western societies. This faith in the "rightness" of the autonomous individual is one reason that liberal Protestantism is such a weak social force today in the West. The Protestant "self" simply cannot bear the moral weight of such social responsibility.

As a way of locating my authority to write this book and yours to read and interpret it, I propose a way of *mutuality*—that you and I truly *are* sisters and brothers struggling to connect through these pages, open to learning as we go. In this learning process, and on this journey in faith and doubt, we are involved with, and in, one another, our communities, and the earth. Moreover, what is in your self-interest—truly for your well-being—is also in mine. If we are seriously interested in our *common* welfare, we will pay attention to the needs of *each* of us; if each of us genuinely wishes to be fulfilled as a person, she or he will contribute everything possible to the well-being of the larger human and creature community. But, in the midst of this ever-expanding network of sisters, brothers, relational dynamics, and truth claims, how can we know anything for sure—about ourselves, one another, the earth, or our creative source? How can we possibly speak with authority about anything?

Spiritual authority is rooted paradoxically in humility. However strong our convictions, humility reflects a realization of our being grounded together in life. Thus, we can speak with passion and compassion only as we move confidently into the storms of opposition, listening and speaking with open minds rather than tightening up and becoming brittle in relation to those who disagree with us.

Spiritual authority grounds our confidence: we know that we can't know everything about anything, including ourselves and especially God, so we can encourage one another to turn our lives over again and again into the mystery.

Even so, we know more than we often imagine we do. And how do we know?

From a *spiritual* perspective, we can know ourselves, one another, the world, and God in at least three overlapping ways: *existentially* we can know ourselves as relational beings, each of us "boundaried" by our skin and life-experiences, and we can study the ethical and pastoral implications of this. We can know ourselves *politically*, shaped systemically and personally by various configurations of social power; we can wrestle with the meanings of this, and often we can act to affect and change these systems. We can know ourselves *mystically*, aware of the transtemporal, transpatial Sacred Spirit present with us, and we can be touched and changed through both this Presence and our awareness of it. Each of these ways of knowing ourselves can be analytical, sometimes poetic, often intuitive, usually requiring study, and always related to the other ways of knowing. None stands alone as *The* Way to know God, change the world, study our lives, or think about JESUS.

Although some will argue that these ways of knowing seem contradictory, the authority of my experience as a relational character on planet Earth assures me that, far from being exclusive of one another, each sharpens and illuminates the others. In this assertion I join Soelle, Buber, and other mystics and activists whose energies have been poured simultaneously into "larger" movements and "smaller" moments in our struggles for social, economic, and personal liberation.

Let me say a little more about these ways of theological knowing, since together they provide the basis of how I have come to the perspectives developed in this book.

We can know existentially. We can know that we are not alone. We can know our connectedness. We can know by noticing the world around and within us. We can feel, think, love, hate, laugh, cry. We can watch and listen and touch. We can taste and smell. We can notice what is what. We can seek to realize where we are, a day at a time, and we perhaps will want to know how we can be even more fully ourselves—connected, that is, in more mutually empowering ways.

There is nothing "self-absorbed" about knowing oneself as a relational being. To the contrary, not to be self-reflective in relation to the world ordinarily leads us to non-reflective self-preoccupations and obsessions. We cannot know much that is true of us or others unless we are noticing and paying attention to what is happening around and within us, and to what it may mean for us and others here and now. Without some honest existential knowing, we are bound to get lost in the fragments of our "selves" and become "smaller" people, increasingly afraid of relating to the world beyond our individual agendas.

We can know politically. We can see, if we are paying attention, that not only are we not alone—we seldom are in right, mutual relation with one another. For many of us, this is especially evident in relation to people whose race/tribal culture is not our own and to those who suffer poverty, hunger, and other socioeconomic oppression more or less than we do. We also may notice wrong relation between men and

women; adults and children; younger and very old people; a heterosexist majority and a sexually "queer"[3] minority; those who are relatively able-bodied and those who are more physically challenged;
Christians and those who observe other religious or spiritual traditions or none at all; and the relation of the United States to other
nations.

We can begin to know ourselves politically—that is, to understand
our social power—as we become aware of our wrong relation with
others. As such, political knowing emerges from our experiences of
the struggles for social justice and change and often also for personal
transformation in relation to justice-work. Political knowing can be a
way of making connections between the larger and smaller places of
our life together—connections based on systemic and structural patterns of power in our midst.

The most creative political knowing is rooted in a commitment to
justice-making; an ability to think critically about power in a particular context of injustice; a willingness to pay special heed to those at the
margins and on the bottom of our common life,[4] and some personal
vulnerability to being touched and changed by what we are learning,
knowing, and teaching. Without critical work, political awareness is
likely to remain superficial and rhetorical. Without personal vulnerability, liberation theologians can become arrogant ideologues, thereby
undercutting our own deeply human capacities to embody and bear
witness to many of the very changes we believe are critical.

We can know mystically. We can know the Source of Life as our own
source. We can know that we breathe this breath of God, that we sip
from this river of compassion. We need no mediator other than our
own intuitive senses of connectedness to all saints and sinners, mar-
tyrs and cowards, all creatures, human and other, who have walked
this earth, and maybe other spheres as well. We can experience the
Spirit as erotically empowering—that is, as the origin of our yearnings to connect deeply with one another, and as source of our own creativity and of our capacities to struggle for liberation.[5]

At the end of *Touching Our Strength: The Erotic as Power and the Love of
God* (1989), I included a small poem about mutual relation and the
sacred power/God that meets us there. The poem grew out of a
dream I had had during an early period of recovery from alcoholism

and bulimia in which I was struggling to make connections between
the more explicitly political dimensions of my commitments (solidarity with people of Central America, anti-racism, women's ordination,
gay/lesbian liberation) and the more traditionally personal experiences (death of my father, vocational struggles, recovery from addiction, and "personal relationships"). The poem, called "Opening,"
signaled my opening into a realm of mystical knowing that would not
so much change, but rather secure, my theological work from that
point on.

> they are so old and many
> the women brown, gray, and wrinkled,
> bent and broken, sparkling, spirited
> some I recognize, many I don't
> and a sprinkling of men, children,
> other creatures with them
> and they gather round me and press
> in close, and lay their hands
> upon me, and touch me with their cheeks
> and paws, and I hear them say
> *you can draw your strength from us.*
> years later, bone-tired
> of stubborn fears, gods,
> words, rules,
> my own resistance, I surrender—*yes.*
> open your hands
> not to hold but to touch
> open your heart
> not to take but to meet
> you will be my sister and
> *you can draw your strength from us.*[6]

In the poem, I am surrounded by others who reach out to me. Not
until I "surrender" my attachment to "stubborn fears, gods, words, and
rules," however, am I able to be touched and changed.

Until the publication of *Touching Our Strength,* folks rather easily
could categorize my theological efforts as those of a "feminist liberation theologian." Certainly, in the larger and deeper scheme of things,
this still is true. But my understanding of everything important—
including the aims of feminism, the work of liberation, and the
ground of theology—has been refreshed by a spiritual intuition and

assurance that everything truly *is* connected, that we really *are* part of one another, and that each of us actually *can* draw strength simply from knowing deep in our souls that we are not alone. Although mystical knowing had been the earliest source of my theological knowledge, it was not until I began to curb my substance addictions, beginning with alcohol, that I began to reawaken to the mysterious path that leads me—and us as we walk it together—more fully into radical engagement with the world.[7]

These three ways of theological knowing inform this work and are "lenses" into our life together on planet Earth. All three ways of knowing, which we can (but seldom do) experience simultaneously—except in astonishing moments of *kairos*—are held together in our lives and work. Existential, political, and mystical knowing together form the basis of a theology that is hard to categorize as being simply "a theology of liberation," or a "liberal," "political," "pastoral," or "systematic" theology.

We know that we inhabit the earth at a moment in history in which many varieties of creatures, along with humans, are endangered. What can we know, and learn, about this crisis existentially, politically, and mystically? What can we know, learn, and teach as spiritual sojourners on this planet?

Existentially, our primary theological wellspring is the capacity actually to *experience* our lives, feel our emotions, think well, drink deeply from the present moment, and know what, in fact, we are doing. Our intellectual focus is on our lives in relation and what we can learn from ourselves—our feelings and fears and dreams—about the world. We may wonder, for example, to what extent we ourselves are endangered and to what degree how we live is putting others in harm's way. We may be aware, through prayer and work and daily lives, of our own connectedness to other creatures, human and other-than-human. We may experience and image God as our Spirit in relation to these others in mutually empowering ways—be they people of other religions, races, classes, or gendered identities, or creatures of other species.

But theologians cannot think simply about our own experiences, our daily lives, our dreams and visions, histories and struggles, our people and the world as we best know it. Without both the political and the mystical dynamics that push and pull us beyond ourselves and what we most intimately may know as ours in any given moment, we get stuck in a framework of reference that is too small for much spiritual enlargement beyond our own personal concerns.

The critique of "experience" as the basis of theological knowledge has been an ongoing accusation against feminist and liberation theologies, usually by academics schooled in European epistemologies (theories of knowledge). There is, as I have noted, some validity in the critique, but not what most of these critics have had in mind. The problem is not that "experience" is merely a "subjective" and therefore unreliable category. After all, *all* theologians work experientially, although most traditionally (patriarchally) educated men and women learn not to recognize the experiential biases of their own work. The problem with much of what has been called "experiential" theology is not that it is "subjective" but rather that its subjects have not been radically relational enough in our work—especially in relation to those whose lives and social locations are different from ours in terms of class, race, culture, religion, and other factors. "Experiential" theology must be critiqued, for example, whenever white Christian feminists like myself fail to take seriously the lives of people and creatures whose experiences not only are not "like" ours, but moreover often challenge the theological affirmations and denunciations that we have come to through our white women's lives.

Over time, some white women theologians have begun to realize the importance of making "experience" a more *dialogical—relational—* category, especially in relation to women with remarkably different experiences and existences from white middle and upper strata Christian women. It has been in this context of enlargement, intellectually and politically, that feminist liberation theologians of different colors, classes, and cultures and of various spiritual traditions and sexual/gender identities have become increasingly "political" in our theological knowing.

Politically, therefore, our primary theological source is our capacity to think critically, to analyze structures and systems of power relations. We do so in order to better understand who has what kind of power in our life together on earth, and how these experiences of power and powerlessness inform—indeed, often actually generate and shape—ours and others' experiences of God, JESUS, other people and creatures, and the earth itself. Intellectually, the focus here is on the larger patterns of connection—the structures and systems—in which all of us play various parts.

Recognizing the theological and ethical problem of endangered human and other creatures as a political problem means that, as theologians, we have to think about such issues as toxic waste not as isolated social problems, but in relation, for example, to racism and classism (into whose neighborhoods are most of our wastes and poisons being dumped?), the economy (why is so much poison being generated and who is profiting from this?), and the complicity (often through silence) of so much of the Christian church. Politically, we may begin to imagine the Sacred Power in organizing creative resistance to the poisoning of the planet—and the related genocide being done to the poor and often dark inhabitants of our cities.

One of the charges leveled against feminist and other liberation theologians has been, from the earliest days of Black (African American) theology in the United States, that it is too "political"—therefore, not "spiritual" enough. This criticism, of course, carries a very different understanding of both God and the world from liberation theologians' assumption that God is, radically, *in* the world and that the so-called "political" and "spiritual" dimensions of our life together not only are inseparable but often refer to the same experience, viewed through different interpretive lenses.

Another concern being voiced today by radical Christian theologians from non-Western cultures, as well as some radical feminists in the United States, is that the Western mind is trained in such highly individualistic (a danger in existential knowing) and/or rationalistic (commonly associated with political thinking) ways of knowing. It is true that we cannot think only in those Western political—socially analytical—modes of thinking in which most white progressives have been educated and be serious about the work of liberation. Feminist and radical Asian and African theologians often understand more clearly than most Euro-American Christians that, of course, *mystical*—non-rational, mysterious, numinous—experiences and the daily existence of each and every person in relation are fundamental theological resources *for liberation*. We do not have to, nor can we, rely solely on

Western political and social theory as a radical theological resource. There is simply not enough psycho-social-spiritual space in most white Western theology for the sort of non-rational—mystical—knowing that often takes shape among people in relation to ancestors who have died, creatures other than human, and dimensions of human experience that we cannot "reach" either through reason or by ourselves.

It was as a four-year-old girl that I had what I would later name as my first mystical experience—the emergence in my life, in 1949, of "Sophie Couch," my imaginary playmate, who took the form of a little Black girl of my own age. She was my first God-image and, as such, my early compass toward the recognition that race, sex, and class do matter in our lives. What I learned through this imaginative childhood adventure is that we can know more than we think we can. We can know more than we can when we are thinking too rationally about what is real or what is happening.

Years later, well into adulthood and early in sobriety, I would reconnect with the Sophie-character—Sacred Power—stirring through life, including mine, and I would know more than I ever thought I could about many things, including the holiness of creation in all its members. Such social problems as the poisoning of the planet not only would interest me ethically and politically. They would begin to shake me at the core of my bodyself. I would know that, like you and with you, I am being poisoned, and that every rock and weed is groaning with us, and I would be moved to listen as carefully to the "language" of the tufted titmouse on the feeder beside the porch as to Katha Pollitt's fine political analyses in *The Nation* magazine.

Just as the political expands existential knowing, the mystical stretches and deepens the political. Yet we cannot simply soar away into realms of mystical imaging and still be grounded theologically in the struggle for right relation, which is what theological integrity involves. Good theology is steeped in and shaped by our godding here on planet Earth, participants in a world that we ourselves help co-create now and forevermore. Theology ought to be neither an escape into a never-never land of fantasies and visions nor an intellectual puzzle that is so often a large step removed from, and cooler than, our passion for justice.

Theological imagination

Existential, political, and especially mystical knowing are tools of *theological imagination*. And what do I mean by "imagination"?

Imagination is, first, a recognition that there is more going on than we can realize. Whatever we know something to be, it is always more than what we know. This is true of JESUS, and it is true of what we know of God. It is true of what we know of the earth, and it is true of what we know of ourselves. We know we are human, creaturely—and yet we are also more than this. Our capacity to see this is "imagination," which is a root of creativity and liberation. Imagination is our primary resource for knowing more than we think we can—about JESUS and with him. Here, as so often when I am thinking theologically, I turn to my good friend and sisterly mentor Dorothee Soelle. In an early work, on the social ethics seeded in JESUS' way of being in the world, Soelle describes what she calls his "phantasy":

> Phantasy is a form of freedom which anyone can achieve during her lifetime. It comes into being like every other virtue as the result of our encounter with the world. It arises out of the education we have received and from the experiences we have had. A person can, during the course of his lifetime, become more imaginative, or, on the other hand, he can give up more and more of his phantasy. He then becomes progressively poorer in his style of living and ever more fixed in that which he refers to as his life-experience or his understanding of people. This growing impoverishment of life takes pleasure in assuming the appearance of maturity. . . . However, it is in fact a surrender of the sense for possibilities, of that phantasy which bursts all boundaries. As a person limits herself to that which she finds, which she preserves and sets in order, her spontaneity atrophies.[8]

Soelle is acknowledging in JESUS a quality of being—"a form of freedom" and "imagination"—that has been sorely lacking in the great patriarchal religions of the world, including the tradition constructed on memories of JESUS himself. No doubt because the church, in the main, has seldom been an advocate of such phantasy as a foundation of Christian life and ethics, Christian dogmatics have tended over the years to reflect little imagination and instead have upheld abstract teachings about God, JESUS CHRIST, and the church—teachings that have been for the most part inaccessible to all but the "most learned" academics.

The mainline churches' theological understandings of both incarnation and atonement, in our own time as well as historically, have been stunted intellectually by the failures of Christian leaders to pick up our beds and walk beyond the boundaries that "right-thinking" theologians have established as necessary to Christian faith. This book is one effort to re-image the heart and soul of Christian theology. To do so will mean pushing boundaries—intellectually, politically, and spiritually—thereby parting theological and political company with many brother and some sister theologians, past and present.

Kwok Pui-lan has coined the term "dialogical imagination" to describe how some Asian theologians are working with biblical texts:

> The Chinese characters commonly translated as dialogue mean talking with each other. Such talking implies mutuality, active listening, and openness to what one's partner has to say. Asian Christians are heirs to both the biblical story and to our own story as Asian people, and we are concerned to bring the two into dialogue with one another. . . . The act of imagination involves a dialectical process. On the one hand, we have to imagine how the biblical tradition—formulated in another time and another culture—can address our burning questions of today. On the other hand, based on our present circumstances, we have to reimagine what the biblical world was like, thus opening up new horizons hitherto hidden from us. . . . The term *dialogical imagination* describes the process of creative hermeneutics in Asia. It attempts to convey the complexities, the multidimensional linkages, and the different levels of meaning that underlie our present task of relating the Bible to Asia.[9]

"Dialogical imagination," a term with roots deep in the soil of Asian Christian experience, is a relative to my understanding of "mutual relation." Both images insist upon the "complexities" and "multidimensional linkages" of real life situations filled with disjunctures and interpretive problems, such as those encountered by Asian Christians who are attempting to study a document like the Bible, which meets them through alien culture and history.

In response to the arrogant theological assumptions of white Western Christians who too often assume that "we" alone know how to do theology, including feminist liberation theology, Kwok suggests that we might open our own minds—indeed become more dialogically imaginative ourselves in the sense of moving beyond the theoretical and political boundaries set by particular interpretive schools as the only, or right, way to god. Otherwise, we Western Christians, regardless of how radical or feminist, invariably will approach theology as a cerebral exercise we (and our Western-styled teachers) are in the process of mastering.

"Dialogical imagination" is also akin to Soelle's understanding of phantasy. Kwok and Soelle both are describing a "form of freedom" that can prevent spiritual and theological atrophy and help generate fresh, liberating theology. I share their desire to hold in creative tension our daily concerns and experiences with those whose embodied experiences of economic, racial, gender, sexual, and other forms of social power are different from our own. Moreover, I believe our theological challenge is to realize that the "politics" of our lives (for example, the many, multiple meanings of being white in a racist society) can be understood most fully insofar as we study our lives in relation to others by means of multiple resources, not just one theoretical tool. More importantly, our lives can more fully embody the struggle for justice.

Cultural history, oral tradition, family albums, poetry, drama, novels, song, dance, and arts and crafts of many forms become serious theological resources—*as* important as anything we may encounter in the great libraries of Western intellectual history. So also do the myriad ways we can learn to listen not only to those people whose voices we may never have heard (or taken seriously) before but also to creatures of many kinds on the earth and in the sky and water.

Minerals and plants and living earthcreatures of many kinds are all children of the Sacred. They are our theological teachers. Their voices and visions become intelligible to us through mutual relation, a way of being that we can share more fully through such relational processes as Kwok's "dialogical imagination" and Soelle's "phantasy." Phantasy, dialogical imagination, mutuality are ways of drawing upon and generating Sacred Power—and of knowing what we know existentially, politically, and mystically. So what do we know—about JESUS and ourselves, God and the world?

Postmodern origins: Pitfalls and possibilities

Long before Foucault,[10] feminists were in a sense "postmodern" philosophers who understood that all knowledge is partial and that

every theory in every field represents a particular standpoint or perspective. It seems that the Christian Right's "standpoint" is that standpoint theory in Christian theology is heretical; that "those who are
right," be they liberal or more conservative, do not accept as legitimate others' perspectives on JESUS, God, or other spiritual and moral
matters. But what of the rest of us; do we not assume that our perspectives are "right"?

For example, I have said that Christology begins with the experience of a loneliness at the heart of things. Do I not believe that I am
"right" about this? Do I not believe this very strongly? Why would I
spend years on this project and pour my heart, mind, and intellectual
energy into it if I didn't think that I'm onto something really significant—"right" indeed! And if I do believe I'm right—and, moreover,
that many other Christian theologians who write books have been
wrong, or at least less right than I am, about JESUS—then what is the
difference between my attitude here and, say, the attitude of Pat
Robertson of the Christian Coalition and Christian Broadcasting
Company, or Bernard Cardinal Law of the Boston Archdiocese?

At first glance, the obvious difference between my work and theirs
is social *power*—by "power" here, I mean "clout"—an ability to move
society, shake things up, and instigate change—for example, simply by
calling the press. Bernard Law and, even more, Pat Robertson have
immense social power, including access to wealth (actual personal
wealth in Robertson's case) and to other men with political, economic,
sexual, racial, and religious power. For either of these men to assume
that he is "right" about anything that matters to others is much more
socially powerful and, in that sense, dangerous than anything most academics, especially lesbian feminist theologians, might write. Without
social clout, arrogance is more a pity than a danger.

But there are arenas in which I, and others like me, do have clout—
in liberal and radical religious circles, among feminists and other social
reformers, in queer religious communities, among academics in religion and gender studies, sometimes in other academic or professional
fields as well. In these contexts, there is nothing, in my judgment, more
damaging to our efforts to build stronger justice-loving movements and
institutions than the smugness and arrogance that we sometimes meet
among sisters and brothers whose values and commitments we share—
indeed, an arrogant attitude that we ourselves at times embody.

There is a vast difference between, on the one hand, the theologian who is excited about her work, knows she's onto something important, and knows she's right about it—and, on the other hand, the theologian who not only is excited and knows she's right but who also assumes that no one else can match her, that others have little to teach her, and that she herself must mentor those more ignorant, less learned, more naïve, or less capable than she. "Those who are right" never think they have much to learn from others, except those who agree with them. They surround themselves with students, assistants, and admirers who constantly will assure them of their "rightness."

Postmodern theory challenges the notion of anyone being "right" about anything, so limited and fragmented is our knowledge, regardless of how expert we may be. I find this postmodern skepticism refreshing. It is helpful to be reminded that our knowledge *is* only partial, especially in theology. Paul said it well—"Now we see only dimly . . . through a glass darkly" —a postmodern perception, if you will.

But it is also true that postmodernism is a philosophy that, if taken to the extreme—wherein everything we can know is so partial that we can never know the whole, only the fragments—seems to challenge the basis of Western *theological* epistemology (or how we know anything at all about what is sacred to us). After all, the very notion of a Christian (or Jewish or Moslem) *theos* (deity, god) denotes a unifying force, spirit, and image. Postmodernism's rejection of the idea of a "whole" and of anything that can be known as "one" would seem to refute faith in a Spirit that moves history and draws us toward something, a realm of peace and unity in which "the lion will lie down with the lamb."

We who work with a great deal of relativity in both the content and methods of what we do need to be aware of how far we may be moving from postmodernism's cynical eschatology—that nothing can ever be known fully or presumably loved completely, for in the end, as in the beginning, all we have, and all we are, is fragments. It may be that, in our theological reflections, we will sometimes find ourselves a little more at home with the epistemology of the Pope or Billy Graham than with those academics who would reject the real presence of a loving Spirit in order, ironically, to protect the integrity (wholeness!) of their commitment to limits and pieces.

But postmodernism's primary contribution to this book (and increasingly to feminist theologies) is in its questioning of the concept of "identity" and "identity politics."[11] From a postmodernist perspective, we are not only partial and limited in our perceptions; we are also partial and limited in who we are—women, for example; white women; white lesbian women; white lesbian Christian women; white lesbian Christian women who raise animals; etc. For several decades now, many feminists, womanists, and other theologians of liberation and justice have enthusiastically endorsed such a notion of "identity" as basic to the theological task. A person's "particularity," we've often called it, virtually shapes her life and work, her politics and spirituality, what she is able to notice and what she isn't. This assumption has formed the basis of a feminist epistemology (theory of knowledge) that has now spanned several generations of feminist theology.

For example, most feminist women, like most people in general, have tended to define ourselves as either "lesbian," "straight," or "bisexual," and, in some cases, as "transgendered" as well. Moreover, we have learned the political importance of identifying ourselves in our work as "white women," "African American women," "Asian women" or "Asian American women," "Hispanic women," "Native women." We have learned that this is the most honest and constructive way we can begin to take some responsibility for the historical shapes and consequences of our own lives. For many a woman, this lingering on the detail of her own racial/ethnic, class, and gendered story has been an indispensable step not only in her own healing and liberation, but moreover in her relation to the liberation of *other* women as well.

Recently, however, some postmodernists have begun questioning the static, well-boundaried shape that "identity" often has taken. In her book *White Women/Race Matters: The Social Construction of Whiteness*, Ruth Frankenberg theorizes that *race* is constructed much like any other ideology and that to ascribe certain characteristics to any people on the basis of race is to naturalize and legitimize qualities that have come to exist through the political and mental gymnastics of oppressors. So too with both *gender* and *sexuality*, which have been constructed as fixed as unchanging categories by those who have stood to gain wealth and other forms of social power by defining "woman" as a certain "kind" of person and by naming "homosexual" as a sick or sinful deviation from "normal" (hetero)sexuality.[12]

Thus, the most significant question being raised today about our "identities" of race, gender, and sexuality is whether in fact they are true. Is it not likely that we humans are much more fluid than these various identities allow? Might, for example, "heterosexual" and "homosexual" be bogus categories, constructed for the purpose of controlling those whose ways of being are not in keeping with the requirements of the dominant culture? What if the ongoing creation of these sexual "identities" over the last century has deepened the divide between "gays" and "straights" so sharply that many of us (both straight and gay) have begun actually to believe that because "God made us this way," we are all stuck with a God-given "orientation" which is fixed and immutable? This naturalizing of sexual identities, or orientations, has become almost a credo of the *liberal* church at the turn of the twenty-first century.[13]

I hope that this book might help loosen us a bit from these fixed, rigid, and very "right" senses of *who we are*. For where our boundaries are tight, there is little room for the creative Spirit to bend us playfully and boldly into whatever we may yet be.

* * *

In my own life, this "loosening" has included my moving away from full-time professional responsibilities. Having labored happily and fruitfully in full-time seminary teaching, I began some years back to realize that my vocational energies needed a re-lease. It seemed to me that the Spirit needed permission to make a new path and find a new rhythm through my work. In order for this to happen, I needed to give myself more time and space away from professional accountabilities; to let myself be more a teacher, less a professor; more a mystic, priest, and writer, less an academic. I had begun to sense that, only insofar as I could get planted in some fresh vocational soil, might I be able to keep working creatively. So along with several other women, I got some land and a few small houses in western North Carolina. After more than two decades on its faculty, I cut back to half-time teaching at the Episcopal Divinity School in Cambridge, Massachusetts, and, with my land-companions, began to form a small, loosely knit community of writers and activists not far from the Pisgah National Forest.

This book is a first-fruit of these renewed theological energies, drawn from the healing energies of the mountains, streams, and woods of North Carolina, in which animal friends and trees, political workers and students, neighbors and construction workers have been my most constant companions. Through ongoing involvement with feminist, queer, and anti-racist activities on college campuses, in churches and other gatherings of local communities; through some political campaigning (on behalf of Harvey Gantt in his second unsuccessful bid to unseat Jesse Helms); through Twelve-Step programs; through relationships and work with church folks and academics in this and other parts of the world in all of our complexities; through ongoing work with students, faculty, and other colleagues at the Episcopal Divinity School, including our shared, sharpened commitment to anti-racist and multicultural foundations for theological education; through quiet times and empty spaces as well as clutter and business; through a spicy combo in North Carolina of National Public Radio, country/bluegrass/Gospel music, and Billy Graham and local Christian broadcasters; and certainly through the faithfulness of family, friends, and collegial companions around the globe, I have been, in Marcus Borg's words, "meeting JESUS again for the first time."[14] And out of our meeting, this book.

3. Our Power in Mutual Relation

. . . . .

Who or what is this "God" whom JESUS loved? What is this Spirit that infused the life of the brother from Nazareth and also fills and spills over in the lives of all creatures great and small, if only we will cooperate? I suggest here that God is our Sacred Power in the struggle to generate more fully mutual relation, in which all of us, not just a few, are empowered to live more fully just and compassionate lives. Injustice, or oppression, is both source and consequence of evil—non-mutual power relations of domination and control. We are urged in and by God to struggle for justice, peace, compassion, and liberation.

And it is not simply we humans who are involved in this Trinitarian (radically relational) "godding"—all creatures are part of the ongoing processes of life and liberation in the world. We humans seldom see this or let ourselves realize it. Our romanticizing of "nature" is one of the ways we avoid taking other creatures seriously as members of our Body.

God's Power and Spirit are ours, as they were JESUS of Nazareth's, insofar as we are making justice-love in the world, in smaller and larger realms of our life together. There is no arena too small, and none too large, for God's power to be shared and celebrated.

. . . . .

There are some standing here who will not taste death until they see that the kingdom of God has come with power.

JESUS, according to Mark

The problem with authoritarian power

It was so hard and sad, holding you as you lay dying, my body pressed against yours, my hands kneading your warm, thick fur.

You, precious beast, were so fully present—vulnerable, unsure, trusting.

You tucked your head beneath my stomach, your face into my left palm. I rubbed your nose.

Bones pressing bones: one body, you and I.

We breathed together in that awful moment, wanting so badly, both of us, to "go with"—the way we'd always done it: the essence of your dogness, my humanness, our friendship.

O Teraph![1] slowly and sadly, it was happening; I knew it (did you?): you were slipping away (or was I?)

Could you tell how much I wanted it to be a gentle passage for you, my beloved friend?

Aware that your breath was weakening, your body becoming still beneath me, I knew I could not go much further with you.

But did you know that something was pulling me into a place I had not been before in quite this way; that in my soul, the place we had grown together, I too gave up the ghost: an illusion that we can hold onto those whom we love?

—Journal, after the death of my dog, 1990

Authority, the "power to authorize" or the "ability to empower," can be held and bestowed in just and unjust ways. Authority is a morally neutral concept, neither good nor evil in itself. By contrast, "authoritarianism," the *hoarding* of authority as power over others, is always spiritually problematic. In creating or submitting to authoritarian power, we abdicate our shared spiritual capacity and moral responsibility to live deeply human lives.

Authoritarian experiences and images of JESUS CHRIST, in which we set Him above us and ourselves beneath Him, are problematic because they distance us from the Spirit that is closer to us than our next breath, that which empowers us to live more fully human lives. Looking beyond ourselves, beyond our humanness and the Spirit in our midst for right answers, we miss the Wisdom here with us now.

When we ascribe all power to a "JESUS CHRIST" who is above and beyond humankind *rather than* among, within, and between us, we step back from knowing and loving the Spirit of life the way JESUS himself did, intimately and immediately.

Putting ourselves under the authority of a deity we have created in the image of kings and lords—ruling tribe men—we turn our backs on the brother who prays in the garden and, in turning away, we allow him to be taken away again to be crucified. Once more we blame ourselves for failing to see what has been going on. Instead of realizing that we do not take our sacred power seriously enough—JESUS' and ours, for he is one of us—we imagine that we do not take JESUS' power over us seriously enough. So we raise Him up even higher and put ourselves down lower, until we hardly can bear the shame. And He reigns on, and we pray that He will forgive us. In this psychospiritual scenario, we are certain of very little, but one thing we know for sure: JESUS is Lord over us, never really one of us.

Lifting JESUS up above us, giving him an authority over us that he didn't ask for and cannot bear, we miss the point of his life, of our lives, and of the life of God.

Am I denying the divinity of JESUS? No. I am denying the singularity of his status as the Son of God. I am affirming the presence of divinity in him and moving through him. I am affirming his participation in the divine life and God's participation in him. I am affirming JESUS' "god-ness." I believe that those who knew and loved him knew and loved God. I also imagine that whenever he knew and loved others, individually and collectively, he too was knowing and loving God. I have no doubt that you and I are as much God's daughters and sons as JESUS was and, moreover, that this has been true not only of human beings but of other creatures too, from the beginning.

An important historical note here: Many African Americans point out the significance, in the context of white racism, of Black people's affirmation that JESUS *is Lord!*—JESUS, not the slave owner, is Lord! JESUS, not systems of chattel slavery or modern racism; JESUS, not the white man or woman, is Lord and Master! This is a primary reason I continue to join in worship that uses authoritarian images of

christological power such as the Lordship of JESUS CHRIST. In singing
or praying publicly to JESUS as Lord, I mean to be standing against
white people as Lord and against other oppressive structures, such as
male supremacy, which also function too often as false gods. I have
serious misgivings nonetheless that the deification of any one human
figure—even JESUS of Nazareth—is a reliable or long-standing spiritual solution to the ongoing theo-political problems generated by the
exercise of authoritarian power—in the Black Church, among feminist Christians, or anywhere else.

Regardless of tribe, gender, or our particular social locations, we
who assume that we and we alone are right about JESUS are relying
upon an authoritarian spirituality in which, even if we do not imagine
JESUS to be an authoritarian power, we ourselves function in this way.
We spare ourselves the complexities and confusions and dialogical
vitality that inhere in all life steeped in Sacred Spirit. It may be true
that those who give JESUS CHRIST all power and glory experience
fewer misgivings about God and the world than those who know JESUS
more as sibling and spiritual friend. But I think it also is likely that
those who know and love JESUS as a brother, rather than worshipping
him as a god, experience the real presence of this man and of others as
well. Still, if we who know JESUS as brother assume that our JESUS
images and Christologies are the *only* ones that convey truth or value,
we are arrogant and authoritarian in our spiritualities.

Authoritarian power has three unmistakable qualities: 1) *Power is
wielded over others.* Some dominant group or individual wields power
over others. The power may be economic or political, psychological or
physical, spiritual or intellectual. 2) *The power remains in the hands of the
dominant party.* It is a static, well-defined "possession" of those who
have it. 3) In this relationship, while the dominant figure remains basically untouched by the dynamic, *the subordinate character(s) are shaped
according to the judgment and will of the dominant.* The JESUS CHRIST of
those who are right wields this kind of power. He is Lord of all. His
power is His and His alone and, whereas those who believe in Him are
affected and transformed, He is not.

Those Christians for whom JESUS is more a spiritual friend than an
authoritarian Lord are commonly dismissed by right-thinking Christians as wrong and misguided in our faith. If we happen also to be fem-

inists, womanists, gay, lesbian, or other queer folk, we are assumed to be worse than simply mistaken—we are seen as contemptuous of JESUS CHRIST, hostile toward Him, and dangerous to His mission.

It is my thesis in this book (as well as a theme of much feminist and womanist theology) that authoritarian relational dynamics are not morally neutral conduits through which either good or evil relationships can be fed. Authoritarianism is itself an evil politic, grounded in the hoarding of power over others and dependent upon the radical subordination of their freedom and imagination, creativity and desire. All authoritarian relationships are morally inadequate, regardless of who the authoritarian figure may be, JESUS or Hitler, the Pope or Pol Pot.

How then can we who are feminists, womanists, and other liberation theologians believe *passionately* both in the Spirit of justice-love and in the particular experiences of JESUS that we cherish without falling ourselves into the very same spiritual arrogance and theological demagoguery we so deplore in the Religious Right? As one whose passion is sometimes interpreted as arrogance by theological adversaries, this is a question with which I have been wrestling pastorally and politically for a long time. The best answer I have found is this: If we really believe that others have at least as much to teach us as we have to teach them about God and JESUS, ourselves and the world, and healing and liberation—we need not worry if our passion for God and enthusiasm for justice is seen as arrogant by those who believe we're wrong.

Mutual relation: Can it be?

Theologian Tom F. Driver urges us to "participate now, in present-future time, in the redemption of the world."[2] To that end, Driver constructed a salient critique of CHRIST as "the center" of creation, humanity, history, church, and society.[3]

> To think of CHRIST as the center, model, and norm of all humanity made a certain sense in the Ptolemaic universe, which had the earth as its center. It continued to make some sense, however strained, in the Copernican universe, which had the sun as its center. Today, christocentrism cannot make sense in the Einsteinian

universe, which has *no center* and in which every structure is a
dynamic relationality of *moving* components.[4]

From a different perspective—attempting to "create a 'women'-
defined feminist theoretical space that makes it possible to dislodge
christological discourses from their malestream frame of reference"—Elisabeth Schüssler Fiorenza also has argued for the removal
of JESUS CHRIST from the center of the Christian story. She proposes
that a community and movement—the ekklesia of wo/men—rather
than JESUS himself, be the focus of our life-energies.[5]

It may seem that this is my effort here as well—with Driver,
Schüssler Fiorenza, and other feminist theologians—to shift the focus
from him to us, and thereby to "dislodge" Christology from its
malestream foundations. Certainly, I share with Driver and Schüssler
Fiorenza the latter aim—I would say, to shatter the patriarchal logic of
Christology as a historical doctrinal focus. But we cannot do this as
long as we are shifting our attention away *from* one *to* another—from
JESUS to present-future CHRIST (Driver), from JESUS CHRIST to the
ekklesia of wo/men (Schüssler Fiorenza).

Over the years I too have wanted to shift the lens—the eyes of faith
and exploration—away from JESUS himself toward the community,
the disciples, all the others within and beyond his immediate circles of
friends, then and now. In the last few years, however, I have begun to
think that this shift from JESUS to others, from him to us, perpetuates
the same problem as the "historical JESUS/CHRIST of faith" debate: It
mirrors our difficulty in finding sacred power *simultaneously* in JESUS,
ourselves, humanity, other creatures, and God; *simultaneously* in JESUS
the human brother and in his risen presence, which is no more or less
divine than his conversations with friends in Nazareth. In fairness to
Driver, whom I regard as the most christologically creative and radical theologian I have encountered, I believe that he means by "CHRIST"
the dynamic of mutuality that we generate together in the ethical
work of justice and he sees "CHRIST" no more or less in JESUS than in
you and me. He never quite makes clear how he understands the connection between JESUS of Nazareth and "CHRIST," and so he leaves me
a little puzzled about what, for Driver, JESUS of Nazareth really had (or
has?) to do with "CHRIST." Still, Driver's view of CHRIST, as I understand it, is very close to my sense of the Christic power that moves his-

tory and redeems the world, a power working through us much as it did through JESUS, who was, in fact, one of us.

I suggest that if we focus entirely on JESUS' humanity or, conversely, primarily on how different he was from all the rest of us, we will not recognize the extent to which he—and we—are called "to god" (I use this here as verb).[6] If we see God as a power incarnate primarily (or exclusively) in one historical (or heavenly) figure, then we miss our own vocation to god.

But there is a much more common spiritual scenario among Christian feminists today, men as well as women: If we experience ourselves as an "ekklesia of wo/men,"[7] as "the Body of CHRIST," or as "Christa/community,"[8] and if at the same time we do not experience JESUS and the saints as actually present with us—in the real, sensual, yearning, talented flesh of one another's bodyselves—we are also missing something: the ancestors, the witnesses, the *real presence* of every justice-loving friend who has ever walked this earth. Without the ongoing (risen) presence of JESUS and all the saints with us, which is passionate and erotic[9] to the core, our power to god does not run deep and is not very trustworthy.[10]

So then we find our sacred power neither "in" JESUS nor "in" ourselves but between and among us. God is *in* the dynamic, sparking movement among and between us, within and beyond us, beneath and above us. God is *with* all of us at once and *with* everyone else as well. This is all true, but there is more. And this "more," I believe, is the key to liberating Christology and saving JESUS:

God is not only *in* or *with* JESUS or us. The Spirit brooding over creation, the One who casts down the mighty from their thrones, this God *is* the movement that connects us all, the whole creation, through all that has been and all that will be, now and forever! This energy for justice and compassion goes among us and between us, within us and beyond us, beneath us and above us, carrying us with Her, transcending our boundaries—crossing over among us, connecting each to all,[11] wherever She goes, now and forever!

That God *is* our power in mutual relation and is not merely "in" our power makes all the difference in the world. It shifts our attention away from the individual entities and "selves" that we are, apart from one another, to the power that is constantly giving us our life together in this cosmos and, even through death, is holding us as one creation. This God *is* our Christic power, the source of all liberation and healing, the root of all repentance and forgiveness. In God is our sadness and joy; in God, our *eros* and creativity.

In the beginning is not JESUS, not you, not me. "In the beginning is the relation,"[12] and in the relation is our power to change the world. In a historical moment marked politically and spiritually by a self-absorption that is intrinsically antagonistic to mutuality, our power in mutual relation is our salvation and JESUS' as well.

My first book on the subject of mutual relation, *The Redemption of God: A Theology of Mutual Relation*, became in its German translation a "theology of mutual *relationships*" (*Beziehung*),[13] and many readers of the English text also have assumed that mutual relation refers primarily to our personal *relationships*. This is not what *The Redemption of God* was about at its core, and it is not what *Saving Jesus* is about.

Understanding relational theology to be interpersonal *rather* than social and political rests in misunderstanding its foundation—mutuality—to be merely about how we act in our one-to-one *relationships*. Mutuality is much more than right relation between friends, lovers, or colleagues. Mutuality is the *creative basis* of our lives, the world, and God. It is the dynamic of our life together in the world insofar as we are fostering justice and compassion.[14] Moreover it is the constant wellspring of our power to make justice-love.

By "relation," I am speaking of the radical connectedness of all reality, in which all parts of the whole are mutually interactive.[15] The term "mutual" has a double and simultaneous meaning, both metaphysical and ethical, mystical and moral. In the first place, "mutual" is almost synonymous with "relation." The white ash, the cat, and I are mutually related—in life together, interconnected ecologically and economically, politically and spiritually, regardless of whether we notice this. In the second place, our moral work as human creatures is to notice this connectedness. We need to help one another learn how to participate in building a world in which the radically mutual basis of our life together will be noticed and desired, struggled for, and celebrated. Ethically, the struggle for mutual relation becomes our life-commitment.

It may be that scientists and artists are more likely than many Christian theologians to comprehend the radicality of our relation. This is because relationality as the heart of God's world undercuts even the notion of a deity that is not *essentially and mutually* involved in the cosmos, the world, and history.

A theology of mutual relation is idealistic in the sense that every life lived well, on behalf of justice and creaturely well-being, *is* idealistic. But it is *not* idealistic in its recognition of the complexities, difficulties, and sufferings that we incur in our life together, including the struggle to be more fully mutual.[16] A theology of mutual relation requires us to study both the presence of our power in mutuality and our fear of it. To understand this power, we have to study our collective difficulties in generating it; hence, a relational theology puts a study, or analysis, of social power at the center of theological reflection. The primary aim of a relational theology of mutuality is to help us reconstruct our life together—systemically and personally—in ways that actually foster mutuality.

Still, it might fairly be argued that, because the concepts of both *relation* and *mutuality* carry such "soft" personal and interpersonal connotations, perhaps they should be avoided in feminist liberation theology. I have wrestled with various images and concepts and, depending upon context, use other terms for "mutual relation": justice and justice-love, compassion, connection, participation, coinherence, and erotically empowering relation. The problem of Christian theological language and interpretation in the West is steeped in the highly individualistic politic and spirituality of modern capitalism and its formative role in shaping our capacities even to think theologically. It is hard for white Western Christians to feel deeply or think clearly beyond the "self's" own interest as we understand it. All of the above synonyms for mutual relation—"justice" no less than the others—face an interpretive[17] temptation among Western Christians to start with the "self" and the self's own God images and, whenever the theological thinking might lead to significant social change, to stop there—stuck on one's self and one's own.

In this social and spiritual context, Martin Buber's work, especially *I and Thou* (1958), has secured my appreciation of the concepts of *mutual* and *relation*. Though often misread as a book simply about interpersonal relations, *I and Thou* is social philosophy. Buber was a Jewish mystic and a social theologian. He ought not to be read through the lens of Christian piety but rather as a radically relational philosopher.

From a liberation perspective, it is not enough simply to affirm "mutuality" or "mutual relation" as our interconnectedness in the cosmos, a state of being, irrespective of our ethics—what we are doing, how we act, what we value, and with whom we stand. It is never enough simply to notice that our lives are connected and that whatever affects any of us touches us all. But noticing—becoming aware of—reality is always a critical step in the process of changing it.[18]

Relational theology should be understood as a metaphysics that is built not merely on speculation but on *experiencing* one another, including the earth and other creatures in the course of our daily lives, work, and love. At the same time, relational theology must be a theo-ethics of *liberation*. It is about *noticing* the real world—our loveliness and pathos, our interconnectedness and fragmentation—and it is about *changing* this world.[19]

What then are some of the *theological* basepoints of a relational theology of liberation from a Christian perspective?

God as relational power

> "Whoever does the will of God is my brother and sister and mother."
> (Mark 3:35)

Like JESUS, we begin in relation.

Relation is not merely a reciprocal dynamic. It is the ground of our being.[20]

When JESUS prayed to God, he was acknowledging the ground of his own being.

When JESUS prayed, the Spirit of God spoke through him, opening more fully to its own purposes—and to JESUS' also, as he went with God.

The Spirit yearns through us all as well, opening through us more fully to itself.

May we pray to be opened through, with, and in God.

Christian theologians historically have worked on the basis of authoritarian assumptions about God and His relation to Man. "Patriarchy" is the hierarchical and usually authoritarian ordering of the world on the basis of the (ruling class/tribe) fathers' rights to control the world and their responsibilities to care for those under their control.[21]

Despite their patriarchal framework, certain of the earlier church fathers understood that God is a relation—a relational power—not a person.[22]

Still, even with this insight into the relational character of the divine, Christian theologians on the whole have refused to acknowledge that neither God, nor JESUS, nor the rest of us can be known and loved in authoritarian—non-mutual —relation. As a system of social control, patriarchy is a system of non-mutual relation. For this reason, love and patriarchy are incompatible. Love is mutual relation. Patriarchy is its authoritarian antithesis. Patriarchy cannot tolerate mutuality, except in matters deemed trivial and of no consequence—like "women's work" and "child's play."

We cannot worship both the radically loving God that infused the life of JESUS and the deity constructed by ruling class Christian men *in their authoritarian image.*

We cannot love both God and mammon.

In the beginning and in the end, God is a relation:

God is not a self-contained entity or a self-absorbed being.

God is love—the constant, immediate yearning and effort to make mutuality incarnate throughout the cosmos.

God is the commitment, against all odds, to justice with compassion.

God is the Spirit celebrating mutuality, the Energy generating justice, the Root of compassion, the Power in the yearning, the effort, and the commitment.

God is radically loving community, ever unfolding, changing, living, dying, and yet ever-living. In a literal sense—embodied, sensual, transformative—God is holy communion.

Thinking about "power"

"Truly I tell you, there are some standing here who will not taste death until they see that the kingdom of God has come with power." (Mark 9:1)

To think about JESUS is to think about power.[23]

Like JESUS, we too are here to bear witness to the realm of God coming with power. This is as true today as ever—and it is also as confounding to most Christians today as it was to JESUS' closest friends.

JESUS was our human brother. One of us. This is not to say that he wasn't divine. The Spirit of God was surely with and in him. The Sacred Wisdom whom Greek-speaking Christians called "Sophia" infused his life. The Source of all life and goodness, which people of the world know by many names and in many images, poured through JESUS' life and death and raised him into the future, where we who come later meet him—and God with him—in one another.

JESUS was divine in the same way we all are—together, in mutual relation with our sisters and brothers. No one of us alone is "God." God is the Holy Spirit connecting our lives, moving with us and through us.

God is our Sacred Power for healing and liberation. God was JESUS' sacred power as well.

We do not know what JESUS thought about his vocation, his call, in relation to God and the world. Did he think of himself as "Messiah," the one anointed by God to play a special redemptive role in the history of Israel? In Mark, we meet an enigmatic figure who prefers that those closest to him "not tell anyone" about him (Mark 8:27-30). We do not know exactly what he, or they, thought was going on. Whatever he might have thought about himself, JESUS seems to have been rooted deeply in a commitment to a Spirit that he experienced as available to everyone; a God who cared more about people's well-being than propriety, customs, or laws; a Source of social and personal transformation; a Wellspring of liberation and healing, judgment, and forgiveness.

JESUS' historical significance—his Christic, or redemptive, meanings—originated in his faith in the power that he experienced in relation to sisters and brothers. Thus, any discussion of JESUS is a discussion of power.

Power is ability; power is energy.

Who "has" power and who doesn't isn't as clear as most power analysts, including feminists, often suggest.[24] No one reading this book is simply "with" or "without" power, as if it were carried, like bottled water, according to one's race, class location, gender identity, age, or ability. All creatures—because we live—participate in imaging and re-imaging power of many kinds.

I may be able to use a chain saw to fell an oak, but the tree has a great deal more power than I to live in the forest amidst many generations of oak with only soil, sun, and rain as its food. I have no power to be an oak, and the tree has no power to be me. But we both have power to relate to one another and other creatures.

But what about "social power"—the economic, cultural, and customary power that certain groups of people have accrued historically, which they use to control—and often to abuse and violate—those who have less, or none, of what they have? In Western history, various particular groups of people—white people, Christians, men, wealthy classes, adults (who are not yet "too old"), to name just a few—have wielded oppressive control over other people and creatures. Such wielding and controlling is an abusive use of social power.[25]

Whenever people use whatever social power they have—economic, racial, sexual, physical, age, professional—to betray, lie, steal, beat, belittle, humiliate, or otherwise violate others, this is an abusive use of power. But it is also true that social power is generated and constructed historically. It *never* constitutes a static, total, or final advantage or privilege, and it ought not to be treated legally as if it should be unchanging.[26]

Social power, like the power of the oak to perpetuate its species and the power of a baby to laugh, is *dynamic*. It is a source of activity and movement. Social power is also specific and limited. A very rich man may have the power to control a town. But if he is in prison for beating his wife, he does not have the power to walk down the street to buy an ice cream cone.

Social power, like all power, is subject to historical change and transformation. It is not simply a given. Male gender hegemony, white racism, advanced monopoly capitalism—none of these sources of social power is simply "the way it is." They have been "constructed"—built, shaped, and given meaning—over time. Whatever has been constructed can be *de*constructed. Whatever has been built can be tumbled. Whatever has power can be bumped against until it falls.[27]

Power is a *dynamic* relational movement against the very boundaries that move against it. It is the water pushing against the dam that is holding back the water.

To argue simply that men have "power over" women, white people have power over people of color, doctors have power over patients, lawyers have power over clients, or teachers have power over students, as if this were all that needed to be said in order to understand these systems of social control, is not only a simplistic analysis of social power. It also disregards the constant, ongoing possibilities for social transformation, for committing ourselves *together* to use power differently, to build different systems and, through processes of conversion, to be "constructed" differently ourselves, as persons in relation, as races, as genders, and as professions (such as clergy, doctors, lawyers, teachers).

Thus, it is misleading to speak of "power over," "power within," and "power with" as if these moments of power were set in stone in our lives, even in our social locations.

Faith is a revolutionary spiritual struggle toward social and personal transformations of power. We need not struggle, or believe in anything, if we have resigned ourselves to the world the way we found it. At the same time (and this is the core of our complexity as earthcreatures) *changing* reality means, first of all, *accepting* it, not denying it, not pretending that it is what it isn't. This means that we must accept the fact that the social order is teeming with violence and abuse set in place through white race supremacy, male gender superiority, patterns of professional greed and exploitation, and many other massive systemic problems.

We ought not to dupe ourselves into believing that we can live in a *utopia* that, in reality, is never where we are yet. And yet, we need to keep the utopic vision alive, a realm in which we are sisters and brothers. We should be crafting our ethics, our laws, our political work, and our spiritual practices in the dynamics and tensions between the vision and the reality.

I believe that, in this creative tension, it is misleading to think of JESUS as having "power over" anyone. For if we "give" him our power, we diminish both his Sacred Power and our own, because *divinity*—his sacred power and ours—is what we generate together in the Spirit. This power is sacred *because* it belongs to no *one* exclusively, certainly not the patriarchal "god" that we have shaped in our image (and then praised for shaping us in His).

It is a mistake to imagine that JESUS had "power within" in a sense that his sisters and brothers do not. If we believe that he was a "better person" than any of us, we sell him short, and ourselves as well. It is also unimaginative to assume that JESUS' "power with" others, then or now, was an unchanging, smooth, or settled way of being in mutual relation. Mutual relation is never "settled" or easy. The struggle for mutuality—which is involved in all real loving—promises tension and turbulence. In this struggle, power is a resource like wind or sun, an energy for life.

All kinds of power can be sacred. Whether economic or racial, sexual or religious, species-based or age-defined, whenever power is used to make justice-love; to struggle for mutuality; to celebrate right relation; to generate more "power with," it is Sacred Power.

The problem with authoritarian images of God, JESUS, and ourselves is that they short-circuit the struggle for mutuality. We are disempowered by these images, made smaller than when we are our most fully human selves—our selves in right relation to one another and to the Spirit that connects us. Only when we are true to our common humanity and, even more basically, our common creatureliness, are we empowered, like the wind or sun, energized for life.

But who are "we"?

We are empowered to god. By myself, "I" am not empowered to god—but then I am never simply "by myself."[28] In the beginning is the relation.

I am not speaking *primarily* of the sort of relational encounters we call "relationships" or "personal relationships" (one-to-one or small groups of friends). I am speaking of the holy ground on which we stand together, we people and other creatures. In the beginning is *our* relation. In this radically relational situation, I am never by myself—although I may *feel* alone, or I may be in solitude.

You and I, as individuals, are forged out of *us*. *We* are the image of God—we women and rocks, we kids and slugs, we men and roses, we whales and waterfalls, we elephants and city streets.

Through *us*, the Spirit roars and spins and whispers and cries. JESUS was one of us. In the realm of Spirit, he still is.

And he is fully human and fully creaturely, and so are we

Is this a ridiculously idealistic image of our selves, beyond our capacities to imagine, much less embody a day at a time?

I think not. It is our reality, who we are here on this planet—people and other creatures together. We need to learn to live as sisters and brothers, in a spirit of mutual respect and shared responsibility for this earth and one another.

To be truly human is to live as "dependent co-arising."[29] This Buddhist understanding, unlike the popular psychological notion of *codependence,* does not refer to an emotional problem. To the contrary, *dependent co-arising* refers to our interconnectedness as creatures. It is the basis of our common life, socially and economically, politically and spiritually. Psychologically—mentally and emotionally—we need to help one another *learn to experience* this in ways that enlarge, rather than diminish, our power in mutual relation.[30] So much traditional and pop psychology, like so much of Christianity, has got it backwards, as if the self, its center and growth, were the beginning of what it means to be fully human.

Neither divinity nor humanity, neither Creator nor creature, is "self-absorbed" when in right relation with all else. Self-absorption and mutual relation are incompatible. The self-absorbed spirituality and psychology of advanced global capitalism and Western Christianity will not allow our power in mutual relation to thrive. The self-absorbed spirituality of those who are right does not permit us to be fully human. There is little room in most of mainstream Christianity today to remember the fully human brother from Nazareth or to live as his brothers and sisters.

The most powerful deity of Christianity in today's world is the Golden Calf of Wall Street, the Lord of profits that is an icon of self-absorption.

Over the past two centuries, the individual-centered anthropologies of most Protestant theologies have fit better with the evolving capitalist political economy than the more corporately based anthropologies of Roman Catholicism and Greek Orthodoxy. As we move into the twenty-first century, however, the gulf between these Christian anthropologies has narrowed to the point that the right Christian attitude has become, increasingly, one that heralds the highest value of the individual human (normally, still the *male* person) in "right rela tion" with his God and his family; his work and his neighbors; his property, his progeny, and his future.

But the Spirit that sparked the life of JESUS leaps among us, threatening to transform us, calling us to god, urging us to move beyond the capitalist spirituality of self-absorption that has captured JESUS and the church.

It is calling us to god

For too long we Christians have imagined that we have very little sacred power, little divinity, little goodness, in and among our human selves. With devastating historical, social, and personal consequences, our patriarchal religious tradition has failed to convey to us the central and most important meaning of the JESUS story—*God is with us, in the flesh, embodied among us, in the beginning and in the end.*

Like JESUS, and in his Spirit, we are created to god.

That is what it means, to be fully human/creaturely—to god.

That is why we are here—to god.

Godding is loving—*justice-loving.*

To live fully in and with humanity is to make justice-love roll down like water!

To live fully in and with divinity is to share the earth and the resources vital to our survival and happiness as people and creatures.

To god is to embody the Spirit that creates and liberates the world, She who is incarnate among us here and now, literally calling us to life moment by moment.

She is calling us to embody the image of (trinitarian) God[31]

Participants together in this fully human life, we reflect the Trinity that earlier Christian theologians presented as an image of God in relation to JESUS and themselves.[32] Despite its androcentric, patriarchal construction, the Trinity is rooted in an *intuition of mutual relation,* rather than self-absorption, as what is most fully divine and fully human. The Trinity is an image of dynamic movement, rather than static unchanging being, as the very essence of God; an image of passion and yearning, rather than dispassion or apathy, at the heart of the Sacred; an image of wholeness and holiness woven through diversity and multiplicity, rather than through sameness.

Those who shaped the doctrine of the Trinity intuited that "something" of God[33] was *in* JESUS; that this "something" had been always, from the beginning; and that this same "something" connected subsequent generations to JESUS and God. What was startling and new about the Trinity was that here were Jews and Gentiles suggesting that this "something" of God—this ineffable divine mystery—was not only beyond human knowing and speaking but was also completely in our midst, fully human and fully divine and fully with us, able to be known and loved, in the flesh.

"What if God was one of us?"[34] goes a recent song. God is not simply *one* of us. God is with and among us *all.* And we can glimpse the mystery, see the face of God, in *any* one of us, not just JESUS. The holy mystery that is our Sacred Power was in the beginning, it was in JESUS, and it is with us now. That is the trinitarian "structure" of God. It reflects the dynamic spiritual movement that *is* God.

In order to distinguish between these historical experiences of this power—the God of Israel to whom JESUS prayed; JESUS himself; and the way JESUS is connected to the rest of us—the early fathers, using relational terms that reflected their own experiences as men in the world, suggested that the One God of All is in "three persons"—Father, Son, and Spirit. (The Spirit is not "personal" in the sense that "Father" and "Son" are, but rather is a way of connecting them with the rest of us.)

Cast in this model of patriarchal social relation, trinitarian thinking in Christian history has functioned unquestionably to hold sexist power in place as ecclesiastical authority—"God is Father, so shall be His priests"; "Only men can conform to the image of CHRIST"[35]—and to contort our images and experiences of God such that they contribute to sacralizing men and boys and worshipping God in their image.

This interpretation dreadfully misrepresents God, JESUS, and the rest of us. Its consequences and causes continue to be the trivialization and too often the sacrifice of women and girls on the altars of male supremacy, "in the name of the Father, and of the Son, and of the Holy Spirit." This blasphemy against the God of love—God of mutuality and justice—is a violation of the Spirit that touches all persons who love God and their neighbors as themselves. It is not worthy of the name of JESUS, nor of your name, nor of mine.

As a theological image the Trinity, rightly understood, should *expand* our God images, not constrict them; it should *stretch* our capacities for wholeness and holiness, not shrink us; it should *sharpen* our religious imaginations, not dull our sensibilities. God as Trinity means that whatever is Sacred is *relational*, never self-absorbed; always moving beyond itself to meet the new, the other, the different, never set in its ways or stuck on itself as the only way.

A trinitarian faith rooted and grounded in the love of God would never require that people be Christian in order to be saved; that only males be priests;[36] or that others be like us in order to be acceptable to God. A strong trinitarian faith, which most surely was the faith of JESUS—in God, in himself, and in others, all in relation to one another—is never acceptable to those who are right, those for whom God must be an authoritarian power.

And how do we live a trinitarian faith? In our struggles for mutual relation, we are breaking free from the self-absorbing and authoritarian religion that distorts the image of what is most fully human and fully divine among us.

He is calling us to be holy

Looping back to my dog Teraph's death, we witness a moment of loving, dying, and letting go that was mutual. That moment, and every such occasion of mutual relation in our lives, reflects who we are created to be together. Ethically, such an image can help sharpen our commitments to building our life together so that persons and other creatures can live and die more fully in mutually empowering ways. Let us look a little more closely:

It is an image of bonding and holding, touching and mutual knowing, between creatures who have grown together as friends—each helping the other to be as really present as possible, one day at a time. It is an image of godding—in which the Sacred is not fastened to either creature but is sparking between and generated by both, and not only by both as individual creatures but as embodiments of social, political, economic, and natural histories.

At Teraph's death, not only he, as one dog, and I, as one woman, came together in this letting go. We brought with us, into the moment, all who had made us who we were as dog, woman, and friends.

How often do we experience such relational "moments" as representative, in some sense, of all who have ever loved, held, yearned, lost? Such an experience is not merely a "subjective," much less a loony, kind of notion. Does it not mark our *participation* with one another in the whole of God's life, an experience of "holiness"?

Such a moment is as real and transformative as anything that happened to JESUS or to those who touched him, like the woman who was hemorrhaging (Mark 5:28-34). Like others of us, this woman was healed *not* by JESUS per se but by the power that moved between them, between JESUS and the woman, and all others who were with them, in person or spirit.

Failing in some basic way to grasp the radically mutual character of JESUS' life, death, and resurrection, the authors of Christian Scripture do not tell us in what ways JESUS was moved and changed in relation to those whose lives he touched. How was JESUS healed, liberated, and transformed by this woman? by John the Baptist? by his mother, Mary? Peter? Mary Magdalene?

The Christian Scriptures and the vast majority of Christians who have taken the Bible to heart have not understood, because church leaders have not helped us understand, that God was no more in JESUS than in us; and that truthfully and wonderfully God really is in, with, and among us—intimately and immediately, here and now, forever and ever. Our spiritual call and ethical opportunity is to welcome this Spirit in our lives, one day at a time.

And so the lives and deaths of those we love—animal companions, partners, friends, children, parents, spouses—are always occasions to go with God again into the gratitude and grief that accompany all real loving, justice-making, godding.

When Teraph died, I entered for a moment with him into that mysterious realm beyond the boundaries of human intelligence in which I caught a glimpse of the sacred truth that both he and I are participants in the life of God, and will be forever. With Teraph, I met the Sacred again. I saw that She was as really present in the dog as in JESUS or me. Through any such experience we can meet and know and love the One who is Trinity:

- She who, from the beginning, has been the source of all loving, dying, and letting go throughout and beyond the cosmos;
- He who—at the same time, in every moment—is embodied through us in our fur and paws, our hands and hearts;
- The same Holy Spirit connecting our lives, celebrations, and griefs to those of persons and creatures in all times and places, strengthening us through the real presence of those who've gone before and those who will come after us.

In any time or place we can glimpse the whole. The entire life and purpose of God—to make justice-love—can take root in each moment of our lives and histories, our cultures and cosmos. Like a mustard seed, small and irrepressible, the Holy One needs only to be noticed and cultivated, struggled on behalf of and celebrated.

And yet . . .

Sometimes it seems that there is more death of Spirit, more death of God, more death of JESUS and of us all, than there is life on planet Earth.

"I cried out loud and none but JESUS heard me!" This was not only Sojourner Truth's experience. It was the collective experience of African American women, men, and children, generation upon generation, and, for many, it is even to this present day: black and white and brown and poor and all oppressed people; those people and other creatures who are sick, afraid, lonely, in despair or danger; those without hope, those without a prayer.

What is the theological root of racism and of other systems and structures of oppression and cruelty, depravity and unjust death? the spiritual source of the violence sealed in the self-absorption of those tribes and cultures, classes, nations, religions, and people who are

right? What of our sisters' and brothers' cries, generation upon generation, at the hands of those who are right? Where is *God* in the midst of
evil? Who is JESUS in the context of this suffering? Who are *we* in these
greedy times and cultures of self-absorption and self-righteousness?
Who or what can save the people and other creatures? Who or what
can deliver us from evil?

4. Evil as Betrayal of Mutuality

. . . . .

Those who are right usually suggest that the solution to the problem of evil is for good people to "obey" those who know what's right. This self-absorbed reasoning serves primarily to hold the power in the hands of authoritarian leaders—especially secular and religious "fathers" and parental figures. This is the basis of patriarchy. I suggest here that evil is rooted in non-mutual, authoritarian relational dynamics that, in the real world, are usually patriarchal.

Drawing on biblical texts, I explore several roots of evil in our life together: fear of our power in relation (which is, in fact, our fear of God); intolerance of ambiguity; denial (refusing to see what is actually happening); and lack of compassion, hence a willingness to do violence to one another, ourselves, and the Spirit of God.

. . . . .

> Woe to you, scribes and Pharisees, hypocrites! For you are like
> whitewashed tombs, which on the outside look beautiful, but
> inside they are full of the bones of the dead and of all kinds of filth.
> So you also on the outside look righteous to others, but inside you
> are full of hypocrisy and lawlessness.
>
> JESUS, according to Matthew

Thinking about evil

Most of us do not like to think about evil. We do not like to think
about evil because, if we are honest in thinking about it, we have to
think about ourselves. If evil is the betrayal of who we are in right relation with one another, to what extent are we involved in the doing of
evil every day of our lives?

Unless we think about evil, what it is and where it is rooted among
us, we make the mistake, often with dreadful consequences, of distancing it from us, seeing it as somehow belonging more to others
than to ourselves. "The Devil," or "Satan," is precisely such a Christian
invention[1]—a device by which historically we have been able to locate
the source of the problem somewhere else rather than in the soil of
our own lives together here on earth.

It is easy to point fingers at the Nazis, at Pol Pot's Khmer Rouge, at
the Hutu and Serbian strongmen who waged genocidal wars against
their people. It is easy to name as evil those individuals whose violent
behavior evokes public outrage: Ted Bundy, Timothy McVeigh, the
"Unabomber," and, even as I write, the three white men accused of
lynching James Byrd in Jasper, Texas, in June 1998.

It is easy to blame systems such as slavery and capitalism; structures
like racism, sexism, classism, and anti-Semitism; and attitudes such as
misogyny and homophobia.[2]

It is harder to examine how our own lives in particular are implicated, often in mundane ways, in the doing of evil, the betrayal of right
relation. But unless we see that we ourselves are never far away from
evil, we cannot participate in its undoing. We Christians routinely
pray, "Forgive us our trespasses as we forgive those who trespass
against us. And lead us not into temptation but deliver us from evil."
This chapter is an exploration of what this "evil" might mean, how we

think about evil and often deny it, and how we are met by images of it through the JESUS story.

Seeking answers to tough questions

There are many morally muddled places in our life together in which most of us are not entirely clear about what is good or evil, though we often have strong feelings and opinions. These often are areas in which the trade off of one "good" or "evil" for another confounds our capacities to pass judgment: Where, for example, is the greater good or evil—in clearcutting the forests for economic growth or in preserving the natural habitat for endangered species? Where is the greater good or evil—in administering justice by executing serial killers or in opposing capital punishment in order to safeguard justice for the most socially expendable among us, poor black men, who disproportionately receive the death penalty in a racist society? Where is the greater good or evil—in teaching young people to fight and if need be kill their enemies in order to protect themselves and others, or in teaching them nonviolence as a strong, effective way of combating enemies?

How do we discern what is more or less good or evil in situations fraught with complexity, tension, and often controversy? And what of questions even closer to home for many of us on a daily basis? Where is the good and where is the evil in our own relationships and work, our choices and commitments, our actions and inactions, our failures to care and our inabilities not to care too much, the countless ways we betray one another through what we say and what we do not say?

Obedience to the Father = the "right" answer

In response to questions of good and evil, authoritarian religion offers the simplest possible answer: *obedience* to the Father, meaning by this both God and His human surrogates here on earth. I have suggested that the image of JESUS CHRIST as Obedient Son of His Father is one of four primary christological images that are implicit in most right-thinking Christian efforts to shape popular consciousness of how our families and societies ought to be ordered.

Socially, this arrangement requires a strong parental figure—a Father or His stand-in—whose role, right, and responsibility are to rule, and children who in turn must obey the rules of their Father/parents. This means that while all humans are "children" in relation to the Father God, some humans, like God, are "father" to most other humans. The human fathers, like God, have a right and a moral responsibility to demand and reward obedience and to punish disobedience. Is it any wonder that so many Christian men and women justify the "disciplining" of wives and children in the Spirit of JESUS and His Father?

In an earlier theological work,[3] I suggested that "erotic power" refers to our deepest yearnings for right, mutual relation. Our erotic power is our sacred power. Through dynamics of domination, however, our erotic power is skewed and twisted. In the patriarchal context of authoritarian religion, it breeds an ethic of obedience. Through patriarchal socialization, many people develop masochistic connections (emotionally, spiritually, and somatically) between the desire for God (to be known, loved, and protected by the very source of our being that we have learned to image as our "Father") and our embodied sensibilities (feelings) that this spirituality requires that we be disciplined for our "sins" (the countless ways we go against our Father, failing to obey His rules, letting him down).

On the other side of this spiritual twist is the sadistic experience shaped out of an identification with the Father God, whereby many men and some women feel deeply the connections between the yearning to be like God through the exercise of male (or surrogate male) headship, parental discipline, and an embodied sense of erotic fulfillment through disciplinary rituals.

In either case, as the sadistic father/parent or the masochistic subordinate, these psychospiritual patterns reflect the authoritarian core of patriarchal Christianity. The doctrine of *atonement* historically has been the primary theological vehicle by which the church has attempted to understand these patterns of father-right and paternal responsibility, specifically of how the father "rights" the relationship between Himself and His disobedient children.[4]

If, however, there is a more fully divine and human dynamic than obedience at the heart of our life in the Spirit, the whole basis of the Christian understanding of atonement and of the cross at its center might be transformed. This intuition is basic to how I experience and understand JESUS as healing presence, and it is central to this book.

Obedience, I am suggesting, is an uncreative, spiritually lazy, and often damaging response to the love of God.[5] While it may be the simplest way to teach children (of any age) right from wrong, it also guarantees that children will not develop the capacities for the inner-discernment and moral-reasoning that accompany mature life in the Spirit. F. D. Maurice suggested that a child who is taught merely to submit to the will or opinion of parent or teacher will "grow up a contemptible coward, crouching to every majority which threatens it with the punishments that it has learnt to regard as the greatest and only evils."[6]

It is, of course, harder to learn how to think ethically, how to determine what is right and wrong, than simply to do what we are told. But suppose JESUS or, for that matter, any of the prophets, saints of God, or others to whom we look for inspiration had simply done what the religious or secular leaders of their times and places had dictated.

And yet, did JESUS not "obey" God, however we may image God— as Father, Parent, Spirit, Mother, whatever? To be sure, obedience is a time-honored image of the relationship between JESUS and the One he experienced as his "Abba" (dad). But we need to be mindful here of the extent to which JESUS used the image of obedience *to God* as a foil to the requirement that he obey religious and secular authorities. Like many African American Christians, JESUS submitted himself to the Source of all Creation, rather than to the rulers of the state; to the Spirit of the law, rather than the letter; to God, not mammon.

We, too, are urged by the Spirit, the One yearning for right relation, She who is hungry for justice to roll down like waters, to obey God rather than the authoritarian principalities and powers of our times and places.

But it is my thesis in this book, following the theological suggestions of Maurice and Soelle, that even in relation to God, "obedience" is a misleading metaphor. It suggests that God is a power *over* us more than a Spirit *with* us; that God speaks *down* to us more than God yearns for our companionship; and that God needs *obedient children* more than friends. It is my thesis here that the Spirit of Life needs us as loving partners, needs us to be spirited participants in a movement for justice-love in the world. In anthropomorphic terms, surely God calls us often to be God's siblings, sometimes God's children, and even sometimes God's parents, for in as much as JESUS was God's child in the world, so too was God JESUS' child, one who came more fully to life through JESUS' faith and work.[7]

What might be a more creative image than "obedience" to characterize our relationship with God, and also a more liberating response to the problem of evil? I am suggesting here that *mutuality*, rather than obedience, is the basis of our life in the Spirit, and that learning to share our power in mutual relation is the most redemptive response we can make to the problem of evil.

Sin, evil, and fear

> we cannot do much
> good, cannot be kind
> or generous people,
> unless we get clear
> about the evil we do:
> the betrayal and demolition
> of whatever is most alive
> through our scrupulously crafted
> self-controls and absolutely
> unwavering
> determinations
> to be perfect

"Scrupulosity" is a spiritual problem: trying so hard not to "sin," not to make mistakes. In contemporary psychological parlance, scrupulosity is "perfectionism," beating up on ourselves because we can't ever seem to get it—life itself—absolutely right. People recovering from addiction often are quick to acknowledge that we represent all who suffer from "the need to be right," and that our drinking or drugging or overeating has been, to some extent, a way of coping with this. Scrupulosity is an exceptionally fussy, petty brand of perfectionism— worrying about every little detail of one's "morality," confessing to ourselves and maybe others every little snippet of fantasy or wrong- doing, constantly needing to be right, utterly self-absorbed with our "sins," trying so hard to be an obedient daughter or son to a Power that is Greater than ourselves.

Those who are right frequently are terribly scrupulous people, attentive in detail to their own—and others'—"sins." This is why they (and we can be "they") can seem so insufferable, petty, and self-righteous.

Scrupulosity is a spiritual problem because it distracts us from recognizing our *real* sin and the *real* evil that we do in it. We are so busy counting angels on the head of a pin—which new diet program to follow, how not to lose our temper next time we are angry, how to purge our sexual fantasies of all lust—that we miss altogether the elephant in the living room: our alienation from one another, which, in contemporary capitalist spirituality, is a problem of radical self-absorption.

Self-absorption is a form of deep spiritual isolation. It is a way of turning in upon ourselves so completely that we come to imagine that our own isolated selves can tell us all we need to know about God, the world, and who we are. Like alcoholism and other forms of addiction, self-absorption is "cunning, baffling, and powerful."[8] Self-absorption does not always seem "selfish." It can take the form of "doing good for others."

Among Christians, this is the form it is supposed to take. We "do" for others, not for ourselves. In fact, this inverted selfishness generates only more of the same spiritual problem that spawned it: a dualistic gulf between "self" and "other" and the objectification of both. You become my object, and I become yours. I act on behalf of your well-being rather than my own, and you act on behalf of me rather than yourself. If we are able to live this way to any degree, we are likely over time to build up resentments, or perhaps become depressed, even anguished, for having given up so much of our own lives. And if, like most people, we are unable to live such "selfless" lives most of the time, yet have long believed we ought to, we're likely to harbor deep senses of guilt and shame.

Most of us do not take to heart each day the fact that, in God, our lives are connected at the root of who each of us is and who all of us are. In this way, I fail to realize that your well-being can only be secured in relation to mine. In fact, the only way we can live really creative, caring lives here on earth, lives rooted deeply in the Spirit, is to learn to struggle together—mutually—to build communities, institutions, and relationships in which everyone's well-being is secured.

Radical self-absorption is indeed the sin of the world, and the source of our damnation—to experience *either* ourselves *or* others as if *either* we *or* they can be experienced apart from one another, objectified and used by one another—*even for doing good*. I am suggesting here that the commandment to love our neighbors as ourselves is commonly distorted through a misperception among Christians that *either* the neighbor *or* the self can be experienced and treated as fundamentally separate beings with fundamentally separate claims to basic human rights and privileges.

But is this largely a Western problem, an understanding of sin that makes the most sense in Euro-American societies, which place a spiritual and social premium on individuality and autonomy, especially for ruling class males?

Certainly, the emphasis on "self" and "other" as separate beings is a modern Western obsession. It is, moreover, the debilitating spiritual foundation of a capitalist political economy. *But neither the West nor the postmodern society holds a monopoly on the difficulties inherent to living as persons in relation and community.* Such difficulties—tensions between "community" and "self" and between real and imagined differences between "us" and "them"; problems negotiating conflicts without violence; historic alienation between groups, tribes, and individuals—provide the context, and often the basis, for human experiences of sin and evil throughout the world.

In this global context, sin is our out-of-touchness with the fact that we are in relation—that our lives are connected at the root and that this is the sacred basis of our creatureliness, our humanity, our lives together on planet Earth. Sallie McFague says sin is "not knowing our place":[9] failing to realize our inherent interconnectedness as the basis of our humanity; failing to realize that our "we-ness" is the material out of which the "I-ness" is forged in each of our lives.

Thus, our sin is in living as if we and others are, or can be, self-contained, well-boundaried, selves set apart from others—in basic spiritual, social, and economic ways on our own. Our sin is to experience ourselves and others with individual "souls" that set us apart from one another in God, "individuals" who, if we "choose," are "free" to live as participants in a common social order. Our sin is in the assumption that, at the root of our humanity and our creatureliness, we are born into the world as strangers to one another and that we are spiritually bound to become more and more autonomous, each of us on his or her own.

Our sin is in failing to know ourselves together, connected at the root of our humanness/creatureliness. It is the massive breakdown of our knowledge of one another, ourselves, and the Spirit that links our lives. It is the basis of our mistaken notion that we are set apart—that by fate, God, hard work, laziness, poverty, or wealth, we are set beyond, above, or below one another. Sin is our "pride" in this "freedom"; our delight in living beyond the constraints and liberating power of the common needs and responsibilities morally intrinsic to social beings. We *all* need food and shelter, education and health care, respect and humor. Sin is our false belief that some can have more right than others to these basic needs, especially material needs like food, health care, and housing.

Sin is a denial of our power *in relation*, our denial of the Sacred Source of our being *together* in life, not as an option but, more basically, as the very ground of our being.

Weakened immeasurably by sin, generation upon generation, we do evil without having a clue that it is *evil* we are doing—the countless ways we betray one another and ourselves: lying to those we love; turning our backs on the homeless; holding racism and other structures of injustice in place through fear, ignorance, or apathy; paying taxes that build bombs and missiles; floating through life in spiritual bubbles that seal us off from experiencing our shared Sacred Power to struggle against the systemic violence undergirding so much of our public policy as we enter a new millenium.

Sin is the false splitness between self and other, and it is the bedrock of our evil. Experiencing ourselves as split at the root, we are self-absorbed and easily afraid of others; fearful of moving together beyond the boundaries of what we believe to be our own self-interest, families, religions, races, and cultures.

Living in sin, we do evil, which is the active violation of one another, ourselves, and the Holy Spirit. Acting against the common good—which always is our personal good as well—we betray ourselves, our common humanity, our creatureliness, our power to live mutually as brothers and sisters.

Evil is what sinners do to one another and ourselves on the basis of our self-absorption and its flimsy ethical corollary, our "interest" in others. Preoccupied with ourselves, "others" become increasingly objects of our lives. (How can they help us? or How can we help them?) But this "us-or-them" basis of our relational lives, and of our ethics, is still rooted in the split between self and other, not in the relational Spirit that keeps before us the question of *how, together, we can help one another.*

What is often called "natural evil"—the damage done by earthquakes, hurricanes, tornadoes, poisonous snakes, sharks, lightning, and the aging processes by which all living things die—is not really "evil" at all. These dimensions of our lives are simply life itself, which includes loss, pain, and death as well as love and joy.

If we were not stuck so deeply in sin and broken so badly by evil, we could live more easily in community, all of us as relatives to one another, able to stand with strangers and friends alike in crises of pain and loss, death and grief, accompanying one another toward realms of peace and strength. As it is, most white Westerners, rather than building community, tend to cover up our pain, hide our grief, and look up to those who suffer without complaint. On the whole, we seek as little help as possible in our living and our dying.

Evil is the establishment of wrong relation—social policies, for example, that hold in place our fear of others, such as the Anglo majority's fear-based responses to Hispanic peoples and cultures, including the dominant culture's resistance to Spanish as one of our national languages.

Evil is rooted in our sin, and our sin is rooted in a fear of "otherness." These three deeply human experiences—fear, sin, evil—are inseparable.

Fear of the other, the different, the stranger is the chief among all the demons that Christian theologians and mythologists have named "Satan" or "the Devil."

Fear shrinks us.
It tightens our muscles,
especially our heart.

It contorts our faces (and
gives us several of them).
It distorts our vision.

We see the world
as too big for us

and ourselves as
too small for
one another
and we turn
inward
seeking safe
space.

We mistake caution
for wisdom[10] and
safety for love.

We see friends
as our enemies,
and we do not see
the enemy at all:

>   the fear
>   that is drying
>   us up—

>   "we are fine,
>   thank you."

and we are
becoming
smaller and
less vulnerable
and more
in control.

Fear shrinks us, but not just any fear—because in certain situations (frequently, those in which we do not belong) it is wise to be afraid of the poisonous snakes, grizzlies, and avalanches we might encounter. It is also wise to be cautious when we are in a violent, or potentially violent, situation. But even in these contexts, we are sometimes likely to mistake caution for wisdom, thereby giving fear the upper hand. Where courage and clear judgment might serve us well in an encounter with danger or violence, fear may cause us to freeze, physically as well as emotionally, and contribute to our victimization.

But it is not fear of violence, catastrophe, or real danger that diminishes our humanity and God's as well. It is our fear of those who are "different" that shrinks us; our fear of the "other," that which we do not know very well, if at all, and therefore that which, in our fear, we are inclined to misperceive as our "enemy" rather than as our sister/brother creature and, potentially, our friend.

This fear is our deadliest power. In the hands of "obedient children," it becomes our motive and energy to destroy one another and violate the Sacred that soars among us; to assault the One who bears our pain, evokes our hope, and encourages us when we are afraid.

Why then does a wise God create beings who can be so afraid of one another and of everything different and new?

Our fear of difference is as deeply human and creaturely as our instinctive fear of falling. We fear what we do not yet know, the bottom we have not yet hit. And this fear—of falling, of others, of the new—*becomes* our participation in sin and our basic spiritual problem. It is a critical issue for our souls, because generation upon generation we lean toward excluding and rejecting, tormenting and destroying, those whom we fear.

It is important for us to realize, however, that the same experience—fear of others, fear of difference, fear of that which we do not know or understand—can motivate us to do evil *or good*. It is at this critical spiritual juncture—in the fear that pushes us to the edge of deeper personal involvement in the sins of the world—that we are able to become "more fully human." At this juncture, we either grow more fully into our full spiritual stature, or we slip further away from ourselves, one another, and the Spirit into the grip of sin and evil.

Our fear of otherness and difference provides opportunities in which we can experience the courage to be really present in life. Without the experience of fear, we cannot take heart—have courage—to engage life in its passionate depths.

Those who know deeply what it is to fear the strange, the new, and the different can embody genuine courage in moving through their fear, becoming thereby more fully human and more fully present in life.

Together with compassion, this courage is our strongest, most reliable resource in the struggle against evil. And how do we learn courage? Through example, mentors, stories, risk taking, trial and error. There are many ways to learn courage. Obedience to those with power over us is not one of them.[11]

God and evil

Christians, like Jews and Moslems, understand God to be the source of complete and perfect goodness and have viewed evil more as a mystery than as a problem that can be solved. Proponents of these three patriarchal religions of the West largely have resisted the notion of an inherent natural or intimate connection between evil and God. They have emphasized that God is the source of good, not of evil.[12] What may seem bad or evil to us either has been attributed to the Devil (as an evil, but lesser, spirit who struggles against God) or has been interpreted as "good for us"—diseases like AIDS, for example, as teaching social deviants a moral lesson.

Through Western eyes, it is immensely difficult for us even to consider the possibility of God's involvement with evil. The idea of a God who "permits" evil is anathema to most of us. To the terrible theoretical possibility that God might be somehow involved in the doing of violence, cruelty, and injustice, questions almost unthinkable press down upon us, such as—does God participate in the raping of children? Was God implicated in the Holocaust? Is God the author of evil? Questions that we simply cannot answer affirmatively if we believe that God is Love.

But not everyone in the world frames the problem of God's relation to evil the way most Western monotheists do. For most of humankind, God is *not* imaged as a supernatural being who acts like a powerful "person": The image of God's involvement in evil-doings suggests that God is like a CEO, the head of a nation, the father of a family, or a military leader—a man or woman with the social power to accomplish certain things and prevent others. The contemporary feminist charge against the traditional patriarchal God of Christianity— that in allowing, even willing, the death of JESUS, God was a child-abuser[13]—reflects this view of God as a patriarchal power who can do whatever pleases Him, and does so, whether it is to stand back and watch as Jews are thrown into furnaces, to actively join in the gang-rape of an eight-year-old girl by her father and his friends, or to nail His own child to a cross.

There are however mystical strands in monotheism, including Christianity, which manage to hold good and evil together in ways that elude those traditions that keep the goodness of God totally separate from evil in order to protect God's reputation. *In these spiritual streams, evil is no less a moral problem but, like goodness, evil is a spiritual mystery deeply embedded in, and not extraneous to, God.*

In this mystery, God is not a supernatural person who is permitting, or doing, evil. Rather, evil is a horrible dimension of a life lived in a Sacred Spirit that is much larger and more wonderful than any evil—or goodness—we can experience or imagine.

God is not involved in evil. Evil is involved in God.

It is not that God is evil but that evil—betrayal, exploitation, violence upon violence—takes place in God's world *despite* the goodness of God. Evil takes root in our fear of many things but mainly of the socially and personally transformative power that is the goodness of God.

Western monotheists have much to learn about evil and God from Buddhism and other Eastern traditions and also from the pagan traditions, especially wicca, which Christianity historically has so feared and persecuted. Could these persecutions—the Christian slaughter of witches in Europe during the fourteenth and fifteenth centuries, and the church's ongoing assaults on women's procreative and sexual freedom—be related to Western Christian men's difficulties in accepting the mystery and vastness of God in relation to everything these men claim to know, including the patriarchal lineage of their authority?

What if this Christian *patriarchy* itself is evil? What if the patriarchal construction of "God" is an evil theological basis? What if God, the Holy One whom JESUS loved and knew, the One who meets us through the JESUS story, is infinitely more vast, astonishing, and creative than any deity constructed in the image of ruling class/tribe men or women could ever be?

JESUS and evil

I am suggesting that the experience of *betrayal* was JESUS' core-experience of evil—his own betrayal at the hands of friends in a context, much like our own, of multiple betrayals being done by people to themselves and one another.

What does it mean, "to betray"? Webster offers several definitions: From the Latin, *tradere*, which means "to deliver," to betray is: 1) to help the enemy; 2) to expose treacherously; 3) to fail to uphold [betray a trust]; 4) to deceive; 5) to reveal unknowingly.[14] Weaving together nuances of these clues, I would suggest that "betrayal" is an act of deception, which always involves *self*-deception, and which results in the delivering of someone or something (often including oneself) into the hands of an enemy whom we seldom recognize *as enemy*.

What distinguishes "betrayal" from other forms of lying or failing to speak truthfully is *the element of self-deception* that invariably moves us in the direction of hurting not only others but ourselves as well. Judas' betrayal of JESUS is an illustration. Not only JESUS but Judas himself was undone by events set in motion when Judas identified JESUS to the Roman authorities who had falsely befriended Judas. When we betray, we imagine that we are right and are thereby justified in our actions.

JESUS' *life and ministry was a struggle against evil—the treachery of betrayal*, a story not only of sleeping disciples, of Peter's denial, and Judas' betrayal but, moreover, of people's general involvement in a socio-spiritual self-deception by which they were delivering themselves, as a society and as individuals, into the bondage of obedience to a corrupt state and feckless religious leadership.

The root of the evil in JESUS' situation was not primarily, if at all, wicked *individuals* set upon destroying anything. It was common peoples' failure to realize their own Sacred Power. The people around JESUS, like most of us much of the time, assumed that they were powerless to do much about anything except perhaps in small ways to take care of themselves and their own.

Evil is the betrayal of our ourselves and one another, one day at a time, in our failures to realize, name, and celebrate the power of God that moves among us constantly, an energy that is sacred *because* it belongs to us all—all creatures, not simply to you, me, those like us, or those we like.

In deceiving ourselves that we have no power, or imagining that we have it all, we betray ourselves, one another, and the One who links our lives. We do so either by becoming passive and obedient in relation to authority *or* by placing ourselves outside the realm of social accountability to one another. While mainstream Christians and "middle America" often represent the former path of self-deception, smaller anti-social groups of survivalists, white supremacists, and right-wing

Christian ideologues represent the latter. Either way, in assuming falsely that we can make no difference anyhow, or that we can do it simply the way we want to—change the world, establish justice, set new rules—we betray ourselves, one another, and the Spirit of Life that binds us together as brothers and sisters.

We betray ourselves, one another, and God, and we secure evil's stranglehold on us when, as either obedient children or socially irresponsible renegades, we live as hostage to the fear of our shared Sacred Power to pick up our beds and walk together into the world as its co-creators, in and with God.

A fear of God who is our Sacred Power in mutual relation is at the root of all authoritarian religion, including patriarchal Christianity, and it is the basis of an ethics of obedience.

Where does this leave us in relation to God and evil?

The temptation to betray: Evil generating evil

JESUS, full of the Holy Spirit, returned from the Jordan and was led by the Spirit in the wilderness, where for forty days he was tempted by the devil. He ate nothing at all during those days and when they were over, he was famished. The devil said to him, "If you are the Son of God, command this stone to become a loaf of bread." JESUS answered him, "It is written, 'One does not live by bread alone.'"

Then the devil led him up and showed him in an instant all the kingdoms of the world. And the devil said to him, "To you I will give their glory and all this authority; for it has been given over to me, and I give it to anyone I please. If you, then, will worship me, it will all be yours." JESUS answered him, "It is written, 'Worship the Lord your God, and serve only him.'"

Then the devil took him to Jerusalem, and placed him on the pinnacle of the temple, saying to him, "If you are the Son of God, throw yourself down from here, for it is written, 'He will command his angels concerning you, to protect you,' and 'On their hands they will bear you up, so that you will not dash your foot against a stone.'" JESUS answered him, "It is said, 'Do not put the Lord your God to the test.'" When the devil had finished every test, he departed from him until an opportune time. (Luke 4:1-13)

We are tempted to make peace with the devil, the evil that surrounds and invades our lives. The temptations are daily and more or less constant:

- to fulfill our bodily hungers, our personal needs and desires, at whatever cost;
- to strive for more and more of whatever we have and want— wealth, status, fame, admiration, achievement, even "love";
- to leap into "magical thinking," stepping off the edge of our own best judgments about what is possible and what is not in our daily affairs.

Each is a temptation to betray not only others but also, always, ourselves as well—ourselves in right, mutual relation—and our power in relation, the sacred energy in our midst. We need to be aware, if we hope to wrestle courageously with evil, that it is a universal, commonplace condition of our life together.

The "temptations of JESUS," as recorded by Luke, illustrate not only the social and emotional force of the evil we encounter in ways small and mundane as well as dramatic and exceptional, but also the *moral purpose of religion*—to help us cope with evil in ways that are healing rather than by betraying who we are; to help us meet evil not with more evil—responding to one betrayal with another—but with love.

The Devil in the story is usually a larger than life "character." In a postmodern world, the Devil is a corporate, impersonal character, seldom a person with a name and face we can recognize. In fact, when we decide that someone is evil—a particular politician, criminal, or business leader, for example—we usually are short-circuiting the more honest and difficult task of finding the even greater evil in the situation.

Citing a leader of the Christian Right as evil, for example, while perhaps not always entirely inaccurate, does little to help foster an understanding of the larger evil forces—social, economic, and political—behind the individual spokesperson for these fear-based politics. The larger public evil today is not the individual right-wing preacher, ambulance-chasing lawyer, or champion of "family values" and tax-cuts, however self-absorbed such people may be. Far more evil, seductive, and dangerous is the massive, elusive structure of the global political economy, which the "haves" keep up with on Wall

Street and which the growing numbers of "have-nots" are being devoured by. It is this global capitalist network that has funded right-wing groups like the Rutherford Institute and Heritage Foundation. And it is these groups that have targeted Bill and Hillary Clinton, ostensibly for their personal flaws and failures, but more truthfully because they are perceived as representatives of the "have-nots" by networks that represent some economically powerful and politically savvy "haves."[15]

It is also important for us to realize that, as we rail against the evil being done by such senators as Jesse Helms and Trent Lott, we may easily miss noticing the evil that *we* do every day in our own lives, per-sonally and systemically, privately and publicly. Moreover, we may eas-ily miss making meaningful connections between *how* evil is driving the Christian Right and its apologists like Jesse Helms and *how* that same well-funded, consumerist, "we can have it all" lure toward self-absorption is driving us in our relationships and our work, our sexual practices, investments, and patterns of life.

The Devil who tempts us, and who tempted JESUS, seldom approaches us with horns and a pitchfork, wearing a swastika, publicly advocating violence, lies, or seduction. Rather, the evil one comes just like we do when we want something—with a smile, in a generosity of spirit, and often, as Shakespeare noted, quoting Scripture!

This Devil always has the same message for us, a message conveyed as "good news":

- *Either* our own needs or those of others matter most. We cannot both matter most, ourselves and others relative to one another, for the Devil does not permit *mutual relation*. Self-absorption is the Devil's birthplace and eternal home.
- There's nothing wrong with wanting more of a good thing—like money—provided we get it honestly and work for it our-selves. We have a right to acquire and possess anything we can.
- God will take care of us if we obey Him. The deity in this schema is a paradigm of patriarchal authoritarianism. He is the Devil disguised as the God of love.

Long before capitalism emerged as an actual historical movement, the Devil was pulling us human folk, with JESUS, into the core of what in our time has become "capitalist spirituality"—the radically distorted spiritual assumption that we can set our own lives apart from the lives, needs, and desires of others and can view their lives and well-being apart from our own.

The temptation to evil is *always* a lure toward setting ourselves and others apart, our own wishes and dreams apart from those of our neighbors, our own fears and sorrows outside the realm of *common* human and creaturely experience.

The temptation to evil is *always* to betray our neighbors and ourselves and God with us. We cannot be in right relation when we are exempting ourselves or others from our common life. Turning to ourselves *or* to others, to our own *or* others' needs as most important, our way *or* someone else's as best, we pull away from the Spirit that is our power in mutual relation, the eternal source of all that is creative, liberating, and healing.

JESUS' responses to the Devil, who was urging him to rise alone above our commonness and be a (patriarchal) god of control and possession, was to remind the evil spirit that the Jewish *Torah* does not permit this setting of one person apart from others by lifting oneself up above the kingdoms of the world—*or* by throwing oneself down.

For JESUS, right religion fosters right relation. The law and observances of Judaism are to be interpreted in such a way as to generate love—justice, compassion, and mutual respect—among all people. Anything less is an act of betrayal—of one's faith, one's people, oneself, and one's God. Anything less is truly the work of the Devil, the essence of evil.

Fear of our power in relation as root of evil: Peter's denial

Why is our fear such a force for evil? Our fear not even of things we ought to fear—violence, cruelty, neglect, isolation—but of relation! Why are we afraid to be ourselves in our Sacred Power? To be who we can be together in the world? What do we fear will happen if we live together as the people we are created to be—sisters and brothers, friends, beloved ones?

This fear of ourselves rightly related has been the psychospiritual underpinning of the anti-socialist obsession that has driven the political

economy of the United States for much of the twentieth century and
that is now driving capitalism as a global movement.

What is this fear about? Psychologists, sociologists, anthropolo-
gists, and biologists tell us: We are afraid of death, of pain, and of isolation. We are afraid of losing control, of falling and having no one to
catch us. We are afraid of our mothers and of our fathers, of being lost
in someone else, and of being lost without someone else. We are afraid
of being shamed, humiliated, and embarrassed; of being noticed at all
by certain people and of not being noticed by others. We are afraid of
God, and we are afraid of being without God. We are afraid of these
contradictions—and we are equally as frightened of being overly sim-
plified ourselves, reduced to superficial, bland portraits of ourselves
by those who would misrepresent us.

We are afraid of living in the contradictions, of holding the complexities that come with living fully in the historical moment. We
reach for quick solutions to social, political, and personal problems—
racism is a primary example (we think we have solved it through
desegregation, voting rights, etc.)—problems that beg to be experienced and understood in their complexity rather than simply "solved"
and put behind us. Indeed, such problems *must* be experienced and
understood in their complexity in order ever to be solved.

We fear complexity, isolation, and death; pain, chaos, and shame,
but more than any of these things, we fear our power, the energy that
always is sacred and always ours insofar as we share it. *We fear ourselves
in this power, which is our own capacity to god.*

And do we not fear our power precisely because we know deep
inside that if we are in it, we will be crucified? Isn't this after all what
the JESUS story shows us —that folks who god get killed? Live like
JESUS, die like JESUS. This is often exactly what happens because, to
paraphrase T. S. Eliot, humankind cannot bear much God.

If we are alive and honest, we experience some fear about what will
happen to us if we put ourselves on the line, if we take a strong stand for
anything controversial. Justice-making, because it challenges systems
and structures that hold unjust (non-mutual) power dynamics in place,
is inevitably controversial in every historical period and situation.

Normally, therefore, we demur from full participation in justice-
making. We are hesitant to leap in with our lives—"Here we are! Take
us!" (to collectivize Isaiah's image of the prophetic response to God).

Most of us play it safe. We are nice. We do not insist upon much of anything. We maintain good boundaries and do our best to stay out of harm's way. We do no evil or violence to anyone, as far as we can tell. We try to stay in control of our own lives and we hope that each person can do the same for her or himself.

We are dutiful handmaids of fear. And this chief demon rewards us in every way it can—relationally and professionally. We have as much nourishment as we need, as many "kingdoms," or realms of control, as we possibly can enjoy, and (we hope) the reward of a long and happy life.

But as frightening as the possibilities of death, pain, and great personal loss are to most of us, the most terrible fear of all is not what will happen to us if we live fully as the brothers and sisters we are called to be. Our most tenacious fear, indeed our terror, is of what we will do, what we ourselves will cause to happen, if we are alive fully in the Spirit; if we embody our power in mutuality; if we become a force for justice-making with compassion in the large and small places of our life together.

More fearful even than death for most people is, I believe, the possibility that we will live! That we will live forever! That we will see ourselves and others as radically different from what we have been taught by the dominant educational, political, and religious forces in Western cultures. What could be more terrifying than learning to see ourselves in the image of the very creatures we have learned, historically and autobiographically, to fear: snakes, rats, and sharks (human and other!)? What could frighten us more deeply than to begin to recognize ourselves in the image of those whom we most hate (violent men, liars and betrayers, arrogant rich white people, reactionary anti-Semites, homophobes, racists, sexists, those who know they are right!)?

I am not referring here simply to the spiritual image of our "oneness" together on the earth, the theological equivalent of an impressionist pastel of how our lives are linked across not only species but also moral chasms. I mean something more outrageous. More awe-ful. I mean that we actually will see and know ourselves—and others—in our goodness *and* our evil, the radicality of our rightness *and* our wrongness. I mean that we actually will experience ourselves together as immersed and drowning in the sin of the world, constantly diminished by it, *and* that we simultaneously will know that together we are liberators of this broken planet, redeemers of Sacred Power, saviors of God and JESUS and everyone else—one day at a time, step by step, in ways as slow and small as need be.

More terrifying to us than the dreadful prospect of dying alone is the strange, emotionally and intellectually challenging promise that we will live together—lamb and lion, friend and foe, victim and abuser, most beloved and most hated. And how frightening to realize that we cannot "make it" or "get there" by figuring it out rationally or by adhering to the "right" religious credo or political platform.

We get there only by moving, as prudently as we can, through our fear of those whom we hate the most. Accompanied by friends and beloved ones, we learn to swim through our fear, one stroke at a time, as if it were the river of life, which of course it is for us, as it was for JESUS:

> Then they seized [JESUS] and led him away, bringing him into the high priest's house. But Peter was following at a distance. When they had kindled a fire in the middle of the courtyard and sat down together, Peter sat among them. Then a servant-girl, seeing him in the firelight, stared at him and said, "This man also was with him." But he denied it, saying, "Woman, I do not know him." A little later someone else, on seeing him, said, "You also are one of them." But Peter said, "Man, I am not!" Then about an hour later still another kept insisting, "Surely this man also was with him: for he is a Galilean." But Peter said, "Man, I do not know what you are talking about!" At that moment, while he was still speaking, the cock crowed. The Lord turned and looked at Peter. Then Peter remembered the word of the Lord, how he had said to him, "Before the cock crows today, you will deny me three times." And he went out and wept bitterly. (Luke 22:54-62)

Had Peter known in his bones what JESUS' whole ministry[16] had been about, he'd have been more confident in the power of the Spirit—JESUS', his own, and ours—to secure him, Peter, publicly and proudly, as JESUS' friend. Perhaps his fear was not simply of being put to death with JESUS but moreover of standing with JESUS in a world in which all men are brothers and all women sisters.

This sacred realm is constantly undermined on planet Earth by crucifixions (violence, unjust death, human cruelty) and by our denials and betrayals of our friends—but it is not eliminated. In God, we meet JESUS *and* Peter as our real brothers, from whom we can learn. In God, we move from one generation to the next, sparking—inspiring—teaching—igniting our confidence in ourselves and one another together as *theotokos*, God-bearers.

In contrast to the Peter whom we see huddled by the fire, the JESUS whom we meet through the gospel narrative was largely confident in the Sacred Power of his relation with others to uphold him as he experienced rejection and denial, betrayal and even death. JESUS did not live a safe life. He was not experienced by those who held religious and secular authority as a nice person. He did not attempt to keep the peace at whatever cost. He was not in control of what happened to himself or others. He was not a respectable man. He did not let the demon fear dictate the terms of his life.

Perhaps through the shameful personal experience of having denied a brother whom he loved, Peter's faith grew. His confidence in the power of his relation with JESUS, their friends, and others grew stronger and more threatening to established authority. Perhaps the seed of this radical personal and political transformation, which would lead in time to his own crucifixion, began to grow for Peter as he "wept bitterly."

> Do not fear those who kill the body but cannot kill the soul: rather fear him who can destroy both soul and body in hell. Are not two sparrows sold for a penny? Yet not one of them will fall to the ground apart from your Father. And even the hairs of your head are all counted. So do not be afraid; you are of more value than many sparrows. (Matt. 10:28-30)

In what sense is our fear of God, our power in relation to the whole created order, a betrayal of ourselves and God? In what sense is this fear also, paradoxically, "the beginning of wisdom"?

When we live in this fear, when we are afraid to embody and show forth the creative, liberating power that is ours by God, we undermine the power of the Spirit in history. We pull against it, as if there were a character named "God" at one end of a long rope and we humans at the other, locked historically in a game of "tug-o-war," pulling fiercely against each other in opposite directions. This surely is how much Christian orthodoxy has portrayed the divine-human relation, and it is not hard to see why. History often looks and feels like a battleground between good and evil, with human beings in the latter role.

But Christian theologians seldom have reflected on God as our relational power; on our fear of God and ourselves, our own godding, as the root of our sin and the evil we do in it; or on evil as an act of betrayal against ourselves, not only God.

Fearing ourselves in our Sacred Power, we split ourselves off from God and one another. We generate oppositional, dualistic images to secure our experiences of fear. This dualistic theological (political, social, psychological) portrait—God over humanity, humanity under God, forces locked in opposition—distorts the integrity of creation and tears at the relational fabric of our lives.

F. D. Maurice is one of relatively few Christian theologians who has affirmed the *goodness* of our "fallen" creation. Without neglecting the force of evil among us, Maurice enthusiastically asserts that "human hearts have a profound sense of [Charity's][17] necessity for them, an infinite craving to possess it, and be filled with it."[18] This "craving" is driven by our relational power, the Spirit of God. It is a yearning for relation that is mutual (of benefit to all), just (right or righteous), and loving (the very essence of God/Sacred Spirit).

Sin, as Maurice sees it, is "essentially the sense of solitude, isolation, distinct individual responsibility:"[19]

> I do not know whether that sense, in all its painfulness and agony, ever comes to a man more fully than when he recollects how he has broken the silken cords which bind him to his fellow; how he has made himself alone, by not confessing that he was a brother, a son, a citizen. . . . The preaching *Repent for the Kingdom of Heaven is at hand*, has always been the great instrument of leveling hills and exalting valleys. It will be so again. The priest and the prophet will confess that they have been greater rebels against the law of love than the publican and the harlot, because they were sent into the world to testify of a Love for all, and a Kingdom for all, and they have been witnesses for separation, for exclusion, for themselves.[20]

Maurice is suggesting that for us to "break the silken cords which bind [us] to our fellows" is to experience the death of the soul (Matt. 10:28) and that this is a greater source of pain and agony than any other misfortune or violence that might befall us. This breaking of the cords that bind us to one another is our betrayal of our own humanness and of the Spirit that makes us fully human. In deserting the well-being of our sisters and brothers, we abandon ourselves.

Falling away from the image of a God who is none other than our power for creating right relation on the earth, we fall into an illusion that each of us is on his/her own, destined to be a separate being in the image of a heroic [and quintessentially patriarchal] God. We mistake individual identity for "soul" and autonomy for "freedom," and we set ourselves on paths that lead us further into social alienation and isolation from one another—and into supposing that, in our privacy, we are most clearly in the "image of God." In this spiritual condition, our sense of powerlessness sets us up, every day, to play the part of Peter as the passion story unfolds.

Intolerance of ambiguity as root of evil: Rejecting the sacred mysteries

> Do not think that I have come to bring peace to the earth; I have not come to bring peace but a sword. For I have come to set a man against his father, and a daughter against her mother, and a daughter-in-law against her mother-in-law; and one's foes will be members of one's own household. Whoever loves father or mother more than me is not worthy of me; and whoever loves son or daughter more than me is not worthy of me; and whoever does not take up the cross and follow me is not worthy of me. Those who find their life will lose it, and those who lose their life for my sake will find it. (Matt. 10:34-39)

There is a deep mystery at the heart of things, and a strong undercurrent of the irrational. Evil takes root in our resistance to that which we cannot fully understand, such as the spiritual necessity of being "set against" those whom we love the most.

We are not set against one another simply because one of us is right and the other wrong, but because we genuinely see the world differently and in our different perceptions—including our views about good and evil—we collide if we are living honest lives. If we are present to life, speaking up, standing to be counted, we will find ourselves set against one another. This is part of what JESUS is saying here.

But there is more. The standard by which we are to be measured by ourselves and one another is our willingness to suffer—bear up—the consequences of living, JESUS with us as brother and spirit-guide, in our Sacred Power. And the context of our daily lives is more one of

mystery and ambiguity than of clarity or certainty. In life, we are invited by the JESUS story not to put our faith in a religious system of
beliefs or rules but rather to "take up the cross and follow [JESUS]."

As many students of Anglican history know, Professor Frederick
Denison Maurice was fired from his teaching post at Kings College,
London, in 1853. Ostensibly, his removal was the result of a dispute
over his refusal to accept the doctrine of eternal damnation, a position
set forth in the last chapter of his *Theological Essays* (1853).[21] As Maurice scholars have noted, however, the controversy that swirled
around this publication reflected the broader theological question that
Maurice raised in his life and that we too need to be raising today:
Should theology and ethics serve our tendencies to set systems of
beliefs and rules above the contingencies and complexities of human
life; or should theology and ethics always be done in more open-
ended, dialogical processes of discovering God in our midst today?

Maurice's chief adversaries at the college in the dispute about eternal damnation understood that the doctrine of hell was an important
ethical instrument of social control, the basis of an ethic of obedience.
(Make people obey by telling them they'll go to hell if they don't, an
adult version of the doctrine of Santa Claus bringing switches to
naughty children). Maurice's opponents feared that any equivocation
of this doctrine would give license to immoral behavior among Anglicans. Maurice also understood that teachings about eternal punishment were related to human behavior as well as divine activity. He
rejected the notion of a loving God who would damn people.

Maurice was concerned that the church's popular teachings on the
subject[22] originated in a distorted experience and understanding of
what God is doing among us here and now, and of ourselves, and of
the divine-human relation. Maurice believed that the church seldom
conveyed as deep and immediate a connection between God and
humanity as is, in fact, the case through CHRIST. Christianity, in Maurice's judgement, is too much a system of doctrine and assumptions
about *future possibilities* and too little a way of life in the immediate
here and now.

For that reason, as popularly conceived among Christians, "hell"
and "heaven" referred to *future* "places" to which people's souls "go"
after our bodies die. Maurice believed that this image of a future-ori-

ented salvation and damnation was mistaken—theologically and ethically—and that "eternity" needed to be understood as an immediate,
present, and perpetual possibility. In essence, if we have fallen away
from our "fellows" today, broken the "cords" that bind us, we are in
hell right now, a spiritual place of damnation, "eternal" in its presence
beyond, as well as in, "time" as we know it. Listen to Maurice on the
subject:

> I know what it [eternal death] means all too well while you let me
> connect it with my present and personal being, with the pangs of
> conscience which I suffer now. It becomes a mere vague dream and
> shadow to me, when you project it into a distant world.[23]

It was not that Maurice rejected the idea or reality of eternal damnation, but rather that he believed that it is a perpetual state of hell into
which we fall as we break our connectedness with our brothers and
sisters. Moreover, Maurice insisted that the constancy of God—the
power and presence of love itself—was eternally stronger than our
capacity for sin and evil; and that this, in fact, was what we see through
the resurrection and eternality of CHRIST, who is the presence of God
with us:

> And if you take from me the belief that God is always righteous,
> always maintaining a fight with evil, always seeking to bring His
> creatures out of it, you take everything from me, all hope now, all
> hope in the world to come.[24]

The significance for Maurice of his affirmation of the *power*, as well
as the goodness, of God should not be missed: God is neither absent
nor powerless in history. The power of God in history, which is the
power of love itself as the cord that binds us to our fellows, is real and
strong *and dependent upon* our faith in "it"—that is, in God's presence
and power with, and through, us. Maurice understood that Christians
name this power and presence "CHRIST," by which we mean both the
risen JESUS of Nazareth and the eternal Spirit of love that we meet in
our love for our neighbors.

The church's teachings not only about good and evil but also about
human experiences of power and powerlessness need to be rooted and
grounded in a shared faith in our own power—through God—to
embody, through our life together, a deep and abiding love for our fel-
low humans.

For Maurice, our sin—the breaking of the cord that binds us—has its own historical roots in an "evil spirit" or "devil," which he experienced as a terribly real and eternal, mighty and mysterious force. Yet, the Devil was, for Maurice, a force that is eternally *less* mighty than the Sacred Power of Love, contrary to most of our rational data and perceptions, then and now, when we consider the depths of human cruelty, greed, slavery, violence, and betrayals of all sorts.[25]

So the primary *ethical* issue between Maurice and his opponents was not whether there is an evil spirit with which we must contend (for both, there was); nor whether there is a place of eternal death into which we fall through our sin (for both, there was); but rather how much license, or freedom, we should give one another and ourselves to contend against evil and to strive for good.

Maurice held out for our freedom, our moral license, to wrestle with moral complexities and, presumably, make mistakes as we live. Such freedom, Maurice believed, provides the basis and substance of our "consciences."[26] His adversaries, by contrast, proponents of an ethic of obedience, assumed that we often can avoid making at least some serious mistakes if we adhere strictly to Christian teachings.

The basic theo-ethical questions implicit in this tension, which is strong and lively among many of us today, are these: How much ambiguity and mystery can we affirm in our life together, especially in relation to our understandings of good and evil? How much license should we grant one another to make mistakes that do (or might) cause more violence, abuse, cruelty, or suffering? To what extent do we need rules and other systems of control to keep us in check? To what extent do we need greater freedom to make mistakes and learn from them?

Not only do I agree with Maurice that such freedom is an invaluable moral foundation, I also agree with him that we cannot teach one another simultaneously to strictly adhere to rules and to exercise freedom in such a way that a strong sense of conscience is developed.

In Maurice's perspective on good and evil and on the divine-human relation, there is an affirmation of the ambiguity and mystery that dwell at the very heart of the reality we share with and in God. The affirmation is not simply of all that we cannot understand. From a moral perspective, it is even more radically a recognition and acceptance of the limits of our capacities to discern, judge, and condemn.

This does not mean that we ought to refrain from passing judgment. We *must* do our best to name what is good and what is evil in our life together, what is right and what is wrong among us. We must do this clearly and emphatically and we must submit one another (including ourselves) to judgment that sometimes needs to be punitive, painful, and hard for us to bear.[27] To propose that we need greater freedom to make mistakes; to affirm the ambiguity and mystery at the heart of all that is, including God; and to accept the limits of our own capacities to discern and judge does *not* mean that we should weaken our senses of accountability to one another for knowing and doing right and wrong. It *does* mean that we should struggle to learn with one another at least three important spiritual and moral lessons:

1. *Our judgments—even of the most heinous, violent acts imaginable—are based on partial and inherently incomplete perceptions and, thus, are imperfect and limited. Even our strongest ethical positions are, and will always be, clouded with much mystery and suspension of certainty if we are honest.*

We really do *not* understand, nor will we ever know fully, the origins or multiple meanings/consequences of such terrible betrayals against ourselves and one another as extermination, genocide, slavery, torture, war, murder, rape, and millions of other forms of violence.

Yet, we cannot justify these evils simply because we do not fully understand them. We are called more deeply into the mystery of God, not toward a super-rational need to understand anything fully. In order to live together on planet Earth with any basic sense of community, we have to name *as evil* such betrayals of the creation and of the creator, of one another and of the Sacred Spirit that connects us. Moreover, whomever we know to be responsible, in whatever historical situation, must be held accountable for what they have done (and failed to do) to us all.

2. *We ourselves are deeply implicated in the evil that is being done, every day. None of us is innocent.*

This includes children and other members of creation as well as adult humans. To be "innocent" would be to be *uncreated*: uninvolved, totally *disconnected*. If we are at all, we are implicated in both the presence and the brokenness of our bonds with one another.

This does not mean that we, individually, are "evil" people, much less that infant humans or plants or animals are individually "evil." It means simply that no one of us can escape being touched by the forces that break and distort us all and that, as we age, each and every creature is, usually unwittingly and mysteriously, a participant in good and evil.

One primary sign of spiritual and moral maturity is the capacity for compassion. Buddhism, on the whole, has done a better job of teaching this than the Western monotheistic traditions, including Christianity. This is partly because Buddhism teaches a stronger sense of community and a less dualistic experience of "self" and "other." Whereas for Christians, "compassion" is often assumed to be a virtue much like kindness and generosity, for Buddhists compassion is the very essence of what many Christians name as the God who is Love.

Whenever people experience ourselves as more deeply bonded together in community, we realize ourselves as more fully involved in one another's lives, including our own and others' capacities to do right and wrong.

3. *We will not undo evil by stomping it out or distancing it from ourselves, but rather by transforming it into a different kind of energy, a force for healing and liberation.*

To co-create this world through the power of a strong, loving Spirit involves getting to know more intimately the fear and other demons that generate the evil that is in the world, including our own lives.

I am convinced that the concept of the "Devil" or "Satan" in Christian theology is itself the result of our distancing the root of evil from ourselves and projecting it onto this "totally other" image, the Devil.

A more honest image of evil—of the Devil, Satan, and the demons that generate our failures to love one another, create justice, and embody compassion—would be simply to name our fear of our sacred relational power as the source of evil, and to acknowledge that this fear is bred in moral complexities.

In this social and spiritual context, the Devil not only has a human face; the Devil *is* our fear of God. And countless "demons"—evils— are spawned by this fear, such as greed, envy, apathy toward the suffering of the world, and our sense of powerlessness in relation to political and other structures that hold the suffering and the fear in place. One such demon is our capacity for denial.

Denial as root of evil: The rich man

> As [JESUS] was setting out on a journey, a man ran up and knelt
> before him, and asked him, "Good teacher, what must I do to
> inherit eternal life?" JESUS said to him, "Why do you call me good?
> No one is good but God alone. You know the commandments. . . ."
> He said to him, "Teacher, I have kept all these since my youth."
> JESUS, looking at him, loved him and said, "You lack one thing: go,
> sell what you own, and give the money to the poor, and you will
> have treasure in heaven; then come, follow me." When he heard
> this, he was shocked and went away grieving, for he had many pos-
> sessions. (Mark 10:17-22)

Most middle strata and affluent Christians have learned along the way
that this story of JESUS' encounter with the rich man, along with the
description of early Christians as "holding all things in common" (Acts
4:32), are not to be taken *literally*. No one really believes that God
requires us to give away all our possessions in order to "follow JESUS"
and walk a sacred path in life. I think there is some truth in what we
have learned—but also something very false.

JESUS' encounter with this man is not about whether a wealthy person can live a faithful life. JESUS confronted the man, whom he loved,
with what he believed to be true. In effect, he said to this person what
he, or any lover of God, might well say to any of us: "You may have
kept the commandments and done good deeds all your life, but there's
something you haven't done. You haven't come to terms with what
you fear, and you can't do this as long as you're hiding from yourself
and everyone else—in your case, cloaked in wealth."

Wealth, in this story as in real life, is a metaphor for denial, and a
powerful one it is. It is also a mechanism that enables our denial. We
often use money as a cover-up—to hide our vulnerabilities, feelings,
deepest yearnings, and certainly our fears, as much from ourselves as
others. When we are hidden from ourselves and one another in this
way, we cannot tap our sacred relational power because we are so
frightened of it. And we fear this God because—like the rich man in
this story—we know, do we not, that if we actually go with this power
in mutual relation, our lives will be changed radically. A transformation will take place at the root of who we are.

So we slip into denial: "Money a problem in my life? What on earth
does that mean? I can assure you I don't love money more than God or

my neighbor. In fact, I use my money for good—I give to the church, to charities, to justice movements, to various causes."

But in our denial, we are out of touch with the sacred. We probably do not know we have much relational power. We may not have a clue what it means—sacred power in relation? What we *do* know is that we have money—and thereby some social, political, and economic power. And here we stand, believing (if we are conscientious Christians or Jews or practitioners of other religions) that we are doing exactly what lovers of God are supposed to be doing: keeping the commandments, worshipping God, living as responsible and respectable citizens, giving to charities, teaching our children right from wrong, doing our best by both God and our sisters and brothers.

Of course, wealth *literally* is an effective means of denial and, in our advanced capitalist society, the accumulation of wealth and the lure of possible wealth are sophisticated mechanisms for keeping the Spirit down and out. It is vital to capitalism that the Sacred *not* be tapped or recognized, precisely because God is the basis of our yearning for mutuality, justice, and compassion—which, if actually embodied and celebrated, would undermine capitalist spirituality. This is why it is even more difficult today than in JESUS' time for the rich to "enter the kingdom of heaven."

Still, the story of the rich man is not, I believe, about wealth per se, but about our proclivity, fearing God and ourselves, to hide from the Spirit that draws us toward mutuality as a way of life. Wealthy and poor alike have many ways of cloaking ourselves in denial in order to protect ourselves from God: We use alcohol, drugs, food, work, sex, shopping, sports, having children, obsessions of many kinds. We become ideologically rigid, wed to certain positions or opinions from which we will not budge. We use violence and war to make our points. We become certain in our narrow-mindedness, or in the arrogance of our open-mindedness, that we are right.

Unaware that our own addictions and self-righteousness are sources of evil in history, rich and poor alike, we are stunned to imagine that we cannot be faithful lovers of God or one another unless we come out of hiding, out of denial. With the rich man in the story, we are likely to turn away instead, grieving that we cannot have it all— our hiding places and ourselves in right relation; our fear of mutuality and our yearning to god; our love of wealth and our love of JESUS.

Or perhaps, in this serendipitous moment, we come out of our denial! And, as we do, shedding our pretensions and masks, we are likely to find ourselves afraid. But this time the fear is not of our Sacred Power, which we are experiencing anew. Our fear is of an unknown future, of all that we cannot control and much that we cannot change, including the likelihood that we will be rejected or worse by those whose ways of being are threatened by who we are and by what we are doing.

In just such a moment, JESUS speaks to us:

> Do not worry about your life, what you will eat or what you will drink, or about your body, what you will wear. Is not life more than food, and the body more than clothing? . . . Consider the lilies of the field, how they grow; they neither toil nor spin, yet I tell you, even Solomon in all his glory was not clothed like one of these. . . . So do not worry about tomorrow, for tomorrow will bring worries of its own. Today's trouble is enough for today. (Matt. 6:25, 28b-29, 34)

Lack of compassion and willingness to do violence as root of evil: The "Holy Innocents"

> Now after [the wise men] had left, an angel of the Lord appeared to Joseph in a dream and said, "Get up, take the child and his mother, and flee to Egypt, and remain there until I tell you; for Herod is about to search for the child, to destroy him." Then Joseph got up, took the child and his mother by night, and went to Egypt, and remained there until the death of Herod. This was to fulfill what had been spoken by the Lord through the prophet, "Out of Egypt I have called my son."
>
> When Herod saw that he had been tricked by the wise men, he was infuriated and he sent and killed all the children in and around Bethlehem who were two years old or under, according to the time that he had learned from the wise men. Then was fulfilled what had been spoken through the prophet Jeremiah:
>
> > "A voice was heard in Ramah,
> > wailing and loud lamentation,
> > Rachel weeping for her children;
> > she refused to be consoled,
> > because they are no more." (Matt. 2:13-18)

Rachel "weeps . . . and refuses to be consoled because they are no more." Many of our tears are for children violated through war, beatings, sexual exploitation, neglect, torture, starvation, murder. *Evil*: We know it when we read about it, hear about it, see it on the news.

But what makes us recoil from the very notion of child abuse even as, more often than most of us can bear to imagine, we ourselves are involved in it, through denial and apathy and, sometimes, as its perpetrators?

It is not simply that children are innocent, although relative to the crimes done against them, they are. Nor is it that they are powerless, although in relation to those who abuse them, they are. Violence against children is especially horrifying to us because it confronts us with our own sense not of power but of powerlessness and, along with our own collective and individual failures, with the apparent powerlessness of God—to do something, anything, to stop the atrocities! Through child abuse, we are met with spiritual questions like those that haunted Elie Wiesel as he confronted the depravity of the Holocaust: where is God as children are thrown into furnaces? Moreover, where are we?[28]

A lack of compassion and, with it, the willingness to hurt others are dimensions of human reality—the reality of evil—that confound our senses of both ourselves and God: Can *we* not do better than this? Is *God* not a holier spirit than one that could "allow" such violence to take over a nation or even a planet?

But again, the scope of the violence done against the children of the earth and against the earth itself is so vast as to propel us into a yearning for saviors to deliver us from our own apparent incapacity not to destroy one another. If we sometimes wonder why sweet, gentle little boys are so drawn to "superheroes" with names like "the Punisher" and "the Avenger," and why babyboomers have been so attached over the years to "Superman" and "Batman," we might think of these fantasy-concoctions as spiritual icons for children who are inheriting an earth filled with evil and violence from which they, and we, need protection. "The Punisher" who, with one mighty swipe, wipes out the evil forces is more interesting—and credible—to a ten-year-old boy than a story about a poor carpenter who tells us to love our enemies.

And what on earth *does* the JESUS story have to say to us, or teach us, about child abuse? intimate violence of any sort? the ravaging of the earth and its creatures? homelessness in the United States? "ethnic cleansing" in Kosovo? genocide in Rwanda? Faced with raw, unmistakable evil in the slaughter of "the holy innocents" by King Herod, what good was the baby JESUS then, and what good is he now?

The point of the JESUS story, then and now, was *not* to lure us away from ourselves toward an adoration of JESUS of Nazareth whom we have named "CHRIST." *Not* to turn us toward "God" as a spirit dwelling beyond us in the heavens. *Not* to empty us of "self-love," nor to alienate us from our sensual, sexual bodyselves, nor to invite us to submit ourselves to a god who desires our selflessness or our suffering.

The JESUS *story is about our relational power.* It is a story told to empower us. A story told to cut through the illusion that we are impotent in relation to evil. The story of the brother from Nazareth and his friends is about making connection among ourselves, building community, for the purpose of rooting and grounding the love of God in the world around and between and within us. That is the only response to evil that has a prayer of working.

The governments of the world, like superheroes, can use muscle, bombs, death chambers, terrorist units, CIA, FBI, more police, more prisons, and many threats in many forms in their efforts to curb evil, the violence being done to us all. But it will be to little avail. For violence generates only more violence.[29] This is what little boys with their plastic spidermen and their guns (toys or the real things) do not realize. It is also what politicians and governors with their capital punishment do not see. We cannot teach one another not to kill by killing those who do. We cannot engender compassion by seeking to hurt people who hurt us.

"No," many will protest, "You're an idealist, a bleeding heart liberal, trying to live in the real world. The only way to curb crime, drugs, and violence is to flex muscle!"

Like JESUS?

The Christian Right, and most of the rest us too, are simply wrong about what kind of power will change the world. Not the power of guns, punishment, or even money, but rather the power of the radical love that is mutuality that is God. In the context of massive violence and evil, such radical idealism is the only solution. Its antithesis is not "realism" but rather the cynicism that reflects a disbelief in humanity's capacity to learn and do what is right.

To believe that we *can* and, moreover, that we often *do*, struggle together to love—and that in our struggle is great redemptive power for us and others—is not to be out of touch with reality. It is to be deeply involved with and in God, "engaging the powers,"[30] changing ourselves, one another, and the world. Only love—the embodied commitment to struggle together for right, mutual relation—can work the miracles required to create justice in the midst of exploitation and peace in the midst of violence. No Batman or Punisher, no god in the image of superman, no "CHRIST" sitting at the right hand of such a god, can help us.

Living in sin, responding to evil

> Love your enemies, do good to those who hate you, bless those who curse you, pray for those who abuse you. . . . Do to others as you would have them do to you. If you love those who love you, what credit is that to you? . . . If you do good to those who do good to you, what credit is that to you? . . . If you lend to those from whom you hope to receive, what credit is that to you? . . . But love your enemies, do good, and lend, expecting nothing in return. . . . Why do you see the speck in your neighbor's eye, but do not notice the log in your own eye? Or how can you say to your neighbor, 'Friend, let me take out the speck in your eye,' when you yourself do not see the log in your own eye? You hypocrite, first take the log out of your own eye, and then you will see clearly to take the speck out of your neighbor's eye. No good tree bears bad fruit, nor again does a bad tree bear good fruit; for each tree is known by its own fruit. . . . The good person out of the good treasure of the heart produces good, and the evil person out of evil treasure produces evil; for it is out of the abundance of the heart that the mouth speaks. (Luke 6:27-28, 31-32a, 33a, 34a, 35a, 41-44a, 45)

JESUS tells us to "love our enemies" and to "take the log out of our own eye" before we "take the speck out of our neighbor's eye." These exhortations, especially the Beatitudes by which Matthew and Luke introduce one of JESUS' earliest and most memorable teachings (Matt. 5:1-12; Luke 6:20-26), have provided the inspiration for a small "nonviolence" movement among Christians and others—most notably, in the modern period, Mahatma Gandhi's work in India and Martin Luther King Jr.'s leadership of the Civil Rights Movement in the United States.

It is sometimes easy, however, for religious people—especially liberal Christians in a society ruled and dominated by Christians—to offer "nonviolence" as a *political* solution to a problem that is *spiritual* at its roots. Gandhi understood that the spiritual basis of nonviolence as a response to evil provides its most tenacious, potentially transformative power. That is why he sought as comrades those who had fought wars or known violence personally. He believed that we can only give up what we've had, relinquish what we've known, create nonviolence if we've known violence deep in our bones.

Like Gandhi and King, JESUS was ultimately concerned with the spiritual basis of our response to evil. This does not mean that any of these three brothers was "anti-material" in his experience of the Spirit, but rather that each understood spirituality as a grounding process, a path into and through the political, social, economic, and other realms of our life together.

JESUS' teachings reflect an assumption that, unless we are allowing the Spirit of love, mutuality, and justice—indeed the Spirit of "enemy-love"—to work through us, nothing we do or say will affect evil, other than to strengthen it.

We cannot undo evil with evil, violence with violence, cruelty with cruelty, fear with fear. This is the heart and soul of JESUS' teachings—and of his life, as it touches ours.

The principalities and powers of domination recognized the revolutionary social implications of JESUS' spiritual teachings and his life. This is why they killed him—to eliminate one more dangerous person, to get rid of one more prophet, teacher, brother, this holy one, this JESUS.

> It was nine o'clock in the morning when they crucified him. . . .
> When it was noon, darkness came over the whole land until three
> in the afternoon. At three o'clock, JESUS cried out with a loud
> voice, "Eloi, Eloi, lama sabachthani?" which means, "My God, my
> God, why have you forsaken me?" (Mark 15:25, 33-34)

The evil done to JESUS was no greater than that done to the people killed in the bombing of the Federal Building in Oklahoma City or to Rwanda's Tutsi peoples, slaughtered because they were born into a particular tribe.

The betrayal of JESUS—by Judas, Peter, and the people—was no different from the betrayal of anyone out of fear, greed, or confusion.

We remember the death of JESUS not because the circumstances that brought him to it were exceptional but because they were so utterly commonplace. Then and now, our crucifixions of one another remain a deep, troubling dimension of our common spiritual predicament. Evil is with us to stay.

And so too is our yearning to make justice-love, a hunger for right relation, a shared desire to embody the passion and compassion of the Spirit. Only with God can we do what is right and strive for what is good—and we are never without this holiest of spirits.

The JESUS story is about re-imaging good and evil and ourselves in relation to both. The story bursts the boundaries of religious understanding that have constricted our images of God and humanity, creation and liberation. The meanings embedded in the JESUS story, therefore, are about the limits of both Judaism, JESUS' own religious tradition, and Christianity, the newer religion named after the messianic title "CHRIST," which the church has usually applied to JESUS himself more than to the Spirit/God that connects us all—which, in truth, is more fully what the JESUS story was all about.

Recognizing our participation in evil and our power to god, we turn now to two primary (frequently oppositional) emphases in traditional Christology: *incarnation* and *atonement,* the former denoting an affirmation of the embodied character of God in JESUS; the latter referring traditionally to God's victory over evil through JESUS' suffering and death on the cross. The oppositional pull between these two emphases in Christian thought has been between "life" and "death"—interest in how JESUS lived versus a more particular focus on how he died—as the primary locus of his redemptive significance.

We will explore, in the next chapter, how either of these emphases set too far apart from the other strengthens the power of evil in history.

5. The Passion of Jesus: Beyond Moralism

. . . . .

In these pages, I am interested in helping us move beyond the moralistic self-righteousness that pretends to know what's right for all persons and creatures in all times and places regardless of how it actually affects real human and creature life. The problem with "moralism" is that it is an abstraction, an idea, usually an absolute, that gets "applied" to actual life irrespective of the consequences.

As a more liberating and compassionate response to the serious, complex moral quandaries and questions of our life together, I interpret the Passion of JESUS as the basis of how he lived in the context of similar quandaries and questions. He lived passionately. By that, I mean that he lived a fully human life—really present, deeply rooted in God, able to be there with and for others, friend and stranger alike. He was able to *be in the questions, share the quandaries*, not put himself outside or above others. There was nothing pretentious about JESUS, and certainly nothing moralistic. He was simply himself, an embodied bearer of hope and faith to sisters and brothers for whom life itself often must have seemed like a quandary of suffering and confusion.

In the midst of it all, JESUS was someone whose Passion for God was his Real Presence in life as teacher, brother, friend, and advocate. His Passion was fueled by his faith in the Spirit that, he realized, was at work in and through him—and through others.

How might we describe his Passion, which is also ours? There are many ways. In these pages, I explore three, all of them "embodied." Each involves our Real Presence as bodies with communities and histories, needs and feelings, hopes and dreams. We are bodies living among other bodies and involved together, collectively and individually, in life, love, work, and struggle. In our embodied life together, our Passion involves our "coming out" for justice-love; our solidarity with the poor, outcast, and marginalized; and often our breaking of

those boundaries that hinder the meeting of human, divine, and creaturely need.

I suggest that, like JESUS and in his Spirit, if we are living passionately, we are participating simultaneously in what Christian theologians have named the "incarnation" (God's embodied place among us)
and the "atonement" (God's redemptive action among us). God is with
us and God saves us precisely by being Really Present with us, among
us, ever a sister or brother in the struggle for more mutually empowering relation.

. . . . .

> If any want to become my followers, let them deny themselves and
> take up their cross and follow me. For those who want to save their
> life will lose it, and those who lose their life for my sake will find it.
> For what will it profit them if they gain the whole world but forfeit
> their life? Or what will they give in return for their life?
>
> JESUS, according to Matthew

Moralism as a spiritual problem

The faith that ought to open our minds and sharpen our perceptions of
the world, the cosmos, and God has too often been used to constrict
our views of ourselves and one another, the world, and God. This is
because we Christians so often are motivated spiritually by fear rather
than faith, except in the most formal sense. Frightened and confused,
we live as sheep without a shepherd.

Moralism is bred in such a spirituality of fear and anxiety. Moralism
is an ideology of rightness and a posturing of certitude that absolutizes
ideas and abstractions rather than actual relationships that are loving
and just. More specifically, moralism devalues mutuality as the basis of
justice-loving relationships.

Moralism holds the idea of "love" above the act of love. This is
because the idea of love is always a relational abstraction by which people do not grow and change, while the act of making justice-love is
always a relational dynamic through which people do grow and change.

Moralism is the conviction that we and we alone know what's right
and, moreover, that we have a moral, or ethical, duty to make others
see things our way irrespective of how actual human, divine, and other
life may be affected.

All of us, not just those on the Religious Right, are moralistic at
times, whether or not our spiritual and political systems and language
reflect this. Whenever this is the case, whatever our politics, we labor
as split people, broken apart from those who are different from us. We
are divided among ourselves (who has it right?), warring with people
outside and inside our ranks, and we are often in opposition to our
own bodyselves, split internally between a "higher" (spiritual) self and
a "lower" (sensual, material, sexual) self.

When I was fourteen, during my own adolescent white girl splitting-
into-sexual-and-spiritual-parts, I gave my life to CHRIST during a Billy

Graham Crusade. Although I still regard Billy Graham with some personal affection, I don't think the "CHRIST" I gave myself to on that occasion had much to do with JESUS of Nazareth. He was more of a coping
device. The "CHRIST"—"JESUS" and "God" all rolled into one—whom I
latched onto at the time became my spiritual beacon, a lure away from
things carnal, sensual, and real, including the real brother who walked
in the Galilean hills.

Fortunately for me, I had met JESUS earlier in my childhood, and in
years to come, through various movements in the struggle for justice,
I would begin to remember him. I would remember him as the free-
spirited character who'd met me in Sophie Couch, my imaginary playmate when I was four and five and still an only child. And I'd met JESUS
in other places too. I would remember Blackie, my snake; the clouds
outside the school; Mrs. Sossaman, who taught the second grade; and
always some new, all-purpose dogs who'd just show up and become
part of the family. Early on, I figured that this JESUS, for whom we
thanked God every morning in our family prayers, had something to
do with dogs and clouds and my parents and me and "the babies" (my
siblings) when they were born—because something about JESUS
seemed to make me glad simply to be alive and part of something
much larger than myself.

Indeed, as a little one, I was beginning to see that "the 'kin-dom'¹ of
heaven is like a mustard seed that someone took and sowed in his field;
it is the smallest of all the seeds, but when it has grown it is the greatest of shrubs and becomes a tree, so that the birds of the air come and
make nests in its branches" (Matt. 13:31-32). Just one story, the JESUS
story, about a person calling us to be larger than our own individual
selves.

The politically active Christian Right portrays JESUS as a deity who
commands and receives obedience from those who are right. But this
same JESUS CHRIST is not only an authoritarian ruler. He is also a self-
righteous moralist who reflects the image of men and women who are
sure that they, and they alone, are right in their religion, their patrio-
tism, and their ideas about right and wrong, especially those that fly in
these times under the banner of "family values."²

As a slogan of the Christian Right, "family values" signals a spiritual and political commitment to clearly delineated, hierarchically

ordered gender relations. Where such values prevail, women know their place and stay in it. Men also know their place and believe that they are obligated morally and spiritually to rule the roost. There is a chain of authority and command in the rightly ordered family— from father to mother to child, and, especially as the children age, from male to female children. This theo-political order, which is the basis of a patriarchal theocracy, is cultivated and preserved through "family values."

These values provide a code of morality fastened so tightly in patri-archal gender relations that it functions as "moralism." Rather than helping secure us in a God who yearns for the right mutual relation that ought to be the root of all morality and ethics, moralism functions primarily to hold us in our fear of mutuality, of one another, and of the God in whose movement we are called to live, love, and work. Stuck in our fear, we become moralistic mannequins who don't know how to cope with the world around us except to mimic the behavior that we believe has been practiced and sanctified by those who are right and have been right from generation to generation.

This moralism is unchanging, unbending, and therefore not open to honest questioning even by conscientious, responsible people. When we are moralistic, we do not wish to have our ideas disrupted by ques-tions or information pertaining to actual human need, feelings, or desire.

Moralism is secured in the assumption that there is only one right perspective and that those who have it are right, period. By contrast, serious discussions of *morality*—learning right from wrong—invite dialogue, questions, information. Whereas *moralism* is fastened in the assumption that there is only one right idea, regardless of how it may affect humans and other creatures, an honest effort to make moral decisions will be rooted in the belief that all of us have something to learn and that no one knows it all or ever will. Moralism is wed to abstractions that can easily be bantered about and laid down as law, whereas actual morality requires our real presence, as sisters and brothers in life, and our willingness to struggle to make right relation.

I have proposed that mutual relation is a creative challenge and redemptive response to the evil that is *always* generated through authoritarian power relations, whether from the political "right," "left," or "center." In the political, spiritual, social, and psychological struggles for a more fully embodied mutuality among all creatures, *our passion for God*—our power in mutual relation—is a more deeply moral and personally transformative response to evil than any moralism can ever be.

Theologically, my point is this: *authoritarian power relations* are the root of evil. Indeed, if the Devil has a human face, it is the face of the authoritarian ruler, the dictatorial father/mother, the prelate who knows it all. In this context, and in the face of such Satanic power, the most salvific response will always be the struggle for social and spiritual, political and personal conditions that call forth and help create mutuality as a way of life, love, and work.

From an *ethical* perspective, where authoritarian power relations prevail, *moralism* creeps over all living things like a kudzu-vine, snuffing out our capacity to breathe in the Spirit of a God who prefers the act of love to the idea of "love" and who respects honest questions and invites us to wrestle seriously with issues of right and wrong. In this spiritually deadening climate, the most socially and personally transformative *moral* response is *our passion for mutual relation*.

This chapter is an exploration of passion as a spirited moral response to evil and a creative alternative to the moralism and self-righteousness of those who are right. I am attempting here to probe the content of incarnation and atonement in human experience, so that we might see more clearly where and how God literally is embodied and acting among us—and how we ourselves "god" in the world. Through studying passion, we are looking simultaneously into where God is among us (incarnation), how God saves us (atonement), and how we participate in the redemption of God.[3]

What is passion?

As an alternative to rigid moralism, *passion* is a fullness of embodied justice-seeking life, the depth and power of an incarnate spirit of compassion; and an openness to risk and struggle in this spirit. Passion signals in-depth engagement, the inability to skim across life's surface, a fullness of life in the Spirit of justice-love, the same Spirit that is our power and desire to struggle for mutual relation.

Those who live passionately in the world do not and cannot avoid suffering. It is not that we "want" to suffer, nor that we think that suffering is "good for us." It is not that we seek out suffering for its own sake—as confirmation of our "goodness" or even simply of our capacity to *feel* and, thereby, to know that we are *alive*. None of these assumptions, which are commonplace among practicing Christians, conveys adequately the truth of why passionate people invariably do and will suffer.

People who live deeply in the Spirit suffer because there are always some who cannot bear them. Like JESUS and many before and after him, people suffer who stand up to be counted in the struggles against oppression and indifference, greed and apathy, rigid moralism, and those traditions and customs (both secular and religious) that take precedence over human needs and the well-being of both creation and Creator. People who live gladly in the Spirit suffer both because, in standing with those in need, they *feel* with them as sisters and brothers and because those who hold unjust power in place invariably are threatened by them and will hurt them.

Atonement, making *right* relation with God, occurs in the context of *wrong* relation—relation steeped in authoritarian, moralistic, violent dynamics. Consider the case of a father who is abusing a child. The father is not God. The father here is a violent man who is doing evil. The child cries out—surely this is the voice of a suffering God. The older sibling steps in on behalf of the child—surely this is an act of a liberating and suffering God. The violent father turns on the older sibling, creating even more suffering.

Whenever God is incarnate (made flesh) in any context of violence or injustice—such as by these children—atonement is underway. And this incarnation of Sacred Spirit *always* involves the suffering of those seeking right relation, both children in this case. Too often, in real life, it involves violence and bloodshed, shedding the blood of those who are struggling for justice-love, mutuality, and right relation and, as such, are acting in solidarity with their sisters and brothers.

The image of JESUS' blood being "shed for us"—as indeed, the blood of all creatures involved in the struggle to make right relation is shed for us—casts a very different light on the divine and human work of redemption from the image of either a sadistic father or a passive, obedient son. JESUS' blood and body, like that of the children mentioned above and especially the older sibling, represent the spiritual and moral power of love and the powerful moral work of acting in solidarity with those who suffer.

For Christians, the cross can be an image of JESUS' *love and solidarity, of what it cost him and what it costs all who suffer because they love.*

The cross has nothing whatsoever to do with a deity who, in the image of a father, would hand his son over to be crucified. Such a strange notion of God could only have arisen, as it did, in the midst of a patriarchal, feudal culture of static, hierarchical relationships, in which people were trying to make sense of both the extent of suffering in their midst and the apparent absence and distance of deity from the whole human drama.[4]

Participation in incarnation and in atonement as the act of solidarity is not only a spiritual event. It is also a political, social, ecological, and pastoral movement of liberation from larger and smaller forces that are cruel, violent, apathetic, or ignorant of what humans and other creatures need in order to live and thrive. Such participation in incarnation and atonement is steeped in a passion that is God's own and that we catch, through glimpses and intimations, in the JESUS story.

In a sense, passion is obsessive—preoccupied by its purpose, fixed upon its mission, filled with itself. No question that JESUS was, in this sense, "obsessed" with God and with justice-love in relation to his sisters and brothers. But in a highly individualistic and psychological climate such as the dominant culture in the United States today, an "obsessed" person is often the very opposite of passionate, for such a person is so consumed with him- or herself that s/he has no sense of connectedness with, or responsibility for, the well-being of others.

What distinguishes the passion of JESUS from such obsessive self-absorption is its roots in a Spirit that stretches us beyond the boundaries of our own skin. JESUS' passion was steeped in his knowledge of a God whose very purpose was, and is, to enlarge our senses of who we are, of what it means to be a person and a creature, by moving us toward right relation with the rest of creation. The God whom JESUS knew and loved never calls us to leave ourselves behind or forget our own worth and, at the same time, calls us never to forget that others matter as much as we do. In God, we are called to hold together our own lives and those of others as equally worthy.

The vision of ourselves struggling for right relation as mutually empowering relation—a vision of ourselves called together into being more fully human and divine—sparked JESUS' passion, and it sparks ours too, in the same struggle.

As we have seen, moving passionately as persons in the Spirit of God into right relation with others and acting with justice-love will entail:

- abandoning moralism and the authoritarian model of relations;
- acting redemptively to bring the spiritual power of love and solidarity to the present moment, while fully aware of what it cost JESUS and will cost us.

As we shall see, acting redemptively also involves:

- *radical embodiment:* building up our common body, knowing that God is in us and we are in God;
- *passionate vision:* commitment to working to build the kin-dom of God in the world;
- *passionate living in the Spirit:* through compassionate engagement, transgressing boundaries, confronting wrong, and accepting the suffering that will follow.

Knowing the body as source of passion

My friend Jim Lassen-Willems, a Christian and a Buddhist in his spiritual practices, suffers from a degenerative disease that is ripping tissues throughout his body. Jim lives in pain. A liberation theologian and passionate believer himself in the sacred character of the body, Jim has learned that *we are both our bodies and more than our bodies.*[5] Through Buddhist meditation, Jim has come to know his suffering as part of the world's own pain and his body as a member of the vast created body of human-and-other-kind. Jim is experiencing in his flesh the fact that whatever more we may also be, we are bodies, like JESUS—bundles of flesh filled with fluids and feelings, organs and orifices, needs and desires that connect us to other bodies in one network of creation. As bodies with basic needs, dreams, and feelings, we creatures are more alike than different. This is true not just among human bodies but among all bodies.

In relation, as social bodies connected to one another, human and other, we know ourselves as more than individual bodies, more than our own flesh and blood and bodily functions. Knowing ourselves as bodies in relation, we can experience transcendence,[6] our Sacred Power in relation "crossing over" among and between us. Together, we can realize that we are communal bodies, creating and destroying one another in countless ways, building up and breaking down our common body, however small (when two or three are gathered together) or large (the whole cosmos).

The JESUS story is, more than anything, about our common body as people/creatures of God. As such, we are, in Paul's words, a body of many member bodies, including JESUS. We are many bodies, human and other. We are different and diverse. Yet we have many common needs and dreams, fears and hopes, which connect us. If we know how to listen and speak to one another, our bodies can teach us much about ourselves, one another, and our embodied power in relation.

Most traditional interpretations of JESUS have not taken our bodies, including JESUS', seriously. They have failed to do so *because* they have not taken seriously our *collective* body or our power in relation as its ground and inspiration. In effect, malestream doctrines of CHRIST—of who and what JESUS of Nazareth was and is—have been constructed historically around the assumption, ancient and modern, that bodies—human and other—are a "lesser" good (if good at all) than *spirit* and are constantly in need of salvation from their own "natural" instincts. Christianity's central doctrines of incarnation and atonement have been shaped around the assumption that our bodies need to be liberated by our spirits.

There is much truth to this, as my friend Jim's condition makes clear, but it is also true that our spirits (the "more" of who we are) need to be liberated by our bodies, "brought down to earth" metaphorically and perhaps literally, as incarnate participants in shaping the kin-dom of the Spirit that calls all bodies and spirits into being![7]

The church has built its history and doctrines, and shaped the lives of its members for two millennia, on the basis of a partial truth—that our bodies need to be saved from sin and death and all kinds of trouble. However, without proclaiming as equally true the fact that our spirits need to be saved through and by our bodies from the sin of disconnection and the death brought on by dispassion, apathy, and loneliness, malestream Christianity historically has become a spiritual cult founded on the "lower" nature of the body (and, not incidentally, also of women, who have been associated with body).[8] Thus, the positive value—including the spirituality—of the body has been largely denied in Christian theology.

The way the body-denying church historically has handled the *problem* of JESUS' *body* and thus the fullness of his *humanity* has been first to deny that he died like the rest of us (he rose from the dead); and second to deny that he sinned like the rest of us (primarily a way of suggesting that JESUS was not lustful or sexually active).

Christian theologians seldom have believed that JESUS was truly and fully human. When they have stressed the presence of God "in" him, they have tended to mean that God was so fully in him that he was not really human, not like us. After all, he was a perfect being, without sin or spiritual blemish.

A half century ago, D. M. Baillie wrote that "a true Christology will tell us not simply that God is *like* CHRIST, but that God was *in* CHRIST."[9] We can be sure that this Protestant Scotsman, who was attempting to clarify the church's historic teachings on incarnation and atonement, did *not* mean that God is in *all* creation in the same way that God was in JESUS—fully in-carnate, seriously in the flesh. Baillie meant what "right-thinking" Christian theologians have always meant: that God was in JESUS CHRIST in a unique way and to a singular degree—"fully"—marking him firstborn of all creation, Son of God, indeed God the Son.

Although I believe that Baillie was mistaken in emphasizing the unique singularity of God's presence in JESUS, he and some other orthodox theologians (often catholic Christians) have been insightful, intuitively and intellectually, in *knowing* that something special, something amazing, something historically significant, was going on "in CHRIST."[10]

I believe that this "something" was not, as many Christians have suggested, the Son's "obedience" to the Father. I believe that it was neither

JESUS' sense of an externalized deity entirely beyond himself whom he followed, nor his sense of identity with God, as if he himself were divine and his own voice the voice of God. I believe that JESUS was following the dictates of neither simply a god above him nor only his own inner voice. I believe that the "something special" about JESUS was his *passion*: the fullness of his embodied life, the depth and power of his embodied spirit, the openness of his body to risk and struggle in the spirit of God. I believe that JESUS lived in this passionate spirit of One who was both with and in him—and *other* than him; the God who was with and in him—and with and in *others*; the Holy Spirit of love in history, the sacred energy moving through JESUS, stirring among the people, acting through them all, and even today as much with and for one of us—JESUS—as for us all.

God was indeed in JESUS just as God is in *us*—as our Sacred, Sensual Power, deeply infusing our flesh, root of our embodied yearning to reach out to one another and bring hope where there is despair, courage where there is fear, justice-love in the midst of apathy, contempt, or violence. This source of our being is not only "like" us; nor is God only "with" us, as liberal and liberation theologians usually insist; She is *in* us, not only in JESUS, making him alone The CHRIST, as Baillie would have it. He is in *us*, literally—you and me, here and now, today and forever, making us all bearers of Christic power.

From a Christian perspective, though never a mainstream one, the salvation of the world did not begin with the birth, life, death, and resurrection of JESUS. Rather, through this sacred story, Christians can see God and ourselves differently from the way we would without the story. The JESUS story can provide a fresh perspective on our relation to the whole cosmos, to the communities in which we live and work and love, and to our own senses of being unique persons, each and all of us. We are invited through this story not to "obey" God, but—like JESUS and in the Spirit that infused him—to pick up our beds and walk, God with us.

If we view JESUS not as the beginning of God's presence with and in us but rather as a window into the eternal, ongoing, presence of the Holy in creation, the JESUS story provides a view into our bodyselves in relation to our Sacred Power. We see that this power is embodied, in, through, and among us—and that it is good.

Beverly W. Harrison speaks of three different, simultaneous levels of our body-experience: cosmic, communal/cultural/historical, and personal/individual.[11] Morally, she notes, the three are entirely inter-active, interdependent, and inseparable. To highlight the sensuality of all three bodies, Harrison speaks of each having its own "skin," a membrane that both connects it and protects it. An individual's experience, for example, of hunger or loneliness, sexual pleasure or playfulness, is related existentially, politically, and mystically to the communal bodies and the cosmic body in which she participates.

The Spirit by which we god as bodies in a world that breaks and bruises our cosmic, communal, and personal bodies is the source of transcendence, our power to cross over between and among our bodyselves. We know that this power is not only with us. It is living and dying *in* our flesh, *in* our bodies, and *in* all that our common body and personal bodyselves experience.

Knowing that God is in our body and that our cosmic, communal, and personal bodies are in God (in mutually *coinherent* relation) sparks our passion for life, for God, for one another, and for the world. It also can form the basis of a Christology in which our assumptions about God, JESUS, and the rest of us are grounded.

This radical acceptance of body is foundational to most Christian liberation, feminist, and queer theologies. Because this affirmation is vital to liberation Christologies, these particular theological movements tend to have strong, passionate Christologies of struggle that are body-celebrating, creature-affirming, and sometimes—especially among queer Christians—erotically empowering.[12]

Passionate vision

The fourth Gospel is textually problematic for many of us today. From a Christian feminist perspective, it is among the most difficult parts of the Christian Bible to read because it seems to spill over with sexist assumptions and racist imagery; it seems rife with anti-Semitism; and it appears to be held together by threads of a Gnostic spirituality that is antagonistic toward the body. Yet this same gospel, with its mystical moorings, manages to convey something of the breadth and depth of the spiritual vision that sparked and sustained JESUS:

> I am asking on their behalf; I am not asking on behalf of the world,
> but on behalf of those whom you gave me, because they are yours.
> All mine are yours, and yours are mine; and I have been glorified in
> them. And now I am no longer in the world, but they are in the
> world, and I am coming to you. Holy Father, protect them in your
> name that you have given me, so that they may be one, as we are
> one. While I was with them, I protected them in your name that
> you have given me. I guarded them, and not one of them was lost
> except the one destined to be lost, so that the scripture might be
> fulfilled. But now I am coming to you, and I speak these things in
> the world so that they may have my joy made complete in them-
> selves. I have given them your word, and the world has hated them
> because they do not belong to the world, just as I do not belong to
> the world. I am not asking you to take them out of the world, but I
> ask you to protect them from the evil one. They do not belong to
> the world, just as I do not belong to the world. Sanctify them in the
> truth; your word is truth. As you have sent me into the world, so I
> have sent them into the world. (John 17:9-18)

The JESUS who is presented in the Gospel of John speaks in a language flavored by the negative valuation of "the world" that is common
to Greek metaphysics. Nonetheless, this JESUS sees a "oneness," a
wholeness and unity, in the realm of God here on earth as well as
beyond what we know as life. Moreover, this JESUS envisions a oneness
constituted by the relational network of all who are "sanctified by the
truth." In other words, what in other places JESUS calls "the kingdom
of God" is not first or simply a spiritual realm beyond the earth and
even perhaps beyond time as we know it. The realm of God, the kin-
dom of the Spirit, is among us here and now, as we are "sent into the
world" by the Sacred Power that sent JESUS himself into the world.

JESUS' vision in the fourth Gospel is of an active band of human
beings spreading "the word" of God in the world. And the word of
God, JESUS and others make clear time and again, is "love." It is "righteousness" or "justice" steeped in love, not in certainty or rigid notions
of "rightness." The passionate vision of the one whom many followers
call "CHRIST" is the making of "justice-love" in a world that is crying
out for it.

In the fourth Gospel's worldview, "the world" is a temporary, material plane—a flat place upon which people dwell largely in spiritual
and material captivity to "the evil one." By contrast, "the word of God"

that is "truth" enables people simultaneously to be "in the world, but not of it." What appears at first glance as well as in many interpretive studies to be the dualism of the fourth Gospel is, I believe, more than simply dualistic. The writer of this Gospel and the JESUS he presents are deeply aware of the complexities and paradoxes in our lives, sometimes even contradictions—"in the world, but not of it," "hated by the world," and, at the same time, "full of joy."

So JESUS' passion is seasoned in a vision of the complexities and contradictions he and we embody as people of God in the world.

Filled with passion about what he has seen through the eyes of God, JESUS' life takes shape: His life is lived publicly, without apology. He announces his mission early on. He is often in the company of people whom secular and religious powerbrokers look down on—prostitutes, beggars, lepers, tax collectors, lots of women and poor people—and he is not there to condemn them but to heal, bless, and encourage them. In order to do this, he breaks social boundaries and religious customs—healing on the Sabbath, touching bleeding women, talking to foreigners, and generally embarrassing keepers of secular and religious law by not giving them the authority they expect. From beginning to end, JESUS' staying power, his capacity to "keep on keeping on," is drawn not from institutional support or public approval but rather from faith—both the power that fuels his vision and the steadfastness of many of his friends, those who stay with him and put themselves at risk by embodying the word of God.

We turn now to a closer look at passion—what it is and how it functions in JESUS' life and our own as a moral mooring. We will see that the passion of JESUS is a thread that weaves together and enables us to re-image and re-create what the church has called "the incarnation" (historically, the embodiment of God in JESUS alone) and "the atonement" (traditionally conceptualized as JESUS' suffering and death on the cross as a "sacrifice" for our sins). By centering solely on JESUS, rather than on other humans and other creatures as well, traditional treatments of incarnation and atonement have functioned primarily to *separate* us from God, JESUS, and one another rather than to *make us one*, which is the prayer and vision of the JESUS we meet in the fourth Gospel.

But why this pointing away from ourselves in order to find God? Why this focus on JESUS rather than on all of us along with JESUS? It has much to do, I believe, with our fear of passion and our aversion to deeply embodied feeling, which is an open window into the God who is with us. We humans can be trained *not* to really experience our lives; *not* to be vulnerable (open) to the needs, desires, and yearnings of our bodyselves; and *not* to realize that the most fully human/creaturely and divine/creative dimensions of our lives are vital links to the sensual, embodied experiences of others.

In its Euro-centric and patriarchal mainstream, the Christian Church has taught us these lessons well. One way it has done this has been through Christologies that have pulled us away not only from our own embodied needs and yearnings but also from many of the most deeply physical and spiritual needs of others, such as the needs for emotional intimacy, tenderness, and presence; for affirmation and celebration of indigenous cultures, lands, and languages; for economic justice; and for time to rest and play. These needs are not add-ons or luxuries. They are not optional for human well-being nor for the well-being of God. Each of these needs—however "material," "cultural," or "political"—is a *spiritual* root and conduit of Sacred Power. When it is blocked or cut off, God's own power is thwarted. And these needs of ours, these roots of God, invariably are blocked by our fear of passion, which is our fear of life itself in its many dimensions.

Christian moralism such as that practiced by those who are right, like the church's mainstream teachings about JESUS, has its origins in this aversion to passion, both as joyful, in-depth living and as suffering.

Several of the central theses in this book are that we humans and other creatures participate in the incarnation of Sacred Spirit; that, in a radically embodied, communal context, in-depth passionate living is abundant with delight, gratitude, and a willingness, if need be, to suffer on behalf of human, creaturely, and divine well-being; that, in this Spirit, our feelings can be openings—windows of vulnerability—into God; and that we can learn to express our needs, desires, and yearnings in mutually empowering ways.

I do not mean that suffering is "good" or "good for us" or that it is "God's will." After all, God is not a giant man or woman who gives thumbs up or down to particular people, places, events, or processes. I do mean that we cannot live fully human lives—an image of incarnation—unless we are willing to share in the world's suffering, close to home and far away; and that, conversely, we cannot become willing to do this unless we are participating more and more fully in the humanity, creatureliness, and divinity of our brothers and sisters—an image of atonement or the making of right relation with God.

And we cannot do any of this—experience joy or sorrow, solidarity or suffering—unless we feel and know that we are alive, or unless someone can feel and know this in our place, as our "representative" to and on behalf of creation and our Creator God. (This is often the case when people or other creatures are without voice, vote, or a way of being present in particular situations or moments.) For Dorothee Soelle, this was JESUS' special role, to be for us and for God, "CHRIST the Representative."[13] This is the role we all are called to play, again and again, to *go with* one another in the radically mutual, interdependent world and creation that we share—and whenever this is impossible (for whatever political, social, physical, psychological, or economic reasons), to *go for* those who are without voice, presence, or the power required in the specific context. To go for others in this way is always to go for God as well.

Passion is a theological term that denotes this "going with" and "going for" God, this godding, this real presence in life and in God. Passion is also an ethical term of agency, or power. As such, passion is our sacred energy for going with and, if need be, going for one another into the joy and sorrow of making justice-love with compassion.

We turn now to several examples of the passion of JESUS as these may reflect our own shared vocation.

Passion as coming out for justice-love

> When he came to Nazareth, where he had been brought up, he went to the synagogue on the sabbath day, as was his custom. He stood up to read, and the scroll of the prophet Isaiah was given to him. He unrolled the scroll and found the place where it was written: "The Spirit of the Lord is upon me, because he has anointed me to bring good news to the poor. He has sent me to proclaim release to the captives and recovery of sight to the blind, to let the oppressed go free, to proclaim the year of the Lord's favor." And he rolled up the scroll, gave it back to the attendant, and sat down. The eyes of all in the synagogue were fixed on him. Then he began to say

to them, "Today this scripture has been fulfilled in your hearing." All spoke well of him and were amazed at the gracious words that came from his mouth. They said, "Is not this Joseph's son?" He said to them, "Doubtless you will quote to me this proverb, 'Doctor, cure yourself!' And you will say, 'Do here also in your hometown the things that we have heard you did at Capernaum.'" And he said, "Truly I tell you, no prophet is accepted in the prophet's hometown. But the truth is, there were many widows in Israel in the time of Elijah, when the heaven was shut up three years and six months, and there was a severe famine over all the land; yet Elijah was sent to none of them except to a widow at Zarephath in Sidon. There were also many lepers in Israel in the time of the prophet Elisha, and none of them was cleansed except Naaman the Syrian." When they heard this, all in the synagogue were filled with rage. They got up, drove him out of the town, and led him to the brow of the hill on which their town was built, so that they might hurl him off the cliff. But he passed through the midst of them and went on his way. (Luke 4:16-30)

One of the first signs of passion in JESUS' life was the *chutzpah* with which he publicly announced his purpose—to proclaim liberation. In effect, JESUS "came out," clarifying that his work would not take place "in the closet," hidden from public view, but would be visible and available to all. Not only did JESUS announce that he had come to preach "good news to the poor" and to proclaim "release to the captives"—implicitly challenging the Roman state—but he did so in Nazareth, his hometown, where, as he realized, this message would likely puzzle people who had known him only as a boy, "Joseph's son." Pretentious, in over his head, flaky—likely impressions of this hometown boy now grown.

Already, JESUS' living, breathing body—through whom the Spirit of Life is speaking—is bearing the tension generated whenever people "go with" and "go for" one another—opening their mouths and speaking up on behalf of the outcast, the poor, the captives.

This boy, our little JESUS, is a prophet—and an ungrateful one at that? When JESUS proceeds to illustrate, with examples from religious history, how unlikely it is for a prophet even to be sent to "his own country," the hometown folks seem to hear this as critique of themselves, and the writer says that they cast him out and take him away to kill him. But JESUS, we are told, manages to "pass through the midst of them" and go away.

These are the early days of a brief ministry in which atonement was underway, as it is always when people are trying to bring more justice-love into this world in actual material ways—feeding the hungry, clothing the naked, freeing the captives, helping the blind and others who are disabled to "see" and "walk" and "talk"—that is, to experience themselves as empowered to live passionate lives.

In this moment of JESUS' ministry, we may catch a glimpse of how it always is. Through the passion and atonement in JESUS' life, we have a glimpse of the passion and atonement in our own.

We see atonement in JESUS' life—in his struggle for right relation with the hometown folks, with the poor and the captives and, through it all, with the Spirit driving him and us to embody justice-love, to be involved in the ongoingness of incarnation. And how? By doing what we can to shape the world in body-feeding and body-nurturing, body-healing and body-valuing ways.

One sign of passion is to be public—come out—with our purpose: to be clear that we will do what we can in the world on behalf of poor and marginalized people and other creatures and, like JESUS, let the chips fall where they may.

To come out as a passionate lover of God and the world does not require an extroverted personality. It requires persons—quiet, reflective, flamboyant, charismatic, scholarly, activist, artistic, hard working, playful, prayerful—who are confident in their own *and* others' abilities to god, and their willingness to struggle together toward embodying the justice-love of God.

Passion as solidarity with the poor, outcast, marginalized

We liberation theologians, feminists and others, have understood that godding involves standing with the poor, the marginalized, the outcast.[14] While we usually have agreed that God is "on the side of the poor," most of us have not been very clear about what we mean by "God taking sides." Does it mean that God actually is *against* rich people and others with power? To respond, we need some power analysis.

But the Christian Bible offers no explicit "power analysis." Nothing in these documents, shaped over centuries and canonized about eighteen hundred years ago, would lead us to imagine that JESUS of Nazareth thought much about "structures" or "systems" of social power. Our contemporary analysis of how power relations are economic relations comes from Marx, not JESUS; similarly, our understanding that all relations are power relations is something we have learned more from Foucault (1980), Gutiérrez (1973), Lorde (1984), and Harrison (1985) than from the authors of Matthew, Mark, Luke, and John.

And yet today, thanks to the meeting places of biblical scholarship, the struggle for justice-love in its many manifestations, and the faith journeys of our communities, many of us read the Bible as a powerful, living critique of both individuals and systems, interpersonal relationships and structures of oppression, our own personal lives and the life of the larger society. We gladly assume that, whereas JESUS was not a "social analyst," his life—as we remember it, through the Christian Bible and Christian history—bears powerful, critical witness to the ongoing struggle to create more justice-loving, people-loving, creation-loving, God-loving societies.

In this Spirit of gratitude, and in an effort to bring our own biases and commitments to the biblical text, many feminist liberation theologians and other liberation theologians bring our contemporary power analyses to the text and find there, often between the lines as much as in them, JESUS' life and ministry as an embodied critique not just of individuals but, even more importantly, of the structures of oppression. Let us take a look at a passage in Mark that is often interpreted by pastors and preachers to be simply about the generosity of a poor widow.

> [JESUS] sat down [in the temple] opposite the treasury, and watched the multitude putting money into the treasury. Many rich people put in large sums. And a poor widow came and put in two small copper coins, which are worth a penny. Then he called his disciples and said to them, "Truly, I tell you, this poor widow has put in more than all those who are contributing to the treasury. For all of them have contributed out of their abundance; but she out of her poverty has put in everything she had, all she had to live on." (Mark 12:41-44)

From a liberation perspective, we might well ask what compels JESUS to "watch the multitude putting their money into the treasury" and even to notice who is rich and who is poor. Why does he care and why does the author of Mark care? There is presumably nothing unusual about this scene in the temple.

Perhaps Mark's JESUS is compelled by the passionate prophetic vision of a God who despises human indifference to human need and all the more so when we think of ourselves as generous contributors to God's work. Perhaps we have here an image of a brother aligning himself with the prophetic tradition of Israel.

We see JESUS positioning himself across from the treasury in the temple to watch for something. I suppose he sees pretty much what he expected: lots of rich people putting in lots of money, and a poor widow who offers a penny.

And in this moment do we imagine that JESUS notices more than simply a poor woman? Does he notices here, as in so many other places in his ministry, what latter day theorists would call "systemic poverty"? Does he notice a "structure of oppression"—the very existence of poverty and the wealth that makes it possible?

JESUS, we can imagine, probably doesn't know any of these people personally—and, who knows, these rich and evidently generous people may be fine individuals, and the poor woman may be a shrew. But let us assume that none of this concerns JESUS in this particular moment. Let us assume what bothers him is the economic injustice embedded in this situation, and all the more so because the religious functionaries play the oppressive system for their own benefit. Mark has just told us that, immediately prior to this scene, JESUS warned his disciples: "Beware of the scribes who devour widows' houses and for the sake of appearance say long prayers" (Mark 12:38, 40).

As I read the Bible, here in this passage and elsewhere, JESUS is driven to "side with" the poor. He is driven by his vision of the Sacred Spirit, which yearns and pushes for right mutual relation. Economic exploitation, like any other form of violence, reflects the antithesis of right relation, the opposite of mutuality. The very existence of poverty—and wealth—must surely have been an affront to JESUS because it is so contrary to the movement of a Sacred Power that fills the hungry with good things.

Does God then "side with" the poor? The God of JESUS is a spiritual movement against the very existence of wealth and poverty, these structures of oppression. It is not that God "hates" rich people and "loves" poor people individually. It is the structures of society, the shape of the world we people are making, that God moves against and, in this sense, "despises." Remember that we are not talking about an anthropomorphic deity who "feels" like we do about these matters. God is a spiritual force, an energy, a drive, and in that sense a relentless yearning for justice.

Regardless of the merits of imaging God in human categories,[15] it is important to keep in mind that the actual power moving the universe, struggling toward right relation, does not play personal preference when it comes to rich and poor, male and female, white and black and yellow and brown, human and other individual creatures on the earth or elsewhere.

The God that JESUS loved passionately was and is a Spirit that compelled JESUS, as it compels us all, to live in such a way that our lives are themselves protests against structures of injustice and exploitation in our religious institutions and in the larger society.

This same God who, we may suppose, compelled JESUS to notice systemic poverty and the indifference of religious leaders to it is available to everybody. All people in JESUS' time and all of us now can draw energy, wisdom, and confidence from the Spirit, which is constantly a wellspring of courage and hope for all who drink from it: rich people as well as poor, men as well as women, white folks no less than people of color, people of all sexual and gendered identities, healthy and sick people, able-bodied and disabled sisters and brothers, human beings and, in ways we probably cannot imagine unless we are wildly imaginative lovers of the natural world, other creatures too.

We all can call upon the Spirit. None of us is "preferred" over the other. This justice-making Spirit that is available to all of us all the time is the God whom JESUS loved, the wellspring of his passion. This Spirit drove him into the wilderness to think about things and encouraged him to put his body on the line—to eat with outcasts, meet with women and foreigners, violate religious rules when they had nothing to do with human need or well-being. This Sacred Power pushed him into confrontation with religious and secular leaders, and it enabled him to accept death at their angry hands rather than betray himself, his people, and his passion for this very God.

Boundary breaking as passionate godding

> He left that place and entered their [the Pharisees'] synagogue; a
> man was there with a withered hand, and they asked him, "Is it law-
> ful to cure the sick on the sabbath?" so that they might accuse him.
> He said to them, "Suppose one of you has only one sheep and it falls
> into a pit on the sabbath; will you not lay hold of it and lift it out?
> How much more valuable is a human being than a sheep! So it is
> lawful to do good on the sabbath." Then he said to the man "Stretch
> out your hand." He stretched it out, and it was restored, as sound
> as the other. But the Pharisees went out and conspired against him,
> how to destroy him. (Matt. 12:9-14)

Rules and customs are agreements that have been established to support the good order of an institution, community, or society. This
good order, in turn, can provide a stable basis of community identity,
or the organization or group's sense of its own purpose, its reason for
being, how well it's doing, etc. To break rules or customs—"boundaries"—that have been agreed to formally or informally can destabilize a community by tossing its clarity of purpose or identity into the
air. Unless order is restored quickly and, if need be, forcefully, confusion may take the upper hand (what's happening? who's in charge
here?) and the fabric of the institution, the Jewish synagogue in this
case, may be torn or shattered.

Throughout my life, I've been taught that JESUS didn't obey the law
when it inhibited the meeting of human need. Perhaps more than any
other, this image of JESUS as a "boundary-breaker" has been held fast in
my consciousness since childhood.

What has not been so widely discussed, at least among progressive
Christians, is the seriousness and respect with which JESUS likely took
the very laws and customs he transgressed, an attitude that probably
intensified the power of his transgressions for JESUS, his friends, and
his enemies. Here, after all, was a practicing Jew, well-versed in Torah,
obviously an unusually bright and aware character, someone who
knew what he was doing. "I didn't come to remove the law, but to fulfill it." We have no indication that JESUS was an "anarchist" in the modern sense, or that his breaking of the law was an "in your face" sort of
petulance.

We have in JESUS more than simply someone in defiance of either
his religious tradition or the state. JESUS' boundary-breaking activities

were motivated by the creative, liberating Spirit of Love. His healing of the man's hand, the disciples' plucking of heads of grain also on the Sabbath, and his general attitude toward religion and state leaders were grounded in this God. That they were perceived to threaten the good order of Judaism was a *consequence*, not a motive or aim, of his actions. That JESUS and, sooner or later, many of the disciples would be put to death as rebels, traitors, and criminals was a *consequence*, not the goal or purpose, of their struggles for right relation.

This distinction here is important to understanding JESUS' passion—the incarnation of God in him and his atoning work that culminates not on the cross but in the suffering that, for him, begins as soon as he begins to suffer "for the sins of the world." The whole point of the JESUS story—the fully human story of us all—is missed if we fail to see, at its core, a passion for *life!* This is not a story about a man who had no respect for law or an aversion to religious tradition. Much less is it a story about a man who sought to suffer and die. JESUS loved life and the Spirit of love, which he experienced as the source of life itself.

If we are seeking to suffer or be killed, or if we are seeking to bring pain or death to others, and if either is our motive in breaking boundaries, then whatever the origins of this personal (or collective) motive, it has little, if anything, to do with the love of God or with the life and passion of JESUS.

There is one exception to this, I believe, and it is both extraordinary and a major, common historical theme that has touched every continent and all peoples, past and present. I am thinking of the revolutionary situations in which people have come to believe that they must either kill or be killed in order to stop a particular evil force working against them or others in the world. What makes the revolutionary situation extraordinary is that, in these situations, such as in the Sandinista revolution in Nicaragua and in the African National Congress in South Africa, people are motivated by a passion for life and the Spirit of justice-love. The motive is not to suffer or bring suffering, to kill or be killed. The motive is to stop an evil power, such as the dictatorial forces of Somoza in Nicaragua and apartheid in South Africa, which evidently can be stopped in no other way. In Nicaragua, the Sandinistas made clear their desire not to replicate the abuses of Somoza; similarly, in South Africa, the ANC has attempted to create a government for

all the people, not simply for the winners of the revolution. In both of
these nations, one testimony to the commitment to create a justice-loving society was the abolition of the death penalty and, in South Africa,
the establishment of the Truth and Reconciliation Commission.[16]

In any given historical moment, there are so many of these revolutionary movements in the world—in East Timor, among the Kurds
and the ethnic Albanians, and elsewhere. Only the passage of time and
the renderings of history by those without much social power can help
us understand more fully which revolutionary historical acts and
movements have been, or are, most truly sacred efforts not only to foil
an evil power but also not to replicate it.

If our purpose is to destabilize society, break rules, or transgress
boundaries because they are silly or obsolete, or even simply because
we can't have our way, then our actions may well be dismissed or punished. But there usually is little revolutionary potential in such a trans-
action, for we seldom pose a serious threat.

If our purpose is to break the law because we, individually, have
happened upon a particular law that we believe to be unjust, it may be
very good to break it. But if we are not participating publicly and/or
intentionally in a larger movement on behalf of justice, then our
action, however bold, is likely to be dismissed or punished simply as
an individual act of defiance. Neither we nor others may be able to
make the connections between what we are doing and what needs to
be done systemically.

Still, there can be, and often is, revolutionary potential in what we
individually do—simply because we have acted on behalf of the larger
struggle for justice, whether or not we have been fully aware of it. The
power of such acts, taken by individuals who may or may not consciously be part of larger movements, should not be trivialized. Like
the actions of Rosa Parks, whose refusal in 1955 to go to the back of
the bus in Montgomery was quite purposely an act representing a
whole movement, one person's boundary-breaking moment may
become foundational to the movement, far beyond what the person
may have imagined.

If we, like JESUS, Rosa, and others, are moved by a passion for the
sacred realm of justice-love—an inherently social, far-reaching relational realm—and if we see what is required here and now—to heal

the man's hand; to respond to thievery in high or holy places when we see it; to name the hypocrisy of religious leaders; to confront governors; to boycott and demonstrate; to refuse to be moved—then our actions will be dismissed only if we agree to stop them. Otherwise, the consequences of what we do will be significant because we are planting revolutionary seeds that will grow. For it is in the nature of the Holy Spirit to expand. "The mustard seed becomes the realm of God."

In each of these revolutionary, boundary-breaking moments, our lives give birth to God, and Sophia (God's wisdom) is incarnate again among us here and now. Because She is here, the foundations of our life together will always be shaken whenever injustice lingers or cruelty and indifference still abound. Insofar as we proceed, God with us, to struggle for mutual relation, we will run into demons of evil like fear and indifference everywhere we turn, including inside ourselves. The JESUS story suggests that, be that as it may, atonement—the making of right relation with God in the midst of evil—is accomplished again and again, historically and autobiographically, in every tiniest moment of justice-making with compassion. In such moments, we not only meet the God whose essence is Love, we actually embody and become the Body of the resurrected God that Christians name "CHRIST." This Christic Spirit is called back to life, risen and incarnate, through our embodied passion.

But how do we distinguish the embodied, boundary-breaking passion of JESUS and his disciples from those Christians who "know they are right"—such as the right-wing ideologues in Operation Rescue? Paul Hill and the late John Salvi, for example, had no question that *they* were following JESUS, embodying his passion, if you will, in their murderous assaults on workers in abortion clinics. Even more complex for those of us on the "left," what is the difference between JESUS in his passionate, non-compromising, struggle against the principalities and powers—and those progressive Christians who are so certain of the "rightness" of our justice positions that we lack compassion for our adversaries and patience with those who may question us or not understand us?

Whether on right or left, among feminists or blatant misogynists, a *lack of compassion* is always a reliable indicator of a serious spiritual malaise. Although I discuss compassion more fully in the last part of this book, it's important to mention it here in relation to the passion of JESUS because compassion is what distinguishes what passion truly is of God, and what is not.

Compassion is *not* simply a feeling. It often is not a feeling at all. Think of those people who have had family members murdered and who have formed groups to oppose the death penalty. Surely their motivation is not often what they *feel* for the individuals who have taken the lives of their loved ones. It is rather a spiritual and political *commitment* to struggle for healing and liberation rather than to perpetuate the spiral of violence.[17] Thus, *compassion is the spiritual, ethical, and political commitment to do no harm, if at all possible, to our enemies, even those whom we may consider the enemies of justice or of God.* I am convinced that compassion is what distinguishes sacred passion from all other experiences and manifestations of strong belief and deeply held conviction.

We have looked at the passion of God as an embodied, visionary, compassionate commitment that moved JESUS, and moves us as well, into special, primary relationship with the poor, outcast, and marginalized. We have noticed JESUS' willingness to break laws and customs in order to embody this sacred passion. We have also witnessed JESUS' perception that God "despises" *systemic* wealth, poverty, and other *social structures* of oppression and cruelty, what the fourth Gospel calls "the world," and that this same God—the power to make justice-love in the world—is accessible to all persons and creatures all the time. We people say *yes* or *no* in countless ways to embodying this Spirit, this sacred passion, in our daily lives.

But on what basis are we able to say yes? We may believe that our strength comes from God, but how does it come? Where do we get our staying power?

Faith as basic resource of human passion

Even here, in the realm of faith, we are not simply on our own, by ourselves.

"Faith" is an embodied realization that God is real, good, and powerful, though seldom on "the world's" terms, and that this same Spirit is the root of our passion. Faith is born through community, intuition, and imagination; it is sparked by our experiences of crisis and struggle, serenity and beauty, friendship and loss, loneliness and hope.

JESUS' power was his own faith and that of his friends—their faith in him, in themselves, and in the Spirit that he called forth in them and that they evoked in him as well. We ought not underestimate the liberating power of *others'* faith in God—their faith in a God who is working through them and us—to help secure our lives in the Spirit that generates hope and raises the dead. Hardly a steady, smooth resource for JESUS, his faith and that of his disciples was at times peppered with frustration and fatigue, doubt and confusion. Nonetheless, this faith—his and theirs—was the crucible of his passion. Their faith was the fuel of incarnation, the human energy that enabled him and them to god. The faith of JESUS and his friends was their confidence, however shaky at times, that God was with them, even through suffering and death.

> They went to a place called Gethsemane; and he said to his disciples, "Sit here while I pray." He took with him Peter and James and John, and began to be distressed and agitated. And said to them, "I am deeply grieved, even to death; remain here, and keep awake." And going a little farther, he threw himself on the ground and prayed that, if it were possible, the hour might pass from him. He said, "Abba, Father, for you all things are possible; remove this cup from me; yet, not what I want, but what you want." He came and found them sleeping; and he said to Peter, "Simon, are you asleep? Could you not keep awake one hour? Keep awake and pray that you may not come into the time of trial; the spirit indeed is willing, but the flesh is weak." And again he went away and prayed, saying the same words. And once more he came and found them sleeping, for their eyes were very heavy; and they did not know what to say to him. (Mark 14:32-40)

It is interesting how little we hear in church about JESUS' fear and frustration—with his disciples and his Abba God. It is too bad we are not educated spiritually to incorporate these very real dimensions of JESUS' humanness into our experiences of his sacred passion. To do so might help us better integrate our own anxieties and fear, our frustrations and confusion, with our experiences of passionate faith in God and one another. As it is, we often learn spiritually and emotionally that we should "swallow our fear" and "have faith!"

But fear is not an enemy of faith. Faith comes into being through fear. Fear of danger, of suffering, of death, and certainly of evil, is our basic embodied "signal" that we may be encountering something that will hurt us or others. To *feel* such fear is to be in touch with reality. Only insofar as we are in touch with reality can we embody the passion of One whose very nature is to be really present. Only through the experience of being actually afraid can we find courage—a power that, like fear, pumps through the heart. Our fear, literally, is transformed into courage. Without it, we can find no courage, take no heart, keep no faith.

But be clear that fear untransformed cannot help us. Stuck in this fear, we shrink,[18] becoming "smaller" persons than we are invited to be, in God. It is especially the fear holding us to perceptions of bogus enemies—"others," those who are "different"—that makes us cowards and actively impedes our faith. Often, such demonic fear is not something we actually *feel* at all, but rather a psychospiritual condition of lethargy, resignation, and eventually despair, which pulls us away from one another and away even from our own desire to god.

But our fear of our own and others' suffering, of unjust death, and of evil, as this fear is transformed, becomes the mightiest fuel for courage and faith. What then is the agent of such transformation? What molds courage out of fear? What takes our doubts and frustrations and, out of these real and universal experiences, shapes our faith? God, of course, is the agent of this spiritual transformation— but how?

The mutuality of our relation with the very Spirit that generates mutuality holds the key to our understanding:

From the beginning, God is our power in mutual relation, its source and resource. It was true before the world as we know it began. We humans are participatory agents, with God, of "more" God—more sacred power, more creative, transforming, spiritual energy.

With this potential, we are born into a world that, from the beginning, has been both shaped by courage (wherever there is mutuality and justice-love) and distorted by fear (wherever there is exploitation and evil). This has been true forever, generation upon generation. It will always be true.

However afraid we may be, however frustrated in any situation, we are nonetheless always *in* God and therefore always able, through the Sacred Power that is constantly with us, to draw God's energy, drink and eat God's nourishment, and through this faith, embody God's power for our godding: our courage, passion, compassion, vision, and faith.

Another way of speaking of the same reality is this: Through God's faith in us, we receive faith. And through our faith, God is embodied in history, one day at a time.

And so while, truly, God is the agent of our faith, its root and source, we humans are agents of God's ongoing incarnation, embodied presence with us. Thus, in a very literal, embodied sense, we humans are a source (not the only source, for there are other creatures in the world and universe) of God's real presence in the world.

Through God, we take heart.

Through us, God does too.

This mutuality is, in reality,

God's incarnate presence.

What then of the disciples sleeping in the garden (they are tired after all, their bodies weary and probably their spirits too) and JESUS' irritability with them? What of other images of JESUS' being frustrated with those whose behavior does not always seem to warrant it—his mother, for example, and the poor fig tree that he causes to wither and die because it is not bearing fruit? And what of the suggestions, by JESUS, that humans are more important to God than sheep and sparrows? Might this holy brother, this embodiment of Sacred Power, ever have been *wrong*? And can "good" Christians even ask such questions? We must ask them, I submit, if we, like JESUS, are real.

The limits of passion

Most Christians expect JESUS to be all-good, completely good, perfect, "without sin," as the tradition has taught us. Either we overlook and ignore things that he did and said about which, if it were anyone but JESUS, we might complain (cursing and killing a fig tree?), we learn to rationalize away the biblical record (he didn't really do this), or we find positive ways of looking at what only appear to be negative images (he's not really belittling his mother at the wedding; he's just trying to stretch and reimage his friends' understandings of "family").

We cannot seem to bear the notion of a JESUS who *didn't* always do or say the right thing.

We seem to think that any error on JESUS' part would automatically diminish his reputation among those who look to him as savior. But the assumptions behind our "perfectionism" support a particular— patriarchal, static, and dualistic—understanding of both divinity and humanity that a more relational apprehension challenges.

The salvific meanings of JESUS and his story are rooted in his *real presence*, which was shaped out of the human condition of limits and partiality. This was as true for JESUS as it is for the rest of us. These limits made him no less fully in God and no less open to God's real presence in him.

There are limits to what we humans know, and many of these limits change with time, but there will always be much that we don't know. This was true of JESUS too. He was a person of his time, for example, in relation to what we call "science." He probably thought the earth was flat—and he was wrong. He was a person of his time in relation to religion. This means that JESUS was more anthropocentric (human-centered) and more androcentric (male-centered) than some of our more contemporary, ecologically aware, feminist sisters and brothers in his understanding of God, humans, and other creatures. JESUS' historically shaped ignorance, his limited knowledge, was part of the fullness of his humanity.

And his divinity? Did that not make JESUS all-knowing? Only if we image God in strictly anthropological terms, as a "cosmic man" who "thinks" and "knows" and "wills" and "speaks" just like we do—except of course *perfectly*. If we image JESUS as this God, then indeed, JESUS was a superman, all-knowing, complete and perfect in every way, utterly unlike any human before or after. This unreal portrait of JESUS *as a magical man* reflects the image of JESUS shared to this day by a majority of Christians, including those most likely to use the name of JESUS as a bludgeon against all who do not share their understandings of either God or the world.

But this magical picture is of a fictional JESUS who never lived and, if he had, would have been neither fully human nor fully divine. For God is not a cosmic man who thinks and knows and wills and speaks like we do except perfectly. God is a spiritual force in which JESUS and the rest of us have our being.

God *is* perfect, in that the Sacred Power, struggling through us to recreate the world in ever more fully mutual ways, is one great Spirit, Whole and "Holy" beyond what we think of geometrically as "whole." The Holy Spirit is spinning and sparking beyond all time and space as we know it, yet fully present with us in every moment of our lives, constantly a resource for us in the tiniest, most mundane questions and in what may seem to us to be the smallest places of our suffering and our joys. This is the same liberating Power that drives the struggles for justice, globally and locally, publicly and in our hearts.

This is the One whom JESUS loved, the God with "whom" and in "whom" JESUS lived a faithful, passionate life, ignorant in ways all humans are, wise beyond most of his fellows in his own time and ours, partial in his awareness of what was happening on any given day, as likely as most of us perhaps to blow off steam when he'd had it with a situation, a day, a friend, a foe; a character of shifting feelings and dispositions who didn't always "get it right" any more than any basically good person does. Throughout, JESUS was more confident than most of us in his larger vision of God's kin-dom coming into the world here and now. "The kingdom" was, as he said, "at hand"—the making of justice-love, in and through the passion of God, as it was in the beginning.

Precisely as a brother with limits like the rest of us, JESUS was able to god in ways that those with ears to hear, eyes to see, or hearts to know could recognize in him and in themselves. "Truly, this man was a son of God."

Passion: Hologram of real presence

On Easter morning 1997 I perched myself on a large rock beside a waterfall I was visiting for prayer and meditation. I had with me a carafe of decaf, four dogs, the New Oxford Annotated Bible, and one prissy cat who had followed at a distance. I opened the Bible and read out loud:

> When the Sabbath was over, Mary Magdalene, and Mary the mother of James, and Salome, bought spices, so that they might go and anoint him. And very early on the first day of the week, when the sun had risen, they went to the tomb. They had been saying to one another, "Who will roll away the stone for us from the entrance to the tomb?" When they looked up, they saw that the stone, which

was very large, was rolled back. As they entered the tomb, they saw
a young man, dressed in a white robe, sitting on the right side; and
they were alarmed. But he said to them, "Do not be alarmed; you
are looking for JESUS of Nazareth, who was crucified. He has been
raised, he is not here. Look there is the place they laid him. But go,
tell his disciples and Peter that he is going ahead of you to Galilee;
there you will see him, just as he told you." So they went out and
fled from the tomb; for terror and amazement had seized them; and
they said nothing to anyone, for they were afraid. (Mark 16:1-8)

What does it mean, I asked, for us to be really present in life? Not
dead and buried but alive and risen?

It means our hearts are opening, not shutting down, and our lives
are stretching toward the new, not fastened in the past as if God were
dead.

It means that we know we matter, all of us, and that we know "we"
means *all* of us, that we are, in this relational sense, one, even amidst
our many differences.

It means that our religion, whatever it is—and our JESUS, if we are
Christian—must empower us to live passionately and compassion-
ately with one another on the earth, not provide escape hatches
through which we can slip away into isolation and self-absorption, or
into a more heavenly place, seeking "'peace, peace' when there is no
peace," "unity" at any cost, a false, untrustworthy unity, not the Unity to
which the fourth Gospel has JESUS refer: "Keep them in my name . . .
that they may be one, even as we are one."

Being really present means that we intuit this oneness, unity,
wholeness, integrity, this spiraling movement and passionate purpose of the Sacred—and we know that we are part of it, here and
now.

It means that whoever we are, wherever we are, and whatever the
condition of our lives, the present moment is ours in which to god.

It means that nothing in the world can strip us of this one holy call
and birthright that we share—to participate in the incarnate and atoning movement of the Spirit in the world.

To be really present means that we say NO to anyone or any thing,
any church or any deity, any JESUS or any religion, that trivializes our
sacred passion for mutuality or disvalues our bodies, our sexualities,
and our struggles for justice-love with and for one another, the earth,

and its many creatures—which are indeed our embodied efforts to love God and our neighbors as ourselves.

Being really present means that *we* are a living sacrament—our bodyselves and our lives, "outward and visible signs of an inward and spiritual grace."

We pick up an acorn and see an oak in it. We notice what someone does and thereby catch a glimpse of who the person really is. And is our knowledge of the oak and of the person a matter of intuition? imagination? inductive reasoning? phantasy? Perhaps a little of all of this. We come to know not only *reality* (the acorn's shape, size, condition, etc.) but moreover *truth*, the always at least partially mysterious *connectedness* at the heart of reality, such as the organic relation of acorn to oak to forest to rain to sun to creatures and so forth.

Might we glimpse in JESUS an image of the whole of us, all of us, human and other creatures, bound by the Spirit that he and we experience as justice-love? Might this image of JESUS' life help us more clearly envision who we are in right relation—as Christians of different denominational traditions and customs; people of different religions, races, tribes, ethnic groups; folks of different genders, many sexualities, and varieties of abilities, ages, and disabilities?

Listening to JESUS, can we hear ourselves?

Finding one, do we discover many?

Noticing the part, can we see the whole?

Loving this brother, do we love one another?

As I sat on the rock, mulling over the JESUS story and what we celebrate on Easter day, an image came to me of the women—Mary Magdalene, Mary the mother of James, and Salome—fleeing from an event they could not comprehend. The women were unaware that soon their fear would become an energy for transformation. This would happen as they began to remember who JESUS was, and who they were with him and one another. Through such "dangerous memory,"[19] these tenacious women would realize that God had been really present with them all along, even before JESUS had come. It would dawn on them that the whole point of this man's sojourning with them was to help them see that, all along, *they,* as much as he, were being empowered by the Spirit to god; and that *they*, no more than he, could be undone by the powers of suffering and death.

Remembering JESUS, they remembered themselves.

Realizing one, they recognized many.

Noticing the part, they saw the whole.

Drawn to JESUS, they found God, one another, and themselves.

This is what Christians are called to do: to remember him and, in so doing, to re-member[20]—heal and liberate—one another. In this re-membering of ourselves—this putting ourselves back together as the sisters and brothers we once have been, we become lovers of God and the world, agents of incarnation and atonement. In this moment—historical and eternal—we, with JESUS, are risen long before we die.[21] And in *this Rising*, in this en-spirited, sacred moment, we are one, an Easter people.

Passion: *Ousia* (essence) of incarnation, way of atonement

We turn now to the *ousia*—that is the very essence, the deepest "being"—of incarnation: what manner of human and/or other crea-turely being is actually God-in-flesh? In one sense this is a Western question, this question of "being." Kwok Pui-lan points out, for exam-ple, that "the Chinese conceive of cosmogony as a dynamic, continu-ous and organismic process in which there is no creator who stands outside the universe."[22] This is one reason many Eastern persons have difficulty conceiving of an incarnate deity, in JESUS or anyone else.

If, however, we Westerners can imaginatively envision "being" not as a static individual human or divine self, but rather as a dynamic interplay of energy, interests, and standpoints, then both human and divine "being" become more active historical forces. And the notion of such divinity being or becoming in-fleshed, in-carnate, through our bodyselves, including JESUS', becomes imaginable.

One of the primary theses of this book is that incarnation and atonement are not inseparable redemptive events or images but rather are the same passionate moment, again and again, throughout history. While "incarnate" describes God's *place* in our midst—with us, in the flesh—"atonement" signals *how* this God-with-us-in-the-flesh is redeeming or liberating us here and now—and, moreover, how we also, in this same moment, are redeeming/liberating God. "In the

beginning is the relation," a mutual relation between Creator and creature, Liberator and those in bondage.

I see at least four "places" in our lives in which God is incarnate and,
in so being, liberates, or saves, us.

1. *In relation to our own individual bodies,* God is in and with our bodyselves, not abstract. God is sensual, not detached from our bodily sen-
sations and feelings. God is yearning for mutuality, not "satisfied" with
anything less.

The problem with patriarchal religion, Christianity and others, I
have noted is that our bodies are not experienced *primarily* as liberating agents that are also themselves in need of liberation. Rather we
learn to think of our bodies more as impediments of one sort or the
other to liberation, or redemption, from evil. In the most dualistic
interpretations of Christianity, which are heretical historically, yet
which hang on from generation to generation, our bodies are themselves evil.

Even when our bodies are interpreted as "redeemed" through
CHRIST and thereby as good and holy created organisms, we who participate in patriarchal religion are inclined to *experience* our bodies as
problematic: sources of lust, greed, gluttony, pride, sins of one form
or another, and, moreover, as "occasions" for illness, decay, disability,
suffering, and finally death. Spiritually and therefore theologically our
bodies are experienced as problematic because, in relation to a deity
who is believed to have power to save, heal, and liberate faithful people, our bodily experiences make no good sense. In fact, they make
bad sense, they make us feel guilty and ashamed, as if we have done
something wrong, or perhaps that we simply *are* wrong, bad, weak in
faith.

We cannot worship such a god and love our bodies/ourselves. This
is the reason, more than any other, I suspect, why so many Christian
women historically have left the church. Women who love their bodies often leave by walking out, renouncing, or denouncing the church,
as is happening today among many highly educated women—white
Westerners and others. Less dramatically and in greater numbers,
women who love their bodies often leave simply by losing interest and
drifting away spiritually, whether or not they "go to church" (which
also is happening today among many white Western women). And

women who love their bodies also often leave patriarchal Christianity
by appropriating what suits them from the church and transforming
it, spiritually and politically, into survival and quality of life resources.
This has happened historically, especially among marginalized
women, and it is happening now.

What then of JESUS' body in relation to the patriarchal God?

If, in JESUS—as in each brother and sister—God was embodied, if
God was sensual, if God was yearning for mutuality, then JESUS most
surely was not the obedient Son of a patriarchal God. To the contrary,
because he was living in relation to a very different Spirit, JESUS was
killed by the god of patriarchy—hung up to die on a cross by people
who were themselves obedient to this master of control. In the context of patriarchal social and religious history, it is true that this
deity—acting through these people—did indeed "sacrifice" (that is,
require the death of) one of them so that the others might come to
believe (through the resurrection of this dead man) in the power of the
patriarchal God to deliver obedient sons (and perhaps daughters?)
from evil.

Thus, in the context of patriarchal religion, the charge of contemporary feminists like Brock (1988) and Brown and Parker (1989) that
the God of JESUS was a "divine child abuser" is accurate. This is exactly
what happened on the cross if indeed the God whom JESUS loved was,
and is, an all-powerful deity whose "love" requires "obedience" from
JESUS and the rest of us.

If, however, this is not the God whom JESUS loved, it is a very different story. What most Christian feminists seem to be missing in their
important critiques of atonement is that a deity who would offer up
his son to die for his own sins—much less for the sins of the world—
is *not*, in fact, the God whom JESUS loved—nor is he God at all. He is
rather a construct in the minds of ruling class men who are frightened
of their own and others' embodied passion, sensuality, and yearnings
for mutuality. Such a god is born in fear, and he, in turn, makes fear
the basis of our experiences of God and ourselves, our own bodies and
those of others, and our understandings of what is right and wrong.

By contrast, the Sacred Power that moves the struggles for justice
with compassion, the sensual embodied Spirit of our yearning for
mutual relation, makes courage the foundation of our lives a day at a

time and is the basis of our understandings of right and wrong. This creative power is "satisfied"—that is, at peace and empowered—not through our obedience, nor the sacrificing of ourselves on altars of collective or individual guilt, but rather by our efforts to honor our own and others' embodied yearnings for mutuality.

2. *In relation to the world*, God is whole, not fragmented, but God is also multiple and various in ways, present and absent.

In God, we become increasingly whole—ourselves, God with us—by embracing our diversity and multiplicity, not by seeking uniformity (sameness of culture, creed, color, or ways of living as diverse peoples and creatures). The more we are ourselves in this multiple wholeness, the more aware[23] we often can be of our right relation with other people and creatures as the root of our very being, and of how it is that we are "fully human" and, in so being, are "fully divine," participants in the fullness of God.[24]

Again, the problem with patriarchal religious traditions, including Christianity, is the *monopoly* that "those who are right" believe that they/we hold on what is spiritually true and morally right. We too often assume that we and we alone have the truth and that other opinions and perspectives are inferior, heretical, sometimes evil. Nothing could place us further from what is true, and really of God, than such spiritual arrogance. This arrogance is born through our fear of differences and, in our fear, the difficulties we have imagining that truth can be both whole and multiple—that is, *always in relation* to everything else. The wholeness, or oneness, of whatever is true is literally the power that holds it together, every participant, each part, all views *in relation* to all others. What this means is that no one of us, collectively or individually, knows or can know the whole truth—about God and the world, good and evil, one another or ourselves.

Racism, like religious arrogance and other historical systems of evil, is constructed out of our fear of otherness, difference, and our resistance to acknowledging, much less affirming, the multiplicity of truth.[25] Racism is the *monopolizing of culture* by one racially self-identified and self-named group—*white* people who are resistant to affirming culture itself as a many-faceted, historically complex, ongoing construction by diverse groups and, within them, by individuals with different opinions, talents, and commitments. As a monopolizer of culture, racism takes on a life of its own, much like an invisible (to white people) tyrant who fabricates and dictates The One Truth about God and the world, good and evil, one another and ourselves.

Those white liberals and post-liberals (probably most folks reading this book) who are tempted to protest, "But I'm not a racist!" don't realize the pervasiveness and depth of racism as an *ongoing*, major historical social problem, collective and multiple in its layers and effects on all of us, not just people of color. White people are white racists because we breathe air that is literally as well as metaphorically *poisoned* by racism. We are racists because, irrespective of our individual wishes, we participate in the monopolizing of culture by white people—because we are white and are part of the group that benefits economically and otherwise by this monopoly. Again, to protest against the charge that we, individually, are racist is to be spiritually mistaken by individualism. It is to miss seeing the strength of our historical connectedness to one another—to other white people and to people of color.

The political problem with the guilt-induced individualistic protest voiced so frequently among white people of good will is that, until we see the moral problem of racism for what it is and see where we stand in it, we cannot effectively resist it. As feminist liberation ethicists Nancy Richardson and Donna Bivens have suggested, the only honest, liberating way white people can struggle against racism is as "anti-racist racists."[26] Seeing exactly where we stand in a "multiplicity of truth" (we are both racist and anti-racist) empowers us to act for good in a world constructed in these multiplicities of truth. We are not above the fray but rather are in the middle of the very muck we so despise.

Seeing ourselves in this way is *humbling*. It is also *liberating* because it strengthens our sense of connectedness not only to those whose racial identity and/or politics are most "like ours" but also to those who are "not like us." This sense of relation to others, including those whose lives we may least understand and/or affirm, is a mighty resource for *compassion*, by which we are less likely to caricature or condemn other racists and are more likely to seek ways of working with these sisters and brothers, agents ourselves of transformation and always, at the same time, being transformed ourselves.

So what of JESUS here? His relation to the world was marked by his participation in the multiplicity of truth and an affirmation of diversity. We have already noted that he was both a faithful practicing Jew and a resister to ways in which his own religious tradition was failing to serve the poor and marginalized. Biblical scholars and church teachers have noted moreover his real presence with all kinds of people, rich and poor, men and women, Jews and others, social outcasts (with whom he was most at home spiritually) and religious and political "insiders."

But what stands out in his ministry is his vision of "the kin-dom of God" as a very spacious "place"—heaven on earth—for those who wish to be with him in it. No one is too "different," too alien to come in. None is denied admission because she is an adulterer, or he is not Jewish, or even because they are rich like the young man, corrupt like the money changers, or arrogant like the Pharisees. Admission into God's realm of truth and blessing is entirely in the hands of those who wish to enter—it is, as Luther noted, a matter of faith alone—not a decision that those with institutional religious power can make for or about others. Anyone doing the will of God—living in the Spirit of justice-love—walks right into the kin-dom of God. Like JESUS, those who enter are participants in incarnation, embodying the Spirit in history. They are also participants in atonement, for they will always pay a price at the hands of a world still fastened in fear and ruled by the patriarchal logic of control and domination rather than by the power of mutual relation.

3. *In relation to history*, God is dynamic, not static; participatory, not uninvolved; accepting, not denying, of what really is happening, here and now, among humans and other creatures, the violence and evil as well as the healing and liberation, and our human involvement in both.

Augustine knew that our understandings of God are related to how we experience time. Although only a few humans probably think much about it, the connection between time and God is foundational to how we experience God, the world, and one another.

"Time" is how we measure the movement of all reality through "space." It is also how we measure change. Everything changes, in time. We are, infant to toddler to teenager, in time. Yesterday, today, tomorrow signal a movement in time in which nothing stays the same, and whatever does not change, in time, dies.

One of the dominating motifs in Christian theology has been to try to save God from changing by locating Him outside of time—as "e-ternal." God is above or beyond time and as such is beyond human history and the natural world. The key here is divine changelessness. A patriarchal deity who is *over* history and nature, ruler of humankind and the world, cannot be subject to change and still be all powerful and all-knowing.

But if God is our power in *mutual* relation, this Sacred Spirit is neither all-powerful (as "the world" thinks of power—controlling, exercising power over) nor changeless in history. In response to the Holocaust, Elie Wiesel, Dorothee Soelle, and others have suggested that God cannot be both all-powerful and all-loving. Historical events would seem to demonstrate this. Most liberation theologians, including feminists, would agree and would come down on the side of God's *love*. Rather than simply concede, however, that God is not all-powerful, it seems to me spiritually and morally more fully true to reinterpret God's power as the *power of love*, a power recognizable not by its control but by its *vulnerability*—that is its openness to being touched and changed by what is happening.

If God's power is God's love, we need to think very differently about "power" than we normally think in a social order founded on the patriarchal and capitalist assumption that power, at its apex, is a combination of "control" and "wealth." We need to be clear that, in such a context, which is the dominant order of Western Christianity, God Himself is assumed to be the pinnacle of economic and social power (sexually, ethnically, and otherwise in charge). Such a view of God's omnipotence has permeated the Religious Right in the late twentieth century: Not only is "America" God's country[27]—hence, the most powerful nation in the world—but we "American" Christians will be rewarded by God, economically and otherwise, in this world maybe, and surely in the next, for our right belief and right behavior.

But if God's power is love, this patriarchal capitalist schema doesn't work. If God's power is love, neither holiness (closeness to God) nor success (achievement of a good life) can be measured by wealth or by the exercise of social control over peoples' beliefs, behavior, or bodies. Both holiness and success are born in our commitments to love one another through participation in history in our own time and place, helping make history a more fully just and compassionate story. And we do so by accepting rather than turning away from reality. We see and accept what is actually happening, including our involvement in systems and structures of good and evil as well as our commitments to helping undo evil wherever we encounter it, in our own lives and those of others, in larger and smaller contexts.

God's *ousia*, the very essence of God's vulnerability—which is also God's strength—is *in* history. As Soelle has noted, we are God's arms and hands in history.[28] This is incarnation. We are God's voices. Her needs are ours. His vulnerabilities are ours. The love we make, whether in bed or in peace work, in shelters or on the streets, if it is really love—mutually empowering—is God's own love. It is also God's power and ours in relation to one another, the whole creation, and our Sacred source.

4. *In relation to evil,* God is suffering with (compassionate), not apathetic; vulnerable, not in control; daring to risk her own safety, not tightly boundaried, or trying to keep out of harm's way at the cost of the embodied yearning for mutuality and the desire to participate in creating the world and history as a more fully just place and time.

God's being is, finally, as much in relation to evil as good. In relation to evil, God suffers—not exactly "like" us because God is not a person or a creature. Yet, because God bears us up through the most wrenching difficulties, God's sacred energy becomes the very essence of our own suffering.[29] This is to say that, in our suffering, we experience the presence of the Sacred with us. We are not alone. Far from it, we are connected through God to every sister and brother who have gone before and who go with us now into suffering and into solidarity with those who suffer. Surrounded by a cloud of witnesses, cradled in the communion of saints, as the tradition would have it, we are empowered through the compassion of God, the suffering of One who is with us.

This suffering God is the same God whose love is power. This means that her compassion, like her vulnerability, is also her power. In God, through and by the love of God, we are empowered to bear with one another. And we become resources of compassion ourselves. We are also opened, made vulnerable, to ongoing personal and social change, not stuck in our opinions, or in places we need to move on from, and not tightly boundaried by fear and rules to protect us from the possibility of harm.

Ethically this means that, in the context of evil and violence, we need to be helping one another risk being vulnerable to life, change, and processes of personal and social transformation, rather than staying closed out of our fear of harm. For violence will not be undone by fear. And neither will other, subtler forms of evil, more nuanced abuses of power.

It is in nobody's best interest to live a fear-based life. It is not in our interest over the long haul to be building professional-boundary cultures in which we are increasingly afraid to touch one another for fear that someone will go too far—be sexual with someone they have power over professionally—and get sued. What ethical or pastoral care can we sustain for long on the basis of fear-based inhibition?

Of course we need to do whatever we can to curb violence in its many forms, including sexual, gender, and racial exploitation, in professional situations as elsewhere. It is absolutely right that we should try to protect one another from harm at the hands of people acting in violent or abusive ways and also that we should punish violence and abuse. My point here is not that we ought not to be doing these things, but rather that we haven't made many attempts to transform the systemic problems that undergird violent behavior. Moreover, until we do become more radically systemic in our approach to problems of sexual exploitation in professional situations, we're not going to get far in curbing it. To defrock or sue a sexually exploitative priest or diocese in patriarchal Christianity is much like putting a bandage on one's head to treat a brain tumor.

Like the criminal justice system, professional cultures—if they are to be moral—must do more than punish the abusers in order to honor the victims. The fact is, we need not only to be struggling together to re-create and transform the systems, such as the church—many of us are already doing this. We need to be weaving our professional ethics out of the warp and woof of our feminist and womanist theologies. We need, for example, to be shaping and sharing public rituals of accountability, in which people who are violent are both held responsible for the harms they (sometimes we) inflict and given opportunities to make amends and, if possible, to move on as transformed members of the community—with the community, not against it or outside it. In such a context of renewal, if we can imagine such a thing, our collective response to violence would be a commitment to mutually empowering relation, a commitment that involves an openness to shared learnings, not an attempt to close ourselves off from these possibilities.[30]

The only way we can imagine such a thing, I believe, is in helping one another learn to see ourselves more as a common people in all our diversity rather than as "us" and "them." To walk a mile in the shoes of an abuser is *not* thereby to legitimate his or her behavior or to soften our condemnation of the violence. What it does is give us a window into the person's humanity. The instant we recognize him as a brother or her as a sister, yes, the very instant we see this, we realize that we are on common ground, together in God. And this recognition stretches us spiritually toward the fullness of our own humanity, which is also the place in which we are most at home with God.

Conversely, in attempting to shut ourselves off from evil, we shut ourselves off from good; in refusing to be open to meeting, even at a distance, the humanity of those who have hurt us, however distorted and ugly this humanity may have become, we turn away from possibilities of healing. This is not because God is evil or a source of harm, but rather because it is only through our vulnerabil-ity to our common life, our openness to learning even from our enemies, and our ongoing struggle for mutuality, that our relational power is sparked and we are able to god.

In godding, we *are* contending against evil, and we are engaged in a struggle that is already won; not because we cannot be harmed or worse but because love is stronger than fear. As history is made, in the smallest moments as well as over the long haul, the power of love cannot be extinguished. This is the message of resurrection, of course, but it is also simply a statement of faith in a power that we have seen or otherwise been touched by in countless, unremarkable ways—our power to live and die and rise again in and through the love of God.

This mutually empowering love is the hope of the world. It is what the JESUS story was all about, our Christic power for liberation. In and through this power, we are moved beyond moralism and self-righteousness into a realm of Spirit that is both gentler and more morally challenging. For in God we come face to face with the meanings and consequences of how we live together in a world being shattered by evil in which we are all involved.

We turn now to the redemptive work of saving JESUS and ourselves from evil—to how it works when we meet in the Spirit of God and are able, one day at a time, to "go and sin no more."

6. Learning Forgiveness: Way of Compassion

. . . . .

In this final chapter, I examine some of the problems with the dominant Christian atonement tradition, which, with other feminist theologians, I also reject as being cemented in the patriarchal logic of
blood sacrifice. Unlike some feminist Christians, however, I reject not
only such violence at the hands of God, but moreover the patriarchal
logic that has produced a deity—Father or even perhaps a Mother—
who reigns above us and seeks our "submission" or "obedience" as children to a parent. Against an understanding of a Lord or Father who
asks us to obey, much less forces us to submit to His will or destroys
us (or an "innocent" in our place), the Sacred Power presented in this
book is One whose very essence is to forgive us, to yearn for our
repentance, and to wait patiently—generation upon generation,
through evils of many kinds—for us to turn in sorrow and repentance
for our failures to love one another.

Aware that forgiveness often is misused and trivialized among
Christians as a way of baiting victims to "forgive" those who have
wounded them, I suggest that we cannot comprehend the Sacred
Power of forgiveness unless we realize that it is, above all, *a moral foundation of our life together in community*. Forgiveness, to be granted and
received in sustainable ways, requires not only that individuals repent
and make amends, but moreover that our communities support these
processes of healing and reconciliation and that all of us seek to build
new ways of living together.

This is something we can only learn, and do, together—with one
another's support and sometimes, in one another's stead, for there are
situations in which it is impossible for particular groups or individuals
to forgive those who have violated them or destroyed their loved
ones, so devastating has been the violence.

In order to give or receive forgiveness, we need solidarity through community and friendship; we need to be involved in the struggles for justice-love because this can teach us compassion; we need compassion (commitment, irrespective of feelings, not to harm one another, including our enemies); we need humility (awareness that the ground on which we stand is common ground); we need to be honest with ourselves about what has happened (what we and/or others have done); we need to be able to imagine ourselves healed, liberated, and transformed; and we need to pray hard and meditate well on these things.

My primary concern as I draw the book to closure is to underscore what I believe to be its basis: the spiritual and political truth that, far beyond being simply a personal option, forgiveness is the hope of the world. Learning it together is the only way we can begin to move beyond the resentments and violence that are tearing our collective and individual bodies apart. Learning forgiveness, if we are, will involve our learning nonviolence as a shared way of life. Nonviolence is, at root, a public, collective commitment, not simply an option for individuals.

Learning forgiveness and teaching nonviolence should become a vocation and mission of the church and other religious organizations and movements. This is the only way any religion can truly be "a light to the nations."

. . . . .

> Father, forgive them; for they do not know what they are doing.
>
> JESUS, according to Luke

Several critical assumptions

In thinking about forgiveness in a world as profoundly broken as ours, where people who have been horribly violated are living in every community, most neighborhoods, and many homes, I want to be as clear as possible about several assumptions I bring to this writing:

- A primary reason we humans need to think together about forgiveness is that the future of the larger social order, indeed the future of the world, is at stake here. Unless we—and I am primarily speaking about us, collectively—learn better how to forgive our enemies and how to ask for and live with (or without) the forgiveness of those people and creatures we have violated, we are likely to destroy ourselves as communities and nations and perhaps as planet Earth.

- I am not assuming that all of us are equally guilty or innocent. To be sure, there are victims of violence and there are perpetrators of violence and abuse. In most violent situations, the two ought not to be confused. (There are certain situations in which it is not as clear—the woman who kills an abusive spouse; warriors who kill other warriors who have killed their families; etc.) Wherever violence happens, it is the fault and responsibility of the abusers, the batterers, the rapists, the torturers, and the war-makers. But much violence in the world is also the responsibility of many others, those whose wealth, social standing, quality of life, or survival is somehow secured by the war that is underway, or the starvation of a segment of the people, or the execution of political criminals. So while I am not assuming that, in any situation, everyone is equally guilty or innocent, and I am assuming that, in many situations, there is very clearly a perpetrator who is responsible and a victim who is not, I do assume that, in the larger moral picture of our life together as a people on this planet, none of us is innocent—not even babies who by the time they get here have begun to be formed by the dynamics of violence that shape us all. In this larger moral framework, each and every one of us needs forgiveness—that is, to be pardoned by our sister and brother creatures and by the God who connects us to one another so that we can get on with our life together, unencumbered by excessive guilt or resentment.

• In the pages that follow, I am not saying that every one of us, individually, should forgive those who violate us if we are to be good people or in right relation. I regard the process of forgiveness much as I do the "coming out" process for gay men and lesbians, bisexual and transgendered people. We do it as we can, when we are ready, and we need to support one another in being wherever we are in the process—whether of coming out or of learning how to receive and give forgiveness. They are both empowering spiritual and political processes.

• I am suggesting in this final part of the book that unless we learn how to support one another in receiving forgiveness (which involves repenting and making amends) and in offering forgiveness (which involves leaving an opening for others to repent and make amends), we are probably doomed as people.[1]

Before we examine forgiveness as a spiritual path and political commitment, however, we need to look at how and why it has become such a distorted and debilitating concept in much of Christian life.

Imaging atonement

And God looked around
On all that he had made.
He looked at his sun,
And he looked at his moon,
And he looked at his little stars . . .
And God said:
I'm lonely still.

Then God sat down
On the side of a hill
Where he could think;
By a deep, wide river
He sat down;
With his head in his hands,
God thought and thought,

Till he thought:
I'll make me a man!

(Johnson 1927, 19–20)

With these words, James Weldon Johnson introduces an African American image of a god who, like any lonely person, wants a friend, someone to keep him company. Not only is this relationship to be a friendly one, it is one of God's great creative acts—the beginning of the human race, created for the purpose of befriending God. I cite this particular theological example because the Black Church in the United States, like some of the more evangelical and pentecostal white Protestant churches, has understood the divine-human relation to be a *friendship*.

While this might appear to run contrary to an experience of God as our relational power, I believe it does not. The image of God as friend illuminates the understanding of our power in relation as sacred.[2] In my theological work on our power in mutual relation, the image of God as *friend* has played a prominent, critical role.[3] *This is because the human experience of friendship is our fullest and most complete opening into the experience of mutuality.* Through friendship with other humans—communally and individually, socially and personally—as well as the rest of creation, we can most fully know our power in mutual relation. To borrow an image from cyberspace, friendship often is our primary gateway to God.

People will naturally ask, "But what if a person really is alone or has no friends? Can that person not experience God?" Yes, such people can experience God. They can do so by re-membering those who have been there too, those who have gone before, and those who are with them even now through the power of the Spirit that has been cultivated and grown by the ancestors and others in the communion of saints in their own struggles for right relation. Buber says, "In the beginning is the relation." We might say also, "In the beginning is friendship." That is how I understand "mutual relation"—as a synonym for "friend"—and this, I suspect, is something like what James Weldon Johnson had in mind in his great poem.

Looking a little further into Johnson's experience of God, we are met by African American history and community at the heart of his theology. Johnson is writing a poem about *creation* in the midst of a community devastated by slavery and its legacy of white racism. In this terrible historical context, the Black poet images God himself as "lonely" and wanting a friend. In the midst of evil, degradation, and a loneliness of the soul, creation *is* friendship—the making of right, mutual relation, whether between races in some utopic time and place, or in the immediate here and now among Black people experiencing friendship with one another in community, as a resource for survival.

Like friendship as a theological image, atonement is not an abstraction that floats free of social and personal experience. In Johnson's theology, much like Holocaust survivor Elie Wiesel's, the making of right relation with God—atonement—if it is to be at all, happens in a context of radical evil, in which what is most evident is peoples' *wrong* relation with God.

The historical context of evil is the crucible of atonement. Wrong relation between groups of people, in which one group is violating and destroying another, or in which people are destroying other creatures and the earth itself—this is the context in which right relation with God always needs to be made. But what does such atonement actually involve? And how does it happen?[4]

We probably cannot envision "right relation" with a spiritual energy the way we can with another person. And whereas God's "being" is basically a spiritual energy or power and not a person, we often catch glimpses of this power in relation to people. For this reason, many of us can more clearly recognize God in relation to one another. We sometimes can image atonement more easily, therefore, if we have a personal picture of God as "one of us"—anthropomorphized, if only momentarily, so that we can notice the relational dynamics of atonement.

In this spirit, let us image God for a moment as one of us: She is devastated that Her human friends have betrayed her. "Again and again you called us to return."[5] Our response to God's call, historically and still today, has been to turn away. We deny our white privilege. We are oblivious to our anti-Semitism. We trivialize our misogyny. We justify our homophobia. We make excuses, always excuses, for ourselves.

What is God's response?

As the source of justice-love, God is also the wellspring of compassion, the creator and liberator of all that is wise and good. Because She knows the secrets of our hearts and our wounded, frightened places,

She also understands that we are not being true to ourselves, one another, or Her. God knows that, in this sense, we do not know what we are doing. Still, She loves us and She yearns for our well-being. She grieves our violence against one another and ourselves. In her yearning and grief, She offers us Herself—as friend. Reaching for us, She longs for us to reciprocate, to meet Her as companion. This is her forgiveness—the YES which is Her yearning, Her grief, Her offering, Her reaching, without ceasing.

God forgives us. But She knows that we cannot "accept" this forgiveness, because we do not experience it. And we do not experience it because we have not turned around to meet Her. We fail to notice that She is with us. In our ignorance or fear, we do not hear God, we do not believe Her, and we do not yet know that we need Her. Instead, we malinger in violence and confusion, guilt and self-justification. Over time, we languish, cut off more and more from others, from ourselves, and from the Spirit, descending to that "place" in ourselves and our world that many poets and religious teachers have called "hell," a place of utter isolation.

Our own experiences tell us that nothing is sadder than to watch those whom we love turn away from us and slowly, or not so slowly, descend into hell. So too with God, nothing could be sadder for God than when we turn away, knowing not what we do, and slip away into hells of our own making.

How then, in this situation, *is* right relation made? Where *is* atonement?

Like forgiveness, atonement has two "moments." The first is eternal: the Spirit is constantly yearning, offering, and reaching for us. There is never a moment in or beyond time and space in which this is not the case. In the second, we are moved through solidarity, community, friendship, prayer, and other resources to go with God, to live willingly in her Spirit. This often involves our repentance, our commitment to turn from the wrong we have done and live differently by turning to God and one another in the struggle for mutuality. But turning to God, going with God, choosing to live in the Spirit of mutuality, has consequences.

For Christians, this is what the cross represents: consequences. It is also what the Empty Tomb points to. Going with God, we suffer at the hands of those who turn away from Her. Yet mutually involved with the Spirit of Life and Love, we are sustained a day at a time through friendship, community, prayer, and other spiritual gifts. Living in the Sacred, embodying its power, we ourselves become agents of atonement, participants in making right relation with God and one another.

This is the historical and spiritual process of incarnation. It is also the historical and spiritual process of atonement. It is what the JESUS story was all about and still is, insofar as we embody it in our lives. In the Spirit that sparked JESUS, we too live. And we suffer *because* we too live passionately in God.

The problem with the Christian atonement tradition

No one whose work I know has done a clearer, fairer exposition of the atonement tradition in Christianity than D. M. Baillie. In responding to "modern man's [*sic*]" question, "Why speak of atonement at all?" Baillie sets out to persuade the modern reader that the good life is "bankrupt without the message of the forgiveness of sins" and that this message of forgiveness "must rest on a doctrine of divine atonement."[6] I agree with both of these assumptions, but Baillie's understanding of "divine atonement" is very different from mine. His position—a modern, neo-orthodox view—illustrates what I believe to be the root problem with how atonement has been presented in Christian tradition.

Baillie charges, rightly I believe, that Western men and women[7] tend to psychologize away both our "sin" and our needs for "forgiveness." He perceives that we have replaced any strong sense of spiritual malaise with what he calls a "moral-failure complex,"[8] which he describes as "an uneasy dissatisfaction with [ourselves] and with what [we] have made of [our] moral opportunity. [We] do not consciously accuse [ourselves], for [we] have a protective pride which is highly characteristic of the whole situation."[9]

Like most of his contemporaries, who were writing in the mid-twentieth century, Baillie trivialized the weight of emotional trauma in shaping human experience. He wrote, for example, "As soon as [the] source of the personal problem in some 'trivial origin' or 'unpleasant experience long forgotten' is discovered and dragged up into full consciousness, it can be calmly faced, it loses its terror, which had no real foundation, and the mind is healed."[10] For Baillie, however, the moral-failure complex is deeper and more spiritually challenging than this. We may assume we can overcome our own emotional problems with the help of psychotherapy or drugs. Baillie knew better.

For him, the moral-failure complex is a malaise of the *soul*, not simply of the mind or body. It has a "foundation which is not trivial or innocent but solid and evil: the fact of moral failure, the fact that a man [sic] has disobeyed his conscience, betrayed his ideals, tarnished his character, lost his battle."[11] He continues, "These are hard facts, and the sting is not taken out of them [unlike psychological problems] when they are faced in the light of day. That makes them look worse instead of better."[12]

At this deep, soulful level of experience, Baillie insists that the solution is not to try to face further into our problems or seek to understand them, "because it is self-centered . . . which is the very root of evil."[13] "There is no solution until we allow the whole situation to be transformed by an orientation towards God," he maintains. "A moralist, as such, can never forgive himself. That is where we see most plainly the bankruptcy of the attempt to have morality without the life of faith."[14]

I strongly agree with Baillie's understanding of our need for God, not just better self-understanding. Except for his dismissive attitude toward emotional trauma as a root cause of human distress, I think he sees rather clearly the problem with our attempts to get on with our lives without coming to terms with our failures. "We have left undone those things which we ought to have done, and we have done those things which we ought not to have done."[15] We may be able to get on with our lives, but our spirits cannot soar. We are weighted down with guilt and shame from which there is no simply rational, psychological, or physical release.

> When it was noon, darkness came over the whole land until three in the afternoon. At three o'clock JESUS cried out with a loud voice, "Eloi, Eloi, lema sabachthani?" which means, "My God, my God, why have you forsaken me?" (Mark 15:33-34)

the greatest danger
in being feared hated
rejected violated
otherwise scorned
or put down and out
is that in our pain
we fall so easily
into shame and so
ashamed of ourselves
we slip downward
into hell: that place
in which we are
inside ourselves
alone.

Come stand together in these times
of violence betrayal and fear.
Do not be undone by the powers
from hell that pursue us most
zealously when we're feeling lousy
about ourselves and others.

"The powers from hell that pursue us most zealously when we're feeling lousy about ourselves and others." This image may give us a clue about what Baillie means by our "moral-failure complex." It is more than simply a "bad time" or "rough day"; more than the moral equivalent of a headache or stumped toe. We are actively pursued by the powers from hell—forces throughout the world/church that prey upon us when we're down on ourselves, stuck in a sense of being unworthy, expecting to receive the "vinegar" we "deserve," feeling increasingly a combination of "nothing" and "alone."

In this condition—which is a massive *social*, not just personal, problem for us today—we often seem to be fine. We work hard and well and are upbeat and even cavalier to all outward appearances. We appear to be successful. We may be well-liked and highly regarded by our peers. In Baillie's words, "[Our moral-failure complex] becomes a repressed complex, festering uneasily under the surface, with the effect of *confusing the whole moral outlook, paralyzing moral endeavor, inhibiting every attempt at a new beginning.*"[16]

One of the great spiritual opportunities for many of my generation of Westerners (several generations younger than Baillie) has been to be faced with the fact—and *spiritual* problem—of our addictions. We should not dismiss "addiction talk" as simply one more way of psychologizing away our afflictions and responsibilities. As a recovering alcoholic and bulimarexic woman, I am clear about the spiritual malaise in which my addictive behavior was and still can be steeped. Like the founders of Alcoholics Anonymous in 1935,[17] Baillie realized that when the spirit is drowning (literally in alcohol or, more figuratively, in life's complexities), we cannot just change our behavior as an act of will. We cannot just say no. We cannot simply figure it out and do life differently. Our emotions and our bodies, as sick as we may be and as badly in need of treatment, are only part of what is hurting. Our souls—the place in us in which we most deeply meet one another and all creation—are weary and afraid and lonely.

The fact is, we need to be able to *experience* our power in mutual relation with one another and creation. In the language of AA, we need "a spiritual awakening." We need to know the Sacred Power in which we live and breathe and have our being.

Forgiveness is our way to God (our power in mutual relation).

Forgiveness is our way to god (verb).

Forgiveness is spiritual liberation from the shackles of the past. It frees us to go forward, "not to shut the door on the past,"[18] and to know peace. Knowing ourselves forgiven by the Spirit of life itself—empowered to go forth, unstuck and able to live each new day with a sense of personal grounding in the Spirit—we ourselves become God-bearers, agents of forgiveness, to others. And that, of course, is atonement—making right relation with God.

> One of the criminals who were hanged there kept deriding him and saying, "Are you not the Messiah? Save yourself and us!" But the other rebuked him, saying, "Do you not fear God, since you are under the same sentence of condemnation? And we indeed have been condemned justly, for we are getting what we deserve for our deeds, but this man has done nothing wrong." Then he said, "Jesus, remember me when you come into your kingdom." He replied, "Truly I tell you, today you will be with me in Paradise." (Luke 23:39-43)

when we are
really present,
vulnerable
with one another
amidst the moral
clutter of our
lives, we are
honest. and when
we are, we see
each other:
I see you
and you see
me.

Let us be honest with one another
so that we can more fully love
and see who we are, you and me.

The problem therefore with the traditional and by far most widely held Christian understanding of atonement as a "substitutionary" and "sacrificial" act of God[19] is that it drives a huge and misleading wedge between how we experience God's love and suffering and how we experience *our own* love and suffering.

Most of what we humans actually *experience* as healing and liberating—justice, compassion, children and family, human love and friendship, beauty of creation, meaningful work, enough to eat, a place to live, animal companions, self-confidence, erotic pleasure and joy, mutuality in relation to others—is assumed by most Christians to be *human*, not necessarily divine, experience.

Whether God is actually present and active in our embodied lives, most Christians believe, depends on the quality of our faith in God through our faith in (the divinity of) His Son JESUS CHRIST. We doubt human experience as a reliable source of sacred meaning unless the particular experience is that of a faithful Christian. Our hesitancy to recognize ourselves and other humans and creatures—regardless of religious affiliations and creeds—as sources of God's love, power, and beauty reinforces the God-over-and-against-us dualism that continues to haunt us and generates our alienation from ourselves, one another, other creatures, and God. It also allows us to imagine that God, since we experience Him as wholly other than ourselves, one "out there" beyond us, actually might be the author of blood sacrifice traditions, ancient and modern.

The older Augustine's somewhat less dualistic faith notwithstanding, mainline Christians continue to reflect his earlier Manichean apprehension of a god who was indeed over and against the world.[20] Baillie and most other Christian theologians following Augustine believe that the *human experience* of God's forgiveness, in and of itself, is not enough. They tend to trivialize it, as well as our other experiences of God's love, as too soft and gentle, not tough enough.

> Is God's love for sinners simply "kindly judgment"? Nay, it is a "consuming fire." He cannot take our sins lightly or treat them with indulgence. "The love that draws us nearer Thee is hot with wrath to them."[21]

Rejecting humanist, secularist, and liberal Christian positions on God's love and forgiveness as morally weak, Baillie and his orthodox Christian colleagues insist that human beings simply do not and cannot know what God is *really* like—"a consuming fire"—unless we realize that He is Bigger, Better, and Other than anything we can imagine or experience, much less help bring into being ourselves through our experiences of mutuality here on earth.

The problem here is in the dualistic assumption that our experiences of mutuality are *merely* human. Baillie and most other traditional Christians begin with an assumption that whatever is human—such as our experiences of forgiveness—is tepid compared to the "inexorable" love of God. Human and other created beings are cast as less loving and less good than God—which is true enough, but too often misleading in its moral and pastoral effect, which is to depress our senses of agency, our power to share and embody the love of God. This is not something most of us do with much consistency, collectively or individually; yet we not only do embody and give flesh to sacred love, it is what we are here to do—the purpose of creation itself, God's plan for us. Human and creaturekind is not un-godly in the eyes of God. More often than most Christians have seemed to realize, human beings are sources and resources of divine love, justice-making, and compassion. It is what we are created to be.

Still, Baillie writes that it is not enough for us to love one another, yearn for right relation, and struggle to go with the Spirit in our daily affairs. This is fine, but for Baillie it is not the spiritual or moral equivalent of putting our faith in a God who loved us so much that He gave his only Son to be sacrificed for us—to undergo a death that we, not he, deserved (and deserve) as punishment for our sins (moral-failures). Baillie and with him much of Christianity maintains that it is precisely God's willingness to punish and be punished (for remember that JESUS is God in this story, both Father and Son)—as a surrogate, in our place—that reveals His relentless love for us sinners.

> After this, when JESUS knew that all was now finished, he said (in order to fulfill the scripture), "I am thirsty." A jar full of sour wine was standing there. So they put a sponge full of the wine on a branch of hyssop and held it to his mouth. (John 19:28-29)

we in the United States
are bearers of much shame:
debilitating senses
that we are rotten
at the core,
and of course we
expect that vinegar
will be offered
to quench our deepest
thirst because that's exactly
what we give one
another in response
to pain fear and shame:
bitterness and beatings,
booze and pills,
punishment and
rejection.

Lead us, strong sister, to streams of cool water.
Kneel down with us to drink. And let us take
the thirsty brother a chalice of fresh water,
not blood, his or ours. Amen.

For us to liberate human bodies and spirits through social movements and personal transformation, to redeem one another from bondage to past mistakes and violence, to temper judgment with compassion and solidarity—this forgiveness is not enough for most Christian teachers, preachers, and pastors.

For brothers and sisters to reach out to us, offering gifts of their experience, strength, and hope, and for them to watch sorrowfully as we turn away into isolation and despair—this forgiveness is not enough for mainline Christians.

For God to wait—simply to wait—with us in faith, hope, and love—this forgiveness is not enough for Baillie's "God."

Very early in the shaping of Christology, the "fathers" (dominant theological forces) realized—rightly, I believe—that our human experiences of justice-making and love, of contrition and forgiveness, of vulnerability and compassion, of loss and grief will not make a perfect world, one without sin and evil. These theologians believed that the completion, or perfection, of creation requires *more* than the struggle for right relation, *more* than one another's solidarity, *more* than our faith in the power of God with us to change the world, and *more* than the patience to wait with one another by the power of this same Spirit. The fathers believed that the *more* required to usher in the realm of God in its fullness is JESUS CHRIST, and that this JESUS must be *more* than merely a good (human) example or "moral influence."[22] Thus, the fathers taught that JESUS was not simply a human brother ablaze with the spirit and love of God. He was God, and not just any god but one who, in the sacrificial tradition of Israel, offered Himself as a blood sacrifice "for the sins of the world."[23]

But why was and is such carnage the will of a God who is love? Because, the fathers tell us, divine love is like that of a really good friend. When we betray a true friend, Baillie notes, we suffer for what we have done.[24] We suffer *because* we realize that we have violated a significant relationship. Moreover, the one whom we have wounded suffers with us because those who love suffer with those whom they love. It is in the very nature of love—to suffer with others. This is true, of course. But what Baillie and most Christian theologians seem not to see is that such a truly beloved friend does not punish by humiliating or destroying those whom he or she loves.

No true lover injures or kills the beloved as punishment for wrongdoing. We do not have to give up our deep sense of the need for forgiveness, a yearning that goes far beyond our capacities to reason or work it out by ourselves, to reject as morally bankrupt the church's atonement tradition of humiliation and destruction. We need to say *no* to a tradition of violent punishment and to a God who would crucify us—much less an innocent brother in our place—rather than hang in with us, struggle with us, wait with us, and grieve for us—forever and eternally if need be.

If God is our creative and liberating power, then this same God is a Spirit of "revolutionary patience."[25] After all, God's creation is unfinished and imperfect. We humans are unfinished and in many ways raw and rough. In our ignorance and fear, often not knowing what we are doing morally or spiritually, we turn away from God and break rank with the sacred Spirit of mutuality. In this real life context, God's healing power is Her presence as a deeply sorrowful God who can do nothing except continue to reach out to us through Her friends and other sacred resources, one day at a time. Continuing to reach out to us, steadfastly refusing to give up, relentlessly pursuing us generation to generation—this is God's forgiveness. And this, perhaps more than anything, is the primary theme of this book.

The deity we must reject is the one whose power over us is imagined to be His love, the god who morally *can* destroy us. Such a concept of deity is evil—a betrayal itself of our power in mutual relation—in a world being torn to pieces by violence done in the name of gods who demand blood sacrifice. Such god-images feed twisted psychospiritualities that normalize sadistic and masochistic dynamics, rape and intimate violence, abuse of children, relationships of domination and control, violence against people and all creatures, and wars justified as holy.

Moreover, in the context of such distorted spiritualities, violence often is experienced as passionately erotic. This is because our erotic energy is at root a yearning for God as our power to make and sustain mutuality.[26] When this yearning twists into a desire for domination or submission—which is what patriarchal relations do to our sacred erotic energies—the desire creates closets in which men (and sometimes women) experience our erotic yearnings for God as violent and often, for this reason, seek God in the convergence of sex and violence.[27]

The deep roots in Christianity of a psychosexual spirituality that links sex and violence are being cultivated to this day by a twisted understanding of atonement that is assumed by most Christians to be right and central to Christian faith. Most Christians do not realize that this central tenet of our religion is steeped in our collective fear of experiencing the power of mutuality—in truth, our fear of God's love for us and of our love for God.

We fear this primary experience of God's incarnation—we fear living passionately. And we fear atonement, which is our liberation from the powers of evil through God's passion working in our lives. We fear our power in mutual relation because if we go with it, we—like JESUS—will suffer, perhaps even die, at the hands of a culture of violence that demands our worship; moreover, *we will live.*

Patriarchal logic and blood sacrifice

The atonement tradition described above reflects a god who is the quintessence of patriarchal logic rather than the wellspring of justice-love from which we draw strength, hope, and our experiences of forgiveness. This tradition, as we see, has been associated with the violence of bloodshed. In Western patriarchal monotheism, ruling class males have constructed theologies in which the shedding of innocent blood is assumed to be *necessary* to making right relation with God. This seems to me an amazing thing! The suggestion that, throughout human history and culture, men (I do not use this word inclusively in this context) have concluded that the only way to get right with the Source of love and justice in history is to offer Him the blood of innocent "victims."

Unfortunately, I am not embellishing one small problematic theme in an otherwise liberating theological heritage. Nor am I being too literal in suggesting that *blood sacrifice* has been established spiritually and politically as *the* way to God/god in Christianity.

In one of her short stories, Ursula LeGuin tells of Omelas, a utopic city in which people are living together in perfect peace, happiness, and prosperity. Everything is absolutely wonderful—except for one thing:

> In a basement under one of the beautiful public buildings . . . there
> is a room [with] one locked door, and no window. . . . In the room
> a child is sitting. It could be a boy or a girl. It looks about six, but

actually is nearly ten. It is feeble-minded. Perhaps it was born defective, or perhaps it has become imbecile through fear, malnutrition, and neglect. . . . It is so thin there are no calves to its legs; its belly protrudes; it lives on a half-bowl of corn meal and grease a day. It is naked. . . . It sits in its own excrement continually. They all know it's there, all the people of Omelas. Some of them have come to see it, others are content merely to know it's there. They all know that it has to be there.[28]

LeGuin goes on to describe what happens when young people are taken, for the first time, to observe this phenomenon:

No matter how well the matter has been explained to them, these young spectators are always shocked and sickened at the sight. They feel disgust, which they had thought themselves superior to.[29]

And the most extraordinary thing of all, according to LeGuin, is that sometimes people simply leave the city.

The place they go towards is . . . even less imaginable to most of us than [Omelas]. I cannot describe it at all. It is possible that it does not exist. But they seem to know where they are going, the ones who walk away from Omelas.[30]

In using this story to teach theology, I try to elicit students' recognition of at least two important theo-ethical matters: the presence of evil in life, even—maybe often—in apparently benign contexts; and the question of moral agency, our power to act in moral ways, given particular situations and limited options. I also try to show that patriarchal logic requires blood sacrifice and creates scapegoats such as the child in Omelas, countless other disposable persons/creatures, and people like JESUS who stand in solidarity with them. We daughters and sons of patriarchy seem to assume that someone *must* be betrayed if others are to live.

But why? Because we sense that it is in the very nature of things? Because from the beginning, God and Satan are struggling for victory over the world? Because throughout their struggle, evil remains as strong as good, demanding from one historical moment to the next that innocent creatures be killed in order to appease the gods or ransom others from the same fate? But is such innocence, readiness, or willingness (in the case of JESUS and many others) to be sacrificed the supreme paradigm of moral goodness, the historical event that best demonstrates the superior strength of good/God over evil/Satan?

In her story, LeGuin seems to reject the logic that would make a virtue of anyone's *willingness* to sacrifice another, even for the common well-being. In telling us about "the ones who walk away" from Omelas, LeGuin seems to be asking if we have the power to "walk away" from the expectation that an innocent should be sacrificed for us.

Womanist poet and theologian Delores S. Williams also addresses the question of sacrifice in the context of African American women's lives. Williams directly addresses us through history, and her primary call and challenge is to the historical *victims* of sacrifice—Black women used as "surrogate" sexual objects, playthings, servants, and nursemaids by white men, women, and children. Over time, through this surrogacy, Williams contends, African American women have become scapegoats of white men's (and women's) sexual desires and representatives of white people's sexual pleasure. Williams enlarges the questions raised by LeGuin by putting them in historical perspective. She challenges the logic that there is moral virtue in sacrificing either others *or ourselves.* The big question raised implicitly by both LeGuin and Williams is why *anyone*—the child in Omelas, Black women, Jews, queer folk, or JESUS—should be subjected to violence.

With LeGuin, Williams, and others, I am arguing that we ought not participate in a social or religious order constructed on the blood sacrifice of *anyone* for the common good. Nor should we worship a god who legitimizes it. We should rather be struggling to expunge from our spirituality and politics the patriarchal logic that such sacrifice is good for us or others. We *must* do this if we hope to be nonviolent people. The rest of this chapter is an envisioning of a Christian faith that does not rest on a theology of blood sacrifice and does not lend itself to the perpetuation of cultures of violence.[31]

Through the eyes of God

Forgiveness[32] is the letting go of resentment or shame that has resulted from wrongdoing, our own or others'. It is a creating, liberating, and life-giving aspiration.

To forgive ourselves, or to accept another's forgiveness of us, is to begin the process of repentance, of "turning, turning, 'till we come 'round right,"[33] a relational journey that must always involve making amends and restitution.

Such forgiveness can happen only inasmuch as we view one another—and ourselves—through the eyes of God.

Of course, we are not God, none of us alone nor all of us together. For any of us, collectively or individually, to assume that we can "speak for God" or "act for God" is always dangerous. More often than not, it reflects self-righteousness and arrogance, and it signals how out of touch we are from the ground of our own lives, those of others, and the life of the Spirit. To assume that we are speaking or acting on God's behalf often accompanies horrific behavior against humans and other creatures. This presumptuous attitude of those who are right is a root of the violence that Christians (and people of other religions as well) have done historically to people of other faith traditions as well as to those within their own religion whom they perceive as deviating from what is right.

Yet it is paradoxically true that, whenever people are struggling to see others in the fullness of these others' humanity or creatureliness—a yearning to recognize the fullness of being in which the Sacred *always* is steeped, in every creature's life—they are in fact perceiving these others through the eyes of God. Through these "eyes"— a metaphor for perception—we see one another as sisters and brothers truly in the Spirit. We come to know one another as we are created, in and by God, to be. This knowledge is the basis of our capacities to receive or offer forgiveness, and it is our best hope as creatures in a world seething with resentment, violence, and the desire for revenge.

A remarkable phenomenon in our time has been the Truth and Reconciliation Commission established in South Africa in the wake of apartheid and chaired by retired Anglican Archbishop Desmond Tutu.[34] The Commission, created by the government of Nelson Mandela to help bring some resolution to the seemingly endless bitterness in a nation torn apart by apartheid, aimed to do some justice in relation to those who had been killed, tortured, or otherwise savaged by their brothers and sisters. In response to confessions of truth and repentance for wrongs done, the Commission granted amnesty, or pardon, to those involved in violent activity during the evil reign of apartheid. Key here was the blanket offer of forgiveness by the state to those who would confess and repent.

Throughout the world many followed with interest the testimonies of people on different sides of this fierce historical battle and were deeply moved by the Commission's effort. The Truth and Reconciliation Commission based its work on a belief in not only the spiritual but moreover the political efficacy—that is, the workability and usefulness—of *forgiveness* in the healing of a nation. In much the same Spirit as Nicaraguan leaders Miguel d'Escoto, Tomas Borge, and Ernesto Cardenal in the period following the Sandinistas' 1979 victory over the brutal dictatorship of Anastasio Somoza, South Africa's current leadership has taken a leap of faith in the power of forgiveness to help mend the political, economic, psychological, and other social and spiritual fractures incurred during and after apartheid.

By sad contrast, if the United States were *as a nation* more forgiving, we would be a truly great moral leader in the world today. But through our public policies, we show that we are not, collectively, a forgiving people. We tend instead to nurse resentments against those whom we experience as enemies, be they other countries like Cuba or people within the United States whose very presence seems to tear at our perception of ourselves as "those who are right." Thus, for example, we lean increasingly on the death penalty as a response to crime; we rely on bombs and retaliation as a response to terrorism; and recently we have voiced self-righteous condemnation and echo rhetorical calls for the harsh punishment of a publicly repentant President whose behavior has shown us mainly how much like the rest of us he is, flawed and inconsistent in his own ways of life and leadership.

The United States is not unique, of course, in forging public policy out of resentments and hostilities that seek retribution and revenge. But our military and economic strength, coupled with our claims to be the leader of the world, make our unforgiving politics, policies, and rhetoric of righteousness especially dangerous to us as well as other humans and creatures.

We must learn a better way, a more forgiving way into the heart of the JESUS story, if we hope to share peace in this world.

when we betray or batter,
lie to or deny, those whom we love,
we rip into the heart of God herself.

the only adequate response,
you say, both yours and ours,
is a sorrow too deep for words,
and a renewed commitment.[35]

> Holy One, help us honor our commitments in ways
> that are honest and kind, so that together and apart
> we might meet you more fully and, through your
> Spirit, learn to love.

JESUS CHRIST as adversary

Alongside images of JESUS CHRIST as authoritarian Lord and righteous moralist is another image often held sacred by those Christians who are right: JESUS CHRIST as adversary, fighter, and finally victor over his enemies, the evil ones who oppose God. The christological image of a divine man who casts opponents into hellfires diminishes our capacity as Christians to imagine, much less experience, the healing power generated not through shame and demolition but rather through forgiveness.

But forgiveness is a badly misconceived notion——especially among those Christians who spiritualize and individualize it, reducing it to the level of a soft, morally vacuous, personal feeling. This is probably what most of us do at least some of the time. Those who go about piously "forgiving" others may be among the least forgiving when it comes to exacting revenge on those who hurt us personally. Moreover, "forgiveness" so often is pared down spiritually to a petty self-righteousness ("See how good I am. See how I can forgive you!"). And in the larger picture, on the front lines of history, countless violent, brutal crusaders for what is right no doubt have experienced themselves as godly, forgiving people in relation to those whom they love.

The point is not simply whether we individually can let go of our resentments toward those who have offended us; nor is it simply whether we can accept the pardon of those whom we ourselves have hurt. The larger question is whether together we can reconstruct the world around and within us on patterns of forgiveness rather than resentment, compassion rather than retribution, peace rather than violence. The future of our families and communities, cultures and societies, religions and nations is at stake here. The future of our love and work, of what we will do and of how we will do it, depends upon our shared commitment to learn forgiveness as a way of life. Indeed, the future of our species and of the earth itself rests more than anything on our capacity, as an earthpeople, to move morally beyond adversarial, hostile posturing in relation to those whom we hate or fear.

Our salvation is not rooted in a JESUS who lords His righteousness over us or a God who will beat us into submission or cast us into a fiery furnace if we aren't right. Whether we are right or wrong in the specifics of lives and deeds, we will be saved primarily by a capacity (that is innate to us all) and a willingness (that can be learned with each other's help) to practice forgiveness precisely because, so often, we "know not what we do." The JESUS we need is the one we have in *learning how to forgive* (for that's where most of us are). We need him to be what he is—through faith, our brother and ally, teacher and friend, spiritual presence and ongoing resource of hope.

Could it be that JESUS himself, like probably every one of us, had a hard time forgiving certain of his adversaries? When he said, from the cross, "Father, forgive them, for they do not know what they are doing," was he asking God to do something that he, JESUS, could not do in the particular moment, so anguished was he?[36] Or was he bearing witness to the possibility that *only* God, in God's own mysterious ways, can forgive? That the Spirit has to work out, over time and through history, how to take away our sins and let the slate be wiped clean?

I am suggesting that, because God is *our* power in the struggle for justice-love, we are indeed able to forgive, provided we realize how truly empowered we are in and through God.

What forgiveness is

Many of us grew up hearing that we should "forgive and forget." Today we often realize that this mandate is badly flawed. We have a sense that if we forget the past, we are forgetting ourselves—where we have been, what we have done, what has happened to us, what it means to us, where we are today and why.

As a matter of fact, to forget a wrong done to us means that we will never be able to forgive those responsible for it.

Christians often commend forgiveness as a panacea for just about all that ails us and our society, as if all we must do to feel better is forgive those who have hurt us. But why *should* we forgive those who have injured us, especially if it has happened in a spirit of malice or greed, violence or contempt? Even more basically, how *can* we forgive violent, hateful acts against us and others?

What *is* forgiveness? Why is it so important morally and pastorally, psychologically and politically, and at the same time so elusive and, at times, impossible, for us to bear as giver or recipient?

Forgiveness is a social, political, and psychospiritual leap out of the past toward the future. It is a passage through obsession with wrongs done. Even in small ways, it is a radical political act because it is the work of justice-love and thereby an indispensable step in peace-making with one's enemies.

Forgiveness is the letting go of resentment over what has been done in order to get on with life. It has at least as much to do with the capacity of those who have been wounded to move forward as with those who have inflicted the injury. We forgive as much for ourselves, our own well-being, as for others. In the image and ways of God, we probably forgive more for ourselves than for others.

Sometimes we suffer more *after* we have been hurt than in the violent act itself precisely because we are unable to move on. Whether as a people or as individuals, forgiveness is the spiritual act of moving on, of not letting betrayals, violence, or pain continue to define us.

But as previously discussed, because we humans are in God's image, we—like God—cannot move fully into right relation with those who have violated us unless they are willing to repent, make amends, and work toward the possibility of making or re-making right relation.

Still, those who have been violated have a great deal at stake in being able to open, however slowly, to the possibility of forgiving those who have wronged them. For it is only through offering forgiveness to those who have hurt us and accepting the forgiveness of those whom we have betrayed or violated that we are able to break the stranglehold of the past and, in a very real sense, begin the pilgrimage back to a peace of mind, however far away it may seem to have gone.

Be clear that this does not happen overnight. We are talking about the passage of time—often months, years, maybe even generations of struggle to forgive. This is the sort of spiritual work that many in the U.S. South (and probably North as well) are still having to do, almost a century and a half after the Civil War. It is the sort of ongoing, long-standing task facing the Tutsi and Hutus in East Africa and the many ethnic/tribal groups in the Balkans and elsewhere around the world. It is of course the terribly challenging work that continues to weigh upon Native Americans, African Americans, Asian Americans, Hispanics, and all of the various Euro-American tribes that have experienced such violent, interlocking histories in the Americas—often because of racism and usually also because of economic, gender, sexual, and religious exploitation.

We Anglo-Americans might ask for forgiveness (though few have done so publicly) from those we have decimated. But we could not receive it, even if those many groups we have violated were willing to offer it to us, unless we were actively seeking ways to make amends and restitution, ways to go and sin no more, ways to put away racism, economic exploitation, and other interlocking oppressions. Maybe then, we as a people of different racial/tribal heritages and histories could begin the struggle for mutual relation at a deeper and more sustainable level than most people imagine to be possible.

Forgiveness is a matter of *not* forgetting. Indeed, it is a matter of remembering as clearly as possible what took place—and only then of being able, possibly, to begin to let it go rather than continue to be defined by it.

Forgiveness is not empowered simply by feeling good. It is generated by the sacred Spirit through some very particular, indispensable roots and resources, including:

- Building of solidarity through community and friendship
- Involvement in the struggle for justice-love
- Compassion and humility
- Capacity to be honest with ourselves
- Imagination/*phantasy*[37]
- Prayer and meditation

Let's examine a little more closely these resources through which, I believe, forgiveness may become more nearly possible:

The forging of solidarity in community with those whom we have experienced as enemy is a cornerstone of forgiveness. Whether as those who have been wounded, those who have hurt others, or, as is often the case, both, the ability to either give or receive forgiveness requires the active, strong, critical support of our friends and community. At one level, this is because evil and good, violence and peace, bondage and liberation have collective roots and communal meanings that require communal response. No one does good or evil outside the social context in which they make meaning of things and in which they have been shaped in many ways. No group and no individual can offer or accept forgiveness with much staying power without the solidarity—the critical support—of other communities and of friends.

Does this literally mean that forgiveness cannot happen unless those who are forgiving and those being forgiven have "a people," an embodied historical community? Yes it does, but not necessarily "in person" here and now. In one of her novels, Gloria Naylor[38] tells of a woman locked in a basement by her abusive husband. She winds up being able to stay sane and finally liberate herself by reading notes left in the basement by her husband's former wife who also had been his prisoner. In this case, "friendship" and "community" are not embodied in a person. Transcendent of time and space, they are created by these women, not one but two women, where their lives meet. Through this meeting—amidst a communion of saints, surrounded by a cloud of witnesses, in the presence of the ancestors—a living, breathing woman experiences herself as not alone and, thereby, as empowered to act with strength, which is her/our Sacred Power. She has a strength that she had not known she had and that, in truth, she did not have alone.

As groups and individuals, our involvement in the struggle for right relation, or justice-love, bolsters our capacities to give or receive forgiveness because, through this struggle, we are working already for the well-being of others, for our own well-being, and often for those who are not like us in ways that are historically and culturally significant (in terms, for example, of race/tribe, religion, language, sexual/gender identity, class, ability, species).

Through struggling alongside others for *their* "survival and quality of life"[39] *as well as our own,* we most deeply realize the presence of Sacred Power with us all. Moreover, we often become aware that this liberating power *is* the power of forgiveness. She is our God. She releases us from ways in which we have been short-sighted, ignorant, afraid, or in other ways disconnected from the needs of sisters and brothers to live in dignity and peace. God frees us from burdens of guilt, shame, and other senses of inadequacy. He gives us a new lease and enables us to start over spiritually. For in the struggle for right relation we come face to face with ourselves as we *all* are created to be. This reckoning with who we are *in* God, this acceptance of ourselves and others, is the warp and woof of forgiveness. It is how we come to realize that we ourselves are forgiven in and by the Spirit that meets us through others' acceptance of our place, alongside them, in the struggle and in life.

Compassion and humility are important cornerstones, along with community and friendship, of our capacities to give and receive forgiveness. As a commitment not to harm others, including our enemies if we can help it, compassion is a primary path into forgiveness, and humility is the psychospiritual ground in which compassion grows. Humility is not a self-effacing quality of personal deprecation or diminishment. It is a confidence that we are sharing the earth with the rest of humanity and creaturekind, including those whom we have hurt or who have hurt us. Humility is at root an awareness that we belong here in life, all of us, no one more than another. Hand in hand with compassion, humility strengthens our yearning for right relation and allows us at least to glimpse one another, however fleetingly, through the eyes of God.

Often in terrible situations in which some awful violence has been done to us, those close to us, or our people, we may not be able to, or wish to, participate *in person—as particular people, collectively or individually—*in struggling for right relation *in person* with the perpetrators of the violence. In such circumstances, compassion and humility can nudge us along over time toward forgiving them through prayer, through a slowly evolving willingness to forgive, and sometimes through the "surrogate presence" of those who, for now, can stand for us, as forgiving people. This is a primary and vital role that community—religious institutions, governmental groups (such as South Africa's Truth and Reconciliation Commission), mediators, chaplains, and neighbors—can play in the processes of forgiveness.

But again, why would we even want to forgive those who have violated us or others in horrible, sadistic, greedy, and other reprehensible ways—like slavery, apartheid, murder, rape, torture, terrors of so many kinds? Why would we even consider forgiving? Because only in being at least open to the possibility of forgiving those who have wreaked havoc in our lives and those of our people can we get on with our lives in the image and by the power of One who is the very essence of that justice-love that *is* forgiveness.

The capacity to be honest with ourselves, which is required for forgiveness, does not refer merely or even primarily to psychological health, but to facing our *spiritual* reality, getting grounded ourselves in God. That so many mental and physical health care providers in the West do not realize the important role of spirituality in the healing process undercuts, in my judgment, the power of their work.

Facing the wrong that has been done to us or by us, we can experience the world around and within us with greater emotional clarity and a stronger possibility for resolve. Feelings give us clues as to what has happened and what it means to us. Feelings are an important path into understanding our experience. We should not be misled by dominant cultural assumptions about the roles of "reason" (positive) and "emotion" (negative) in knowing what we know. *Honest* emotion does not diminish clarity or mute reason; it strengthens our capacities to think and understand. Emotional honesty secures our capacities to reflect on our experiences of violence and pain, whether as those wounded or those who have inflicted the injury.

We do not necessarily have to express ourselves honestly to those who have violated us. This is bound to vary greatly from one situation to another. Indeed, it can be unwise, even unthinkable, to have anything to do, personally, with those who have hurt us or others—or whom we have wounded. But we must be honest with *ourselves* and, if we do have good friends and community, we can turn to others with honest feelings about the violence that has been done.

To *feel* hurt and angry does not have to undercut our capacity to forgive. To *feel* guilty and remorseful does not have to inhibit our ability to accept forgiveness if it is offered. In fact, it is in refusing, or being unable, to feel such pain—yet stuck politically and socially, physically and mentally, in its effects—that we are more likely to throw up barriers to forgiveness and not know what we are doing or why we are doing it in relation to those whom we can only hate.

Imagination and the phantasy (the mix of imagination, intuition, and freedom that we have discussed earlier) is a creative energy for envisioning what may be possible, some day—ourselves as forgiven and forgiving people. Upheld by solidarity in community and friendship, strengthened by compassion and humility, emotionally honest with ourselves and with others where possible, we can catch glimpses of ourselves in right relation—even if we are not there now and are unlikely ever to be in the particular situations that we envision. We can see how it could be and might be someday for others, if not ourselves. We see our children and others who will inherit from us the strength to break the stranglehold of the past and let it go. We see our usually very small part in the relational movement of making justice-love in the world—both in the larger sweep of history and in our own more personal situations. We see that our part is to extend forgiveness to those who have harmed us—even if they cannot receive it because they are not repentant—and to accept it from those we have harmed.

Again, please be clear that I am not leveling all wrong relation, as if everyone were somehow equally guilty of violating others. This would be absurd and outrageous. I am suggesting that none of us is a stranger to wrong, broken relation. This assertion reflects the foundation of our life together as social, historical, communal characters. We live together in a badly distorted, damaged and damaging, world in which we and our people all are involved. No one born into this world is untouched by wrong relation and the evil we do in it. We pass on this evil, from one generation to another, from culture to culture and person to person, usually in ways that we don't recognize as evil.

In this world, *prayer and meditation* are spiritual foundations of our abilities both to forgive and to let ourselves be forgiven by God, even where other people may refuse to forgive us the wrong we and our people have done. By "prayer," I mean an intentional opening of our hearts and minds and bodyselves to the presence of the Spirit. Prayer is an active reaching, or speaking, to God, in which we talk and sing, whisper and scream, laugh and cry with the Sacred One in our midst, and we also become silent in its presence and listen for what may be said to us. In prayer, we struggle with the Spirit as we might our best friend. In the life of this Western Christian, meditation is a less verbally and cognitively active process. It is a way of becoming vulnerable in the Spirit, more of a letting go of ourselves "into" God than a conversation "with" God.

In the old Gestalt image of "ground" and "figure," prayer usually is "to" the figure whereas meditation is "in" the ground. For me, both are important ways of becoming more aware that we are rooted and grounded in a Spirit that empowers us at least to imagine that we can forgive one another and also receive the forgiveness offered by the Spirit—even if, in particular situations, our brothers and sisters here on planet Earth cannot or will not forgive us.

And how does the Spirit offer us forgiveness even when others don't? The Spirit empowers us through a variety of natural and human resources—such as community, books, art, music, stories, including the JESUS story. Through these gifts, God invites us to remember ourselves and one another as sisters and brothers. We remember that each of us is a wounded, flawed, and fragmented character who, as such, is involved in betraying right relation. Even so, broken and morally ragged ourselves, we are able, with the help of those who are there for us, to draw from the wisdom of those who have gone before and get on with our lives in the Spirit, never forgetting where we have been and what has happened.

Is repentance absolutely necessary?

breaking the stranglehold
of the past we risk being
toppled into a startling
new perception of those
we've harmed and also
those who've harmed us
and we see we can't make
false peace with them

and we see also that
this surely must be
the root of God's own
pain: accepting
that nothing
can be done
to make things
right with those
who turn away.

Can "nothing be done to make things right with those who turn away"? Liberation theologians have insisted that there can be no real forgiveness where there is no repentance. What are we to make of this?

When we have no remorse for our wrongdoing or perhaps do not believe we have done wrong and therefore are not repentant, we cannot accept forgiveness. Through our ignorance, denial, greed, false sense of pride, false sense of loyalties, "hardness of heart," and nearly always our fear in one form or another, we place ourselves beyond the experience of forgiveness.

In such situations, God's forgiving power is always present and ready for us, but we do not experience it. I am thinking, for example, of white folks who do not believe that we are complicit in racism; of people who do not see anything wrong with homophobia; of U.S. military leaders who do not think they are doing wrong in authorizing the bombing of Iraqi and other people. In such cases, we do not realize the extent to which we are at odds with the Holy Spirit, and we do not see either ourselves or others very clearly through the eyes of God. We may assume that we are living good, moral, maybe even holy lives, and in some ways we may be. But we also are living in sin—in alienation and disconnection from our sisters and brothers. We are pulling against the Spirit, the Sacred energy that connects us to one another in mutually empowering ways.

It is important for us to keep in mind several things about forgiveness and repentance:

1. We are always involved—actively or passively, knowingly or unwittingly—in violence of one form or another against others: animals, earth, hungry people, members of other tribes and religions, those whom we don't like, those whom we fear, those whom we disregard.

2. We seldom realize that our repentance is always being called for, if not by those whom we've wounded, then surely by those lovers of the Spirit and of the world who reach for us somehow—in person, or through history, literature, prayer, art, phantasy.

3. Like all others living in sin, we too stand always in need of compassion rather than contempt to help move us through alienation and violence toward right relation.

4. Making right relation always involves repentance.

> Unless we are repentant
> for the evil we are in
> and the wrong that we do in it
> we are not trustworthy
> in relation to anyone
> Including ourselves
> and if we cannot be trusted
> who are *we* to speak of
>   love?

Although unrepentant people cannot accept the forgiveness that would help move them/us spiritually toward right relation, we who experience ourselves in certain circumstances as unforgiving or as unforgiven, or perhaps as not needing forgiveness, need more than anything to be treated with compassion.

Remember that I am not speaking here of sweet, nice feelings, but rather a radical act of relational solidarity. Compassion, an active mode of relational presence, is steeped in the faith that *all* people can be touched by the power of the Spirit and stirred toward the repentance that makes right relation possible. It is never too late for anyone, from the most wretched abusers to the young girls whose only personal experiences of wrong relation may be their shame about their competence and relational power, a shame that reflects a social brokenness that is not of their own making and is in no way their own fault.

As spiritually complex as the problem of being unrepentant ourselves is the quandary of our relationship with those who have violated us or our ancestors and who are not, as far as we can tell, repentant.

Can we—how can we—forgive them? We as particular tribes, genders, or religious groups? We as individuals?

Of all human situations, this one, I believe, most fully images
atonement, because it is the situation in which we *know* we experience
and share God's own predicament—being violated and wounded by
people who are not repentant for what they have done and, probably,
are doing. Such a situation draws us deeply into God. It also casts in
bold relief the theological and moral problem with the Anselmian
doctrine of a god who requires "payment" (JESUS' crucifixion) for the
sins of the world (ours). In a word, the most basic ingredient missing
from the church's traditional teachings on atonement has been *compassion*. Anselm's god, which the church has adopted as its own, has had
little, if any, compassion.

It is hard for most of us Christians to realize what we must if we are
going to practice compassion as a spiritual and political commitment:
We have been taught, and too often shown, the wrong kind of god.
Can we turn this situation around and get on with our lives in the
Sacred Spirit of compassion, which was the God that JESUS surely
loved?

Compassion and nonviolence: A spiritual path

None of us, including JESUS, needs to be destroyed so that the rest of
us can live holy lives. We are envisioning in this chapter a spiritual path
that leads us *away* from blood sacrifice as in any sense acceptable to the
God whom JESUS loved.

We have reflected on several problems with the mainstream Christian atonement tradition:

1. It is steeped in the trivialization and deprecation of human experience as ungodly.
2. For this reason, it represents a more radically dualistic apprehension of the divine-human relation than most mainline theologians will admit.
3. It is built around an image of a deity whose "inexorable love" is
   experienced by human beings as punitive, shaming, cruel, and
   even sadistic in relation to people whose psychospiritualities
   have been shaped, to various degrees, by images of a god whose

love is violent—toward others, toward His Son, and toward Himself.

4. It promotes blood sacrifice—that is to say, the sacralizing of violence against others and oneself—as a (or even the) way of spiritual liberation.

5. Finally, it reflects a deity made in the image of human impatience with one another, ourselves, and our Sacred Source. In the best, most mutual relationships that have been broken—relationships not only between individuals but also supported by strong, respectful friends and community—those who have been violated and those who have done wrong often can find ways to restore what has been lost or at least some significant part of it. In relationships more like the one that most of us actually experience between ourselves and God—in which time and again we turn away from the vocation to love justice and show mercy in our relations—it is hard to imagine how we might restore a right relation with the Spirit of justice-love and compassion. Furthermore, it is not hard to understand why so many Christians, like Anselm, Baillie, and countless others, have imagined that surely God had to exact a harsh penalty for the terrible sins of the world.

What these Christian believers have lacked is faith in God's inexorable patience as a significant dimension of God's love.

To be sure, the evil among us is rampant, exacting tolls too high for many of us to pay or even imagine. And we humans must do everything in our power to protect one another, ourselves, and other creatures from the violence that invariably results from the fear-based betrayals of our Sacred Power in mutual relation. This means that, in this real world of ours, we will always be looking for better ways of protecting ourselves and one another from violent people and from others whose fear, greed, dishonesty, or rage threatens to harm us or disrupt the relative stabilities we are able sometimes to create as communities and cultures.

But we must not confuse protecting ourselves and those we love with inflicting upon our enemies the same torture and brutality that they may have inflicted (or wished) upon us. Contrary to the prevailing religious, moral, and political sentiments on the Right today, might does *not* make right. Justice makes right relation. Justice-love *is* right relation. We do not need an "almighty" god, except insofar as God's love—Her justice-love, Her compassion—is Her strength and Her power.

Putting our faith in God's patience with us in this imperfect, morally cluttered, and often evil world generates greater social and spiritual space for us to be honest, gentle people with ourselves and one another—space in which we are able to cultivate humility rather than fear as the basis of our life together and thereby become more deeply moral people. We need more images of a patient God who loves the world so much that She gives her people time and resources like history and culture, human friends and animal companions, work and play, mountains and water, food and music, memory and reason, imagination and talents, and prayer and worship, and as many chances as we in our fear may need to come to our senses.

We need not sacrifice one more child to the bloody god who needs innocent victims, one more person or creature to a deity who must punish either us or himself in order to love the world.

There is another way to god, in which compassion replaces honor and even self-respect as the highest good and in which nonviolence becomes a way of life, a liberating response to the ongoing savaging of ourselves and one another.

It is my thesis in this book that these twin commitments—compassion and nonviolence—are *living sacraments*, outward and visible signs among us of an authentically liberative atonement tradition.

Compassion, nonviolence, and loneliness

Let me say it again: *compassion* too often sounds to us like a soft feeling. It rings of pity and often patronizes those who are, or seem, "poorer" in some ways than we ourselves. In the prevailing reactionary political climate, for example, compassion often is used by liberals as a synonym for our own politics. In the realm of public policy, we "liberals" have compassion and "conservatives" don't. Not surprisingly, conservatives, in trying to present their own politics as compassionate, are likely to define their brand of compassion as "more realistic" than that of liberals. I dare say that no one who supported the "welfare reform" bill of 1996—not a single senator, congressperson, or President Clinton himself—thinks of him or herself as short on compassion; whereas those of us who were appalled by this "reform" believed that it lacked compassion. In short, we liberals are seen by conservatives as too soft, not realistic enough in our commitments to the common good, whereas we on the left view more conservative folk as very hard on the poor and as not idealistic enough to even envision a *common* good.

Compassion challenges this prevailing liberal-conservative split. This does not mean that compassion is a non-political "spiritual" quality, as some folks might suggest. It means that compassion is not simply, as many liberals assume, an individual's free-floating emotional and mental inclination to "be for" any people and creatures who might need some help. Nor is compassion a harder-edged belief that those who think they know what's best for others can forge into public policies to benefit the common good regardless of what most commonfolk might want, need, or think about this.

Compassion is not primarily a feeling or a spiritualized state of being. It is not a package of patronization for the poor. Genuine compassion is a shared—communal—commitment to do everything in our power to struggle toward the well-being of all people and creatures, including our adversaries, and especially those whose ways of being in the world we do not like or understand. In a potentially conflictual, perhaps even violent, situation, compassion is a commitment to do no harm to our enemies if we possibly can help it.

We learn compassion through community and friendship, usually to the extent that we ourselves have benefited from it. Insofar as we have known compassion, as its beneficiaries, we can more likely embody it as a trustworthy personal commitment. Otherwise, "compassion" usually will float freely "in" us as a feeling (as in much liberal spirituality), or it will stick in our gut as an obligation to the "less fortunate" people (as in some conservative politics).

Nonviolence is a first fruit of compassion.[40] *It is also a collective, public force, seldom an option for individuals who are in harm's way.* Nonviolence is the practical effect of the commitment not to harm our enemies if at all possible. The qualification—"if at all possible"—is intended to allow for *spontaneous* and *last-resort* defense of one another and ourselves that can find no other solution. Even in such situations, violence

should be as minimal and nondestructive as possible. Here I am referring both to large-scale defense, like armed struggle against oppression, and to smaller encounters, such as a woman's defense against an
abusive spouse.

It is important to keep nonviolence, as a movement, in historical
perspective. I cannot over-emphasize the fact that nonviolence is a collective public force, seldom a practical or very real option for individuals. It is true that we often associate the names of individuals with
it—for example, pacifist Congresswoman Alice Paul, who cast the
lone vote against U.S. entry into World War I; Mahatma Gandhi of the
Indian struggle against British colonialism; Martin Luther King Jr. of
the Civil Rights Movement in the United States; Mohammad Ali, Mus-
lim pacifist who refused to fight in the Vietnam War; and the Vietnamese Buddhist monk and activist for global peace, Thich Nhat
Hahn. But these persons have not been merely iconoclastic, boundary-
breaking individuals. They have represented—and, in that sense,
embodied—movements, communities of activists, public forces larger
than any single person's commitments. This relational basis has been
the source of their strength.

Nonviolence is not merely a political strategy, although it is certainly often that. It is never only a private opinion, although we may be
strengthened and shaped individually in significant ways by our shared
commitment. Nonviolence is a shared way of life that invites "a dialogue."[41] By "dialogue," I do not mean simply "talking." I mean acting
together in mutually empowering ways. "Dialogue" in this sense refers
to a way of proceeding in life—dialogically, mutually, in such a way
that all parties can be beneficiaries.

Nonviolence is dialogical. It is an effort not to act unilaterally. It is
steeped in the presupposition that all others, even our enemies, are
worthy of dignity and respect. It is a yearning for peace that will not
settle for peace without justice because such "peace" is not peace at all.
It is a way of life with roots in solidarity (really a public manifestation
of compassion), in community and friendship; in *phantasy*; in prayer
and meditation; and in humility. Like forgiveness, nonviolence is
imaginable *only* through our power in mutual relation.

In our world today, a nonviolent way of life with its communal basis
is also, paradoxically, a lonely life.

Looping back to our resources for forgiveness, let's look into this paradox to notice both the loneliness and the serenity, the sorrow and the joy, at the heart of the matter.[42] Earlier I suggested that solidarity through community and friendship, together with humility, are cornerstones of our capacities to forgive and to accept the forgiveness of others in such a way that it makes a difference in our lives. I noted also the roles of the struggle for justice-love, emotional honesty, imagination and *phantasy*, and prayer and meditation in the spiritual and political work of forgiveness. What is it, in this way of being, that promises us lives filled with a "peace which passeth understanding" and yet moves us also into what John of the Cross called "the dark night of the soul"?[43]

Community and friendship provide the joy and peace of knowing that we are not alone in life but rather are participants who share a common way. Ideally, this is a role of family, as our most intimate companions, not "family" as defined narrowly in the limited, modern, capitalist, and non-biblical sense that the Christian Right embraces with such enthusiasm. Family is, in reality, wherever we find ourselves at home in a womb of compassion.

> Meanwhile, standing near the cross of JESUS were his mother, and his mother's sister, Mary the wife of Clopas, and Mary Magdalene. When JESUS saw his mother and the disciple whom he loved standing beside her, he said to his mother, "Woman, here is your son!" Then he said to the disciple, "Here is your mother!" and from that hour the disciple took her into his own home. (John 19:25b-27)

> family is
> wherever
> we find our
> selves at home
> in a womb
> of compassion.

> Let us behold one another as sisters
> and mothers, fathers and brothers,
> grannies and grampas, lovers and spouses,
> animal companions, friends, and beloved
> children: family. Amen.

Through this sense of "beholding" one another, whoever and wherever we are, we cannot escape sorrow. Drawn by love and held intimately in connection with those whom we love, we experience death and loss and grief, and also the often less ultimate but no less dreadful experiences of betrayal, disappointment, and relational wounds of a thousand kinds. Our family is vast and global and at the same time, for most of us, a much smaller experience of simply being at home with those whom we love. In both larger and smaller arenas, compassion and humility are lenses through which we who are family learn to view one another. In these contexts of joy and the sorrows that come with it, nonviolence becomes a way of experiencing ourselves and one another.

We may experience nonviolence as an aspiration even if, in our particular contexts, we do not and cannot practice it with much consistency. Our inability even to imagine being a radically nonviolent people has much to do with the sad reality that our communities are so broken and so weak.

Even with nonviolence as only a desire and a prayer, however, we can become a more serene people, able to be more honest with ourselves and others and more fully at peace among and within ourselves. Conflict and pain do not disappear, but we more easily can take them in stride, not becoming undone by them. And as we become less afraid of anger and conflict, more grounded in compassion and nonviolence, our staying power gets rooted. We become better able to participate for the long haul in the ongoing struggles for justice, those closest at hand and sometimes those more national or global movements for liberation and freedom. We are likely to discover here, in the midst of social struggle, a stronger sense of personal peace and well-being.

This paradox is strengthened through the practices of prayer and meditation and the gifts of imagination and phantasy. Bearing witness to the power of Martin Luther King Jr.'s "dream," we are surrounded by clouds of witnesses, upheld by the communion of saints, empowered by the ancestors. Along this path, we come to know the world and one another, ourselves and the Spirit, more fully and honestly as family.

By no means is it ever a solitary struggle. We are never alone in it.

And yet, it is a lonely place for each and every one in it. It is lonely because it is so *radically* at odds with what it means to be either human or divine in the dominant patriarchal culture that is shaping the world around and (always to some degree) within us.

It is a lonely place because twenty-four hours a day the dominant world/church is pressing upon us definitions of "community" and "friendship," "compassion" and "humility," "justice" and "love," "God" and "world," "self" and "other," "struggle" and "serenity" that—if we accept such definitions—will exhaust us because they tend to be so individualistic, adversarial, and impossible to embody in healthy or holy ways. In this context of constant social and psychospiritual disappointment, loneliness is a protective wrapping for our souls, the place in us in which we meet and most fully love one another, ourselves, and the Spirit that is our power to love.

Though our lives may be filled with friends and intimacy, love and struggle, public participation and personal relationship, there is *always* a place in us that no one can reach or know. If people know us well, they know this place is there in us—and that they cannot reach it, not because we do not trust them, but because none of us (not our friends, and not us) can escape the yearning and the loneliness that comes with living passionately in God. Our best friends know this, usually from their own experiences as well, and they accept the lonely place for what it is: a spot that keeps us well on *our* terms, not the world's, rooted and grounded in a Spirit that "the world does not know."

The loneliness paradoxically is indispensable to our loving one another, ourselves, and God without needing to know everything about anyone or anything, including God. It is the taproot of our capacity to accept the mystery and unknowable dimensions of all that is, especially God.

What keeps forgiveness from being idealistic?

Speaking as one who knows deeply the fatigue of wrongdoing as both subject and object of betrayals that tear at the fabric of our human and creaturely well-being, I am all the more persuaded that learning forgiveness, however long it may take us and our people—learning to be its givers and recipients—is more than anything what we need in order to make right relation with one another throughout the world and to live more fully in the Spirit that empowers us.

Our very life as a planet and as communities of people and creatures depends upon it. A willingness to learn forgiveness is not an option for people who are serious about survival and quality of life. Forgiveness makes quality of life possible for its givers and recipients. Without it there will always be, as LeGuin recounts, some child kept in its own filth in a house at the edge of town, someone hanging on a cross, some innocent offered up yet again as a living sacrifice for the rest of us.

When we are in conflictual situations, in which we and others honestly see things differently, and especially when some have been badly wounded by others, we are very near the heart of God—because this tends to be a real and honest, deeply human situation in which we and others are yearning for some healing and liberation.

This critical moment is often when some one(s) will get hung on a cross. It is also the moment, the "Eternal Now," in Tillich's language, in which the Spirit urges us to walk away from the violence in search of a better way.

We can find our way beyond violence only with those who are unwilling to offer us, themselves, or others as a living sacrifice for anything or anybody and certainly not for a God who surely recoils at the very notion of such sacrifice.

Along this spiritual path we may be destroyed, but it will not be because we have sacrificed ourselves or others. Whatever suffering comes our way will be because we have lived as fully as possible into our power to god, and because God has lived as fully as possible through us.

> It was now about noon, and darkness came over the whole land until three in the afternoon, while the sun's light failed; and the curtain of the temple was torn in two. Then JESUS, crying with a loud voice, said, "Father into your hands I commend my spirit." (Luke 23:44-46a)

aware that he was slipping
away JESUS entrusted
himself to the spirit
of an open future.

there was I guess no shutting
down of pain no casting out
of doubts no
rejection of those who had
hurt and betrayed denied
and crucified him.

there was simply I
guess a turning
of himself over
into the life love
and ongoingness
of the One whom he
trusted.

in turning ourselves
over we make
a relational trust
from which we and
others too can draw
courage and wisdom
serenity and hope
a day at a time.

Epilogue

Saving JESUS: Twelve rubrics

1. Pray and meditate. Make time and space for silence every day.
2. Cultivate community. Use institutional resources where you can. Build new ones where you must.
3. Speak truthfully, and tell honest stories.
4. Be kind. Treat your body, and others', tenderly.
5. Think about power relations, and let this analysis inform your faith, secure your compassion, and season your commitments.
6. Name evil and act toward its transformation. Be an ally, in solidarity with those who are violated and oppressed.
7. Remember, in the struggle, to take your friends along.
8. Know the difference between the things you can change and the things you can't.
9. Keep things in perspective, including yourself. Don't let things become larger or smaller than they are. Out of this wisdom grow patience and humor.
10. Do not be ashamed of your anger at oppression, injustice, violence, cruelty, and other manifestations of evil.
11. Strive to live nonviolently in all realms by cultivating compassion and practicing forgiveness as recipient and giver.
12. Keep your courage (Robert DeWitt).[1]

Liturgical Resources: Celebrating Resurrection

. . . . .

I have included several liturgical resources here that I have written for particular occasions over a period of more than twenty years. The reason I have added them is to demonstrate that, yes, it is possible to move away from "right thought" about JESUS (various orthodox and classical Christologies) in order to celebrate the Sacred Spirit and the JESUS, as well as the humankind and creaturekind, presented in these pages! It can be done liturgically. Much of it is being done all over the Christian world by feminists, womanists, *mujeristas,* and other theologians of healing and liberation. These few liturgical pieces represent one small effort in this direction, celebrating our lives in God, a people risen through faith, hope, and the struggle for justice-love.

. . . . .

1. Blessing the Bread: A Litany for Many Voices (1978)[1]

In the beginning was God,
In the beginning
   The source of all that is,
In the beginning
   God yearning,
   God moaning,
   God laboring,
   God giving birth,
   God rejoicing.

And God loved what she had made.
And God said,
   "It is good!"
And God, knowing that all is good is shared,
Held the earth tenderly in her arms.
God yearned for relationship,
God longed to share the good earth,
And humanity was born in the yearning of God—
We were born to share the earth.

In the earth was the seed,
In the seed was the grain,
In the grain was the harvest,
In the harvest was the bread,
In the bread was the power,

And God said,
   "All shall eat of the earth,
   All shall eat of the seed,
   All shall eat of the grain,
   All shall eat of the harvest,
   All shall eat of the bread,
   All shall eat of the power!"

God said,
   "You are my people—

My friends,
My lovers,
My sisters,
And brothers,
All of you shall eat
Of the bread
And the power,
All shall eat!"

Then God, gathering up her courage in love, said,
"Let there be bread!"

And God's sisters,
Her friends and lovers,
Knelt on the earth,
Planted the seeds,
Prayed for the rain,
Sang for the grain,
Made the harvest,
Cracked the wheat,
Pounded the corn,
Kneaded the dough,
Kindled the fire,
Filled the air,
With the smell of fresh bread.
And there was bread—
And it was good!

We the sisters of God say today,
    "All shall eat of the bread
    And the power.
    We say today,
    All shall have power
    And bread.
    Today we say,
    Let there be bread!
    Let there be power!
    Let us eat of the bread

And the power!
And all will be filled
For the bread is rising!"

By the power of God,
Women are blessed.
By the women of God,
The bread is blessed.
By the bread of God,
The power is blessed.
By the power of bread,
The power of women,
The power of God,
The people are blessed,
The earth is blessed,
And the bread is rising!

2. A Eucharistic Prayer (1980)[2]

A. May God be with you.
B. And also with you.
A. Open your hearts.
B. We open them to God and one another.
A. Let us give thanks to God.
B. It is right to give God thanks and praise.
A. It is right and a good and joyful thing to stand open in the presence of God and one another as thankful people, lifting our voices in chorus, with those who have gone before us, and with men and women throughout the world today, singing,
All: *Holy, holy, holy God,*
   God of power and might,
   Heaven and earth are full of your glory,
   Hosanna in the highest!
   Blessed is the one who comes in the name of God!
   Hosanna in the highest!
A. Wise and gracious God, Creator of all good things, Redeemer of this broken world, you who bless your people and the earth itself, Holy is your name.

B. You are the source of love in the world, the wellspring of justice in history, the resource of peace on earth. Holy is your name.

A. We pray to you, God of our fathers and mothers; God of the judges, prophets, and priests of Israel; God of the Old Covenant and of the New Covenant; God of Mary and JESUS; God of the church. Holy is your name.

B. Elohim, you are God. You lead your people out of bondage into freedom. Holy is your name.

A. Following JESUS, we call you *Abba*, for you love us. Guiding us, you are insistent, patient, protective, encouraging, comforting. Holy is your name.

B. God our father, your will be done, on earth as in heaven. We thank you for giving us the bread we need. Holy is your name.

A. You hold us in your strong arms like a mother with her newborn infant. You have raised your children from generation to generation, planting seeds, harvesting grain, baking fresh bread, preparing meals, feeding your people, holding us up when we are too weak to walk on our own, teaching us how to walk and empowering us to go forth in the world as your daughters and sons. Holy is your name.

B. God our mother, you are the matrix of our power, our tenderness, and our courage. We forget too often that you are God. Holy is your name.

A. We know that your names are as numerous and varied as your people, to whom you reveal yourself in different ways so that we may be your co-creative, imaginative lovers in a world abundant with redemptive images.

B. We see you in the sun and the moon, the rain and the wind, coming with power.

A. We see you in the liberation of humanity from injustice and oppression. We see you, coming with power.

B. We see you in our friends and lovers, our spouses and children. We know your passion, your patience, your commitment to right relation. We experience you, coming with power.

A. We see you in the bodies of hungry people, broken people, tortured people, and a tortured earth. We tremble, and we believe that you are coming with power.

B. We believe in you, and we know you are with us, because we remember the power you revealed to us through the life of JESUS, our brother.

All: *We remember that on the night before he was executed by those who feared both him and you, he ate a Passover meal with his friends in celebration of your liberation of people from bondage. Remembering your power, he took bread, blessed it, broke it, gave it to his friends, and said, "Take. Eat. This is my body which will be broken for you. Whenever you eat it, remember me."*

After supper, he took wine, blessed it, gave it to them, and said, "Drink this. It is my blood which will be shed for you and for others, for the forgiveness of sins, to heal and empower you. Whenever you drink it, remember me."

Remembering JESUS *and the power of your love revealed through him, we ask you, Father and Mother and Friend of all, to bless this bread and this wine, making it for us the body and blood of* JESUS CHRIST. *Bless us also, that we may be for you* CHRIST's *presence in the world, people in love with you and your creation. All this we ask in your holy name, that with* CHRIST *and in* CHRIST *and by the power of your Holy Spirit, we may live forever as your people, O gentle God of power and grace.*

3. Variations on a Sufi Prayer (1992)[3]

Let your heart beat strong among us
Let your hands be ours this day
Let your will infuse our purpose
And your joy inspire our play
Let your wish be our desire
Let your act become our deed
Let your word become our speech
And your love become our creed
Let our plants spring forth your flowers
Let our fruits produce your seed
Let your need become our struggle
And our lives become your creed.

4. Blessing (1983)[4]

Tender God, touch us,
Be touched by us,
Make us lovers of humanity,
Compassionate friends of all creation.
Gracious God, hear us into speech,
Speak us into acting,
And through us, recreate the world.

5. The Great Thanksgiving: A Rite Based on the Song of Mary (1995)[5]

(This rite is based on Luke 1:47-55.)

A. May God be with you.
B. And also with you.
A. Open your hearts.
B. We open them to God.
A. Let us give thanks to God.
B. It is right to give God thanks and praise.
A. It is a right and joyful thing to stand in the presence of God and one another, trusting as we do that where the Spirit of God moves among us, we are beckoned as lovers to present ourselves as partners in the holy work of creation and redemption, for God's sake and for our own.
B. We proclaim your greatness, O God. We rejoice in you, our Savior.
A. We rejoice in you, merciful Father, for remembering us, even in our forgetfulness of you. We give thanks to you, patient Mother, for remembering us, even in our dis-memberment of you.
B. For your regard has blessed us, ordinary men and women who serve you. As you have blessed us, so too will all generations remember us as your people.
A. We your people, whom you have chosen as friends, recall the splendid array of gifts you have set before us: the breath and sensuality of our bodies; the food on our tables; the warmth and

comfort of shelter; the support and solidarity of friends; the intimacy of lovers, family, those who reach out to us even in our fear and denial.

B. You, Beloved One, have raised us up to befriend. Touched and moved by you, we are empowered to love the world you have made. Because your power is great, so too is the power of your friends.

A. Gathered in friendship, we remember what you have done to bring us here: we remember your commitment to your people, your commandment that we love one another, your liberation of our forebears from injustice and oppression, your steadfast promise that you will not forget us.

B. Your mercy is on those who fear you throughout all generations. You have showed strength with your arm.

A. But most of all, you have shown compassion toward us and all humankind. You have shown that you are with us and that your movement can be ours as well. This we see in JESUS, our brother, our friend, our savior, for we remember his life, death, and resurrection as a sign and a promise that your love cannot be crushed, your justice cannot be undone, your ways cannot be thwarted, and your life cannot be taken away, as long as we your people are faithful to you in the same spirit that JESUS CHRIST was your faithful son.

B. You have scattered the proud in the hearts' fantasy. You have put down the mighty from their seat and have lifted up the powerless.

A. We remember, O God of Power, that your son JESUS, on the night before he died for us, took bread, blessed it, and gave it to his friends, and said, "Take, eat; this is my body, which is given for you. Do this in remembrance of me." After supper, he took the cup of wine, blessed it, and gave it to them, and said, "Drink this, all of you. This is my blood of the new covenant, which will be shed for you. Whenever you drink it, remember me."

B. We remember his passion, O God, and your justice: that you fill the hungry with good things and send the rich, empty, away.

A. We are hungry people, and so we ask you, O God of justice and mercy, to bless this bread and this wine, making them for us the body and blood of JESUS CHRIST, in whose Spirit we are called and sanctified to live holy lives.

B.　You, gracious God, remembering your mercy, have helped your people in all generations, as you promised Abraham, Sarah, and Hagar; now stand with us, blessing those who share this feast of love, that we may go forth from this place, empowered to join with you in your ongoing creation, liberation, and blessing of the world.

All: *All this we ask in the name of* JESUS CHRIST. *Feed us daily, hold us fast, send us forth boldly, joyfully, and ever faithful in your Spirit. Amen.*

And now in the Spirit of CHRIST *we pray:*
Our Father, Our Mother, you are in heaven. Holy is your name. Your justice come. Your will be done on earth as in heaven. Give us today the bread we need. And forgive us our sins as we forgive those who sin against us. Save us from the time of trial, and deliver us from evil. For the goodness, the power and the glory are yours, now and forever. Amen.

6. A Eucharistic Litany of Mutuality and Solidarity (1999)[6]

[People, singing and bearing gifts of their lives and labor, gather 'round the altar.]

A:　We are here to celebrate life!

B:　We come alive and prosper spiritually only in shared resistance to all that thwarts life's promise.

A:　Sisters and brothers, we are here to remember the root of our resistance and the source of our celebration.

B:　We are here to remember the brother from Nazareth, his story and our own in the struggle for justice-love.

A:　We remember that in the beginning
　　　　is the relation—
　　　　a relation so sturdy
　　　　a relation so certain
　　　　a relation so deep and so wide
　　　　it will never be entirely broken.

B.　We remember the relation.
　　　　From it, we draw a story
　　　　of community and suffering

faithfulness and betrayal
a story of Life generating life,
of creation and destruction
birth and death
yearning and struggling
for bread and justice.

All: *A story of love and hope against the odds.*

A: Into this turbulent tale
of people wandering
in search of home and justice,
into this community
of prophets and poets
covenant and lament,
JESUS was born.

All: *Faithful Jew, poor brother, political problem, one of us.*

B. JESUS lived deeply in God,
God lived deeply in JESUS.
May we live in this same Passionate Spirit,
in love with the Holy One
which is our Power for making justice-love
and the Wellspring of our hope.

A: Seeking to live more fully in you, O God,
he was ignorant in ways common to us all
and wise beyond most words we use to describe him.
He had strong confidence
that your Sacred realm
was coming with power.
With him, we believe that it is!
With him, we believe that radical love
Is a dangerous and serious business.

All: *We rest in his Christic Spirit which is none other than your*
Sophia.

B. In your Wisdom, he stayed with his cause,
which was yours.
In your Courage, he died for his cause,
which is yours.
May we, in your Spirit, god[7]

one day at a time,
in the struggle
for compassion and hope
freedom and justice
healing and liberation
bread and roses!

>All: *With* JESUS, *we are called to embody you, share you, cele-*
>*brate your gift of life, and pass it on!*

A: Remembering that he died because he loved you, O God of life
and justice, we gather round now to share food for the journey
and strength for the struggle.

B: We are told that shortly before he was arrested and executed as an
enemy of the state, JESUS shared a Passover meal with his close
friends.

>All: *We imagine he said something like this:"When you eat this*
>*bread, remember me—and who you are with me. When you*
>*drink from this cup, remember me—and who we are*
>*together."*

A: We remember him
and ourselves with him.
as we gather here in you
to celebrate this story,
which is his story
and your story.

>All: *It is also our story, by the power of your Spirit.*

B. We have come
and we will go
bearing witness to
our intimations and glimpses
of your abiding Power
that connects us deeply with other humans
and, mysteriously, with creatures of all kinds
in your Realm of Peace—
in which the hungry are fed
and the prisoners freed,
in which the oppressed are liberated
and the wounded and sick are healed

in which the lion and the lamb are friends

in which we study war no more—

      All: *All of this by the transformative Power of your Presence.*

A: We thank you, gracious God, for the opportunity you have given us to join in co-creating the world!

B: In particular today [we thank you for the gift of our co-creative sister and colleague, teacher and friend, mentor and partner and beloved companion, Bev, whose life and love and work makes your Presence so real and near to us. Bless this beautiful woman as she prepares to leave this seminary home for the Southern hills where she will rest and write, play and delight!]

A: Bless this food which we now share, and bless us all as we seek to go forth from this place, refreshed and alive in your liberating Power!

B: May we be strengthened through faith to live boldly and kindly in this world at this time, knowing that we are here on this earth to voice your passion for justice, embody your loving presence, drink deeply from your living waters, and sing your praises with our lives.

      All: *This we pray, remembering* JESUS, *who called us friends, and said, "Follow me."*

[People will then feed one another in the Spirit! Hymns may be sung, drums played, music made, animals enjoyed, and everyone delighted!]

Notes

Preface

1. Ruether 1979.
2. Driver 1981.
3. Chung 1990; Adams 1995; McFague 1993, 1997; Spencer 1996; Rasmussen 1996.
4. Chung 1990; Kwok 1995; Fabella and Oduyoye 1988.
5. There are some important christological tasks that I am not attempting in this book, either because, in my judgment, numbers of us have paid enough attention to the concerns or because other theologians are better equipped than I to address certain issues from within their specialized theological disciplines.

In the former instance, for example, *I am not interested in probing further the tensions between "JESUS of history" and "CHRIST of faith" emphases in the development of Christian doctrine.* This historical pull serves to underscore every generation's efforts to reconstruct "JESUS" or "CHRIST" in its own image, not in itself a problem, but dangerous. I reflected on this danger a decade ago:

> [The] tendency to create divinity in our own image is, to some degree, universal. It is not wrong to create theological and christological images of ourselves. . . . But . . . it is destructive of the . . . world we share to leave the matter there—stuck on one's own "JESUS" or "CHRIST" image. It is wrong to close the canons at the end of one's own story or that of one's people. . . . [In] attempting to correct such mistakes, both CHRIST of faith and historical JESUS images have . . . [moved] the debate in a circle, back again into a self-defensive posturing which signals the drawing of Christological boundaries around our own sacred icons. . . . (1989b, 19–20)

Even to *think* about taking sides in the "JESUS of history" and "CHRIST of faith" debate, I had come to realize in the mid-1980s, is to perpetuate the patriarchal logic of "either/or" solutions. Not that most thoughtful Christian theologians over the years have intended to do this—as they (I should say, we) have chosen either the human "JESUS" as our focus or his divine life as the "CHRIST," in either case unwittingly downplaying the spiritual significance of the "other side."

We Western Christians do not know very well how to think about power in non-dualistic ways. We normally cannot think of "humanity" and "divinity" in ways that do not imply the "existence" of two different entities or "beings." Ontology, or the study of being itself, as Kwok Pui-lan has noted, is a very Western (dualistic) philosophical interest that runs contrary to much Asian understanding of reality. Assuming that Western Christians cannot simply step outside our historic cultural legacy, in which we have learned so deeply to *experience* our selves, the world, and God as, in some important ways, separate "beings," how then can we even imagine living life or engaging the JESUS tradition in a non-dualistic manner? *The key to this quandary, I believe, is a radically relational experience, perception, and understanding of being itself—and of doing.* This requires us to move on beyond the JESUS of history/CHRIST of faith discussions. This movement is what I am attempting in this book.

The book also is not primarily sociology, psychology, history, or a biblical study. I am not trying here to produce a social, historical, or psychological study of JESUS or the rest of us. Others (usually biblical scholars) have done this, sometimes very well indeed, producing interpretations and assessments of the JESUS story that both challenge and assist large numbers of teachers, students, and others seeking to better understand the staying power (for better and worse) of Christian faith.

For example, I have often heard recently from people in local parishes about how exciting they find Marcus Borg's book, *Meeting Jesus Again for the First Time* (1994), in which we are invited to "meet JESUS" as a "spirit person" and ourselves as well. Feminist students and colleagues often take note of Elisabeth Schüssler Fiorenza's work, including her 1994 book, *Jesus: Miriam's Child, Sophia's Prophet,* in which she continues to build a case for "the ekklesia of wo/men" as a "discipleship of equals," in which JESUS participated as one of us. Many students of radical biblical, feminist, (and other) liberation theologies have been energized during the last decade by John Dominic Crossan's *Jesus: A Revolutionary Biography* (1994), in which, employing a sophisticated method of comparative textual analysis, Crossan presents JESUS as an itinerant peasant who lived and taught a simple, but revolutionary, spirituality and politic. Easier to overlook on this side of the Atlantic is a compelling, informative study on the social history of JESUS' time and place, *Lydia's Impatient Sisters* (1995), by German feminist biblical scholar Luise Schottroff. I mention these particular books because each of them is making an important difference in contemporary discussions about JESUS among academics in religion, especially biblical scholars. This discourse continues to be largely white, although, in the United States especially, increasing numbers of people of color are taking part.

It is not intended to be a book simply of special interest to other white lesbian feminist Christians. In these times, the voices of theologians of color speaking about JESUS are present and clear among us—and, still, they are marginalized in the pretentious, *systemically* racist realm of religious studies. As long as the academic guilds and mainstream religious institutions like churches and seminaries continue to be predominantly patriarchal and Euro-centric in shape and substance, the explicitly christological work of such theologians as James H. Cone, Jacquelyn

Grant, Kelly Brown Douglas, Delores S. Williams, Rita Nakashima Brock, Chung Hyun Kyung, and Kwok Pui-lan will continue to be "received" within the academy as well as by mainline churches as representing "special interests" rather than all of us.

Like many sister and brother theologians of color, I too teach, speak, and write with a special *hope* that "my people" will be empowered by my words *and* that "other folks" will study their lives in relation to what I am doing. I *want* my theological work to reflect my being a white middle-class lesbian feminist Christian priest and academic, and I am satisfied that these details of my identity infuse this book. Still, like Delores Williams, Kwok Pui-lan, our gay brother Robert Goss, the peace activist Jim Douglass, and others who do Christology that is either issue-oriented (queer justice, peace, etc.) or intentionally reflective of our social locations (African American, Asian, queer, etc.), I am aware that my work is still "received" by many in the academy and mainline churches as the "special interest" pleading of a lesbian feminist.

Elisabeth Schüssler Fiorenza has been critical of many women theologians on this very question of whether we make our claims strongly enough for the universal validity of our work. What Schüssler Fiorenza evidently fails to see is that almost all theologians who clearly articulate the social bases of our communities, identities, and theologies do so in order to *strengthen* the universal import of what we are saying. Her complaint is disingenuous, coming from a sister who has helped put *women-centered* biblical studies on the map. Schüssler Fiorenza, after all, is clear that *she* does not intend to exclude men from her "discipleship of equals," hence her term "wo/men," which is meant to signal gender inclusivity. So too do I, in this book, mean to reach everyone I can—everyone who is able and willing to reach toward me.

This particular project does not seek to hold primary attention to the social constructs of my being white, female, lesbian, middle-class, relatively able-bodied, or even Christian. So, while it is true that *Saving Jesus* is not written simply, much less only, "to" or "for" or "about" "people just like me" (an odd and imprecise notion!), this is still a deeply lesbian text. It is a transparently white and middle-class book, and it is very much the handiwork of a Christian woman who prays and walks dogs and hikes and tries, in person and on paper, to trouble the waters of the dominant social order in and well beyond the church. Whatever broadbased appeal the book may have will come, if it does, through my efforts to be true to these very particular roots of my life—the specific communities of people and creatures who make me who I am—in relation to JESUS and everything else.

6. Soelle 1977.

1. Origins

1. I am grateful to Joanna Dewey and Beverly W. Harrison for raising these questions with me.

2. Soelle 1995.

3. Heyward 1982.

4. On "love," see Soelle and Cloyes (1984); Harrison (1985); Cooey, Farmer, and Ross (1987); Brock (1988); Heyward (1989a); the General Assembly Special Committee on Human Sexuality, Presbyterian Church USA (1991); Nelson and Longfellow (1994); Gilson (1995); and Ellison (1996).

5. Buber 1958.

6. See the General Assembly Special Committee on Human Sexuality, Presbyterian Church USA, especially Chapter 1, Part B: "Faithfulness to God . . . requires seeking justice-love or right-relatedness with self and others. We intentionally connect justice and love in this way, to emphasize that genuine caring for concrete human well-being is never content with a privatized, sentimentalized kind of loving, but rather demonstrates a devotion that enables persons and institutions to flourish in all their rich complexity. Such love, such justice, such passion for right-relatedness seeks to correct distorted relations between persons and groups and to generate relations of shared respect, shared power, and shared responsibility. Justice-love knows full well that where there is injustice, love is diminished" (1991, 14).

7. Maurice 1853.

8. McFerrin 1990.

9. Heyward 1982.

10. I wonder if this insight was at the heart and core of the early church's debates, especially at the Council of Chalcedon (451 c.e.), in which theologians concluded that JESUS was fully human and fully divine.

11. By "right wing," I mean those political forces (parties, organizations, and individuals) that today represent an effort to restore the social power of the "private sector" (e.g., religion, family, private schools, small businesses). More specifically, right-wing politics are committed to freeing *males of the ruling tribe* from social and public accountability by making everything except women's lives "private," and by subjecting women's bodies and lives to public [legal] constraints. The anti-abortion, anti-homosexual, anti-taxes, and pro-gun politics of the right wing underscore its efforts to secure the power of white men in their own homes. The most ardent right-wing spokespeople in the U.S. today (e.g., Pat Robertson, Pat Buchanan, Beverly LaHaye) and the most blatantly racist, sexist, heterosexist, and anti-Semitic organizations (e.g., Christian Identity and other neo-Nazi groups) are *theocrats*: advocates of a "Christian nation" in which the "private" realm of Christian fundamentalist religion actually becomes the dominant "public" force and, either literally or via its clout, takes over the executive,

legislative, and judicial branches of government. In the United States this has happened throughout the 1990s at local levels (e.g., school boards) and in a number of state Republican parties. See Berlet (1995), Diamond (1995), and Lienesch (1993).

12. Many religious fundamentalists, not only Christians, throughout the world today have theocratic aims. It is also important to note that not all Christian or other fundamentalists share the theocratic political interests and aims of groups such as the Christian Coalition. See Marty and Appleby (1991, 1993a, 1993b, 1994, 1995).

13. I first heard Dorothee Soelle use the term "Christofascist" while I was a doctoral student and she was a faculty member at Union Theological Seminary in the late 1970s. In that context, she was referring to the behavior of those Christian seminarians who seemed absolutely sure that they, and they alone, understood the meanings of the Christian gospel.

14. Miller 1996, 121.

15. Readers should realize that, as categories of power analysis, neither "whiteness" nor "maleness" refers primarily to individual Caucasian men but rather to the historical processes of social construction that have bestowed economic, religious, psychological, political, cultural, and other social privileges on certain groups and withheld them from others. While many white men have little privilege in a white racist and sexist society, many more men of color and many more women have little or none. See Lorde (1984), Frankenberg (1993), Ignatiev and Garvey (1996), Harrison (1985), Phelan (1989), Cone (1986), and Williams (1993).

16. Pat Buchanan's presidential campaign of 1996 illustrated the tensions among right-wing Republicans between economic isolationists, like Buchanan and Phyllis Schlafly, and others, like George Bush Sr., Jack Kemp, Dan Quayle, and Ronald Reagan, as well as "moderate" Democrats like Bill Clinton, who support—more than justice, wherever there must be a trade-off—the global growth of capital generated in the United States.

17. Rich 1986.

18. Charles Williams' novels include *War in Heaven* (1965), *Place of the Lion* (1965), *Descent into Hell* (1949/1973), and *Greater Trumps* (1950/1976), all published in the United States by Eerdmans of Grand Rapids, Michigan.

19. Note the racist imaging—darkness and blackness to denote evil as over and against lightness and whiteness, which traditionally have represented good, in most Christian literature. As epistemological and spiritual problems, racism and dualism always reinforce each other.

20. It is tempting to advocate our own spiritual path as the Right path for each and every one and therefore not to object to the state's help in establishing our way as best via the institutionalizing of public holidays, like Christmas, and the legitimizing of dominant religious symbols and values through public display,

such as the Madonna and Child on postage stamps. Such issues as the display of a crèche in a public space have been debated in recent decades. It is important to keep such questions of what should be public, of what serves the common good—of what we believe is "right" for most people—open to new input, especially, always, from those whose lives have been marginalized and whose voices have been silenced historically (from women, racial/tribal minorities, queer people, children, sick and disabled folk, and practitioners of non-dominant religions, and—as Wisdom opens our minds and lives—from other-than-human creatures as well).

21. The organization ACT UP was founded in the United States in the late 1980s by people (primarily white gay men) with AIDS and others in solidarity with them to demonstrate publicly against social, political, and ecclesial policies that contribute to the demonization of people with AIDS and the trivialization of AIDS itself as the personal concern of only those people who are HIV-positive.

22. Beverly W. Harrison has named and discussed this "capitalist spirituality" in conversation, classes, workshops, and lectures in recent years and is currently writing on the subject.

23. Maurice 1853.

24. See Heyward 1989a for elaboration on "erotic power" as our desire to taste and smell and see and hear and touch one another. It's our yearning to be involved—all rolled up—in each other's sounds and glances and bodies and feelings. The erotic is the flow of our senses, the movement of our sensuality, in which we experience our bodies' power and desire to connect with others. The erotic moves transpersonally among us and also draws us more fully into ourselves.

> *Although, to some extent, everyone's eroticism is distorted by abusive power relations (of domination and control), the erotic is the sacred/godly basis of our capacity to participate in mutually empowering relationships.*
>
> Abusive power relations teach us to be afraid of our erotic power— afraid, that is, of one another and of our own creative/liberating power in relation. In learning to fear the erotic, we resist relating intimately with one another. In addition, we are cut off from knowing and loving ourselves very well, because self-knowledge and self-love, very much like the knowledge and love of God, is available only in right, mutual relation with others. (Heyward 1989a, 187)

25. I prefer the term "Christic," an adjective descriptive of JESUS' (and our) power in mutual relation, to the term "CHRIST," the title commonly ascribed to JESUS that normally is taken to set him apart from and above the rest of us. See Heyward 1989b.

26. Several feminists who have written about "last things" are Ruether (1985, 1998), Grey (1990), Isasi-Díaz (1993), and especially Keller (1996), who creatively and wonderfully taps the roots of things that are not yet in the midst of our present life/struggle in relation to all that is, has been, and will be.

27. See McFague (1993) for more on "knowing our place."

28. Johnson (1992) cites the difference between Moltmann's understanding of *God's* suffering (1974) and Schillebeeckx's belief that God is with us in *our* suffering (1979, 1980). This seems to me a misleading distinction insofar as it presupposes a *necessary* difference between divine and human suffering. The distinction between Moltmann and Schillebeeckx on this point, however, does represent a primary tension in much liberal and liberationist Christian faith and history—that is, between the experience of God's transcendence and presence, on the one hand, as "radical immanence" (see Driver 1977; Heyward 1982; Keller 1986) and, on the other, as God's *participation* with us. The latter view, which allows for a greater distinction and difference between Creator and Creature, or God and the world, has been the more dominant view both traditionally and in contemporary liberal and liberation theologies.

I am arguing in this book (as less explicitly throughout my earlier work) for a third position in which there is less difference between God's immanence and God's participation, God's *being* among, between, and within us, and God's *going with* us as friend. I suggest that radical *immanence* (which is very close to pan-en-theism) and radical *participation* are by no means mutually exclusive experiences or images of divine and human and creaturely involvement. I find helpful Charles Williams' understanding of co-inherence (1949/1973)—or the mutual being-with and being-in one another. This is what the doctrine of the Trinity is an attempt to illuminate. See Chapter 3, note 31.

29. In earlier drafts I referred here also to the "imperfection" of creation. Two readers of the manuscript, Lisa Gray and Jeanne Tyler, during a 1999 summer session course at the Graduate Theological Union in Berkeley, California, helped me see two specific problems associated with the notion of *perfection* and *imperfection:* (1) the faulty assumption that whatever is unfinished, and even chaotic, cannot in its own way be "perfect"; and (b) the linguistic difficulties raised by the concepts of *perfection* and *imperfection* for people with disabilities who frequently hear that a disability is an "imperfection" (in contrast to others who are not disabled and are, therefore, more nearly "perfect").

30. Among the most pervasive interactive historical movements of evil and suffering in Western Christian cultures have been:

- *Hetero/sexism:* ruling tribe male definition, domination, and placement of women. Hetero/sexist institutions, religions, and social orders actually create "woman," "man," "femininity," "masculinity," "heterosexuality," "homosexuality," as *social categories of persons*, not simply as biogenetic forms, descriptions, or dispositions; I use "hetero/sexism" as one word to underscore the inseparability of sex and gender "issues," of the oppression of women ("sexism"); of gay, lesbian, and bisexual people ("heterosexism"); and of transgendered sisters and brothers.

- *Racism*: tribal supremacies that, in United States history, have taken the form of white/Euro-cultural ownership, thereby creating "black," "white," and "other" as greater than black and lesser than white;

- *Classism*, arrogant anti-populist attitudes, customs, and institutions shaped around complex interactions of wealth, race, gender, education, religion, and other "identity" variables.

- *Anti-Semitism*: the most peculiarly "Christian" evil of all, in which the scapegoating of Jews as evil has set the stage over two millennia for the relentless persecution of Jews by Christians "in the name of CHRIST" (and by others, such as Moslems, whose own anti-Judaism has been strengthened by Christian anti-Semitism).

31. Soelle 1977.

32. It's important that we be aware of both the racism and the classism in these terms and that we take seriously the depth of their roots in Euro-American cultures.

33. I recall an incident several years back among children in my neighborhood. When asked by a young girl why the latest cub in "The Lion King's" family couldn't be a girl, a nine-year-old boy responded instantly, "Well, he *couldn't* be a girl, 'cause he has to be king, and girls can't be kings!"

34. Gilligan 1991.

35. Heyward 1993.

36. See Altizer and Hamilton (1966), Van Buren (1963), and Soelle's first book published in English (1967), written as *An Essay in Theology after "The Death of God."*

37. Brock 1988.

38. Schüssler Fiorenza 1993.

39. Hunt 1991.

40. Williams 1993.

2. Speaking with Authority

1. In 434 C.E., the monk/theologian Vincent of Lerins wrote what would become a basis in Catholicism for the evolving concept of "tradition": "In the Catholic Church . . . all possible care must be taken that we hold that faith which has been believed everywhere, always, by all. For that is truly and in the strictest sense 'Catholic,' which, as the name itself and the reason of the thing declare, comprehends all universality" (132). A hermeneutic of generosity might suggest that in the fifth century, what would become known in time as "the Vincentian Canon" was an important safeguard against heresies. But a wiser hermeneutic in this case, one of suspicion, would suggest that, in the fifth century as at the turn of the twenty-first, "heretic" often referred especially to those whose social marginalization and political views either rendered them

voiceless or—more truthfully—intentionally muted their theological voices. Such a hermeneutic of suspicion is foundational to feminist and other theologies of liberation.

2.   My thanks to womanist theologian Lisa Anderson, who asked, "How can one truly love what one refuses to see?" at the meeting of the American Academy of Religion in San Francisco, Nov. 23, 1997.

3.   Not all heterosexual people are hetero*sexist* and homophobic. But most of us—gay, lesbian, bisexual, and heterosexual—are, in fact, both heterosexist and homophobic in our deepest fears and feelings. Hence, I am using the term "queer" in this book not as a synonym for gay, lesbian, bisexual, and transgendered people, but more broadly for all people, whatever their own sexual identity, who stand in public solidarity with gay men, lesbians, bisexuals, and transgendered/transgendering sisters and brothers. To be queer is to struggle enthusiastically without apology against heterosexism (*not* heterosexuality) and homophobia.

4.   Liberation theology's "epistemological privilege" of the poor ought not be interpreted as a romanticization of the poor's capacity to know what is right or wrong, anymore than other folks do. The epistemological privilege of the poor is, rather, the *ability* (or "privilege") to know first and best what it is—to experience the call and push of God against poverty, against the economic system and social structures that generate poverty, and against the greed and ignorance and stupidity that hold poverty in place. The epistemological privilege of the poor also puts a moral and political mandate before the non-poor—that is, the rest of us—to listen to the poor; to take seriously what we hear and see and learn; and to act in solidarity with the poor in the struggles for bread and justice. See Gutiérrez (1973), Cone (1986), and Ruether (1985).

5.   See Jantzen (1995) for a compelling presentation of Christian mysticism as a social and political protest/movement, especially among women, in the context of religious and other forms of oppression.

6.   Heyward 1989a, 157.

7.   Four friends have accompanied me in special ways along this path. My beloved Angela of the Clare Community in Stroud, New South Wales, Australia, is an artist, visionary, and—much like St. Clare herself—a courageous sojourner in the Mystery; Jim Lassen-Willems is a beautiful brother priest in the Christian tradition, teacher of meditation in the Buddhist tradition, and Seer of much Wisdom; and Janet Surrey is Buddhist and Jewish and my most steadfast and purposeful companion on a journey into ever-deepening study of our Sacred Power in relation. And then there is one who is utterly baffled by all this talk of "mysticism," yet who is herself deeply immersed in the Magic of Connectedness with All Creatures—Beverly W. Harrison, my longest-term companion (32 years so far), a lover, a life-partner, and an exceedingly Wise WomanFriend without whom nothing in my/our spiritual life or my/our theo-ethical work would be what it is.

8. Soelle 1968/1995, 51.

9. Kwok 1995, 12–13.

10. Several examples of contemporary feminist theologians' earlier "standpoint" perspectives before most of us knew much, if any, "postmodernism" were the Cornwall Collective's (1980) and the MudFlower Collective's (1985) works on education; the volumes on feminist theologies and spiritualities edited by Christ and Plaskow (1979, 1989), Heyward (1984), Harrison (1985), Keller (1986), Thistlethwaite (1989), Thistlethwaite and Engel (1990), and works by women theologians of color in the United States and elsewhere, such as Cannon (1988), Isasi-Díaz and Tarango (1988), Fabella and Oduyoye (1989), Chung (1990), and Grant (1992). Several presentations of feminist theology as consciously postmodern include Welch (1985, 1990), Chopp (1989), Cooey (1994), Fulkerson (1994), Tanner (1992, 1997), and Keller (1996).

11. See Phelan (1989) and Spelman (1988).

12. See Heyward (1984), Harrison (1985), Weeks (1985, 1991, 1995), Nelson and Longfellow (1994), and Ellison (1996).

13. See McNeill (1976, 1995) and Spong (1988) as two examples of liberal Christian (and liberal psychological) understandings of sexual "orientation" as innate to the individual. This essentialist view is more widely held among gay men and male theologians than among lesbian and feminist theologians. Mollenkott (1992) is probably the best known (and certainly one of the most courageous and articulate) lesbian feminist liberation theologian who shares the essentialist perspective.

During the last decade, increasing numbers of gay, lesbian, bisexual, and transgendered activists and academics have been exploring gender and sexuality as fluid categories that are more descriptive than definitive of human experience. Resources include Anzaldúa (1987), Bergmann and Smith (1995), Bornstein (1994/1995), Feinberg (1996), Pratt (1995), Sinfield (1994), Warner (1993), and Weeks (1995). Theologians working along these "fluid" lines include Elias Farajaje-Jones, Marvin M. Ellison, Anne Bathurst Gilson, Renée Hill, Daniel T. Spencer, Robin Gorsline, Beverly W. Harrison, J. Michael Clark, and increasingly many working on academic and/or activist projects relating to gender and sex.

14. Borg 1994.

3. Our Power in Mutual Relation

1. Teraph was my fourteen-year-old collie-shepherd dog, who died on March 19, 1990. I wrote this piece to him several days later.

2. Driver 1981, 11.

3. Ibid., 50–52.

4. Ibid., 56.

5. Schüssler Fiorenza 1994, 3.
6. See Tillich (1951, esp. Part 2, 163–210; and 1952), Daly (1973), Driver (1977), Heyward (1982), Soelle and Cloyes (1984), and Mollenkott (1987) for clarifications of God as verb.
7. Schüssler Fiorenza 1994.
8. Brock 1988.
9. See Brock (1988), Heyward (1989a), Gilson (1995), and Spencer (1996) for more on "erotic" power as sacred.
10. This is my lament in relation to some white feminist, as well as nearly all patriarchal, theology—it's too self-absorbed and small or too linear, dry, and "academic" (pretentious and unfeeling). It so often lacks soul, passion, and, it would seem, any sense of accountability to real flesh and blood people and creatures. It seems largely to mute rather than spark our erotic power.
11. See Driver (1977) and Heyward (1984) for discussions of "transcendence" as radical immanence (Driver) and crossing-over (Heyward).
12. Buber 1958.
13. *The Redemption of God* was published in German in 1986 by Kreuz Verlag in Stuttgart as *Und Sie Ruhrte sein Kleid an*.
14. See Jordan, et al. (1991) for psychological explorations of mutuality by the Stone Center for Developmental Studies at Wellesley College in Massachusetts. Janet L. Surrey, a Stone Center Associate and an originator of its relational psychology, has been an invaluable resource for my work in relational theology. We have talked through nearly everything in this book.
15. Catherine Keller's image of a "web" (1986) is close kin to my understanding of mutuality, but "web"—while a beautiful, strong metaphor for connection—does not convey adequately the passionate *commitment to action* on behalf of mutuality. Similarly, other process theologians, like Cobb (1972, 1975, 1976), Suchocki (1981/1989), and Griffin (1973), building on the insights of their philological mentor Alfred North Whitehead, describe a relational process much like the movement imaged in these pages.

With the emergence and increase of liberation theologies (Black, Latin American, Hispanic, Asian, feminist, gay/lesbian, et al.), various contemporary theologians might well describe their work as rooted in both process and liberation commitments. Brock (1988, 1996), Keller (1986, 1996), Sallie McFague (1982, 1987, 1993, 1997), and Suchocki (1982/1989, 1994) exemplify this simultaneity of perspectives. Similarly, with heightened consciousness of the environment—an awareness that earlier process theologians helped generate—process theology is becoming increasingly a theology of the environment. John Cobb's ongoing work and Sallie McFague's contributions illustrate this theological evolution.

Moreover, whether or not we realize it, most feminist theologians—certainly all relational theologians—are indebted to process theology, understood broadly as a theology of connection, movement, and change, a philosophical companion to major scientific discoveries/realizations of the twentieth century, especially Einstein's work on "relativity" and all that has followed. Driver (1981) points out that most Christian theologians are still living out of a Copernican worldview rather than an Einsteinian.

16. My writings on "erotic power" (1989a) and, especially, on "boundaries" (1993) have been critiqued as failing, among other things, to realize the tragic downside of eros (Sands 1992; Skerrett 1996) and, consequently, of expecting mutual *relationships* to sort of magically happen because we want them to and because they would be nice. These critics seem not to notice the primary place in my *theological* work of evil and suffering and my intense interest in the constancy of contradictions and ambiguities inherent in mutuality and in the struggle to bring it more fully into being (1976/1999, 1982, 1984, 1985, 1986, 1989a, 1989b, 1993, 1995). My attention to erotic power and boundaries as theo-ethical themes belongs to a larger struggle to understand more fully how mutuality may function as a liberating and healing response to evil (understood as abusive power relations).

17. Perhaps even more basically, the temptation to start with the "self" is an *epistemological* problem for most Westerners, or an issue of how we know what we know. On the whole, we simply do not know how *not* to start with our "selves" as disconnected in a fundamental sense from other "selves." How often do we hear, "We're born alone and we die alone," when, in reality, we are born—and we die—in relation to an entire cosmos of persons (beginning with our mothers) and in relation to multiple histories and possibilities, which most of us simply learn not to notice.

18. One of the remarkable roles Mary Daly has played for over thirty years among religious feminists is in calling us to *notice* what's happening in patriarchy. Many of us have been critical of what we have perceived to be her failures in taking the next step—joining in the struggle to bring down the patriarchal church, society, and world. But I have come to realize that Daly's very presence in the universe as a Wicked Shrew and a Canny Crone is itself the "next step," and the next, and the next . . . and that simply by writing her books and daring to release them into the midst of us, Daly lives and works as a Fiery "Elemental Feminist" Activist here on this planet at this time—and maybe in other places and times as well! See Daly (1973, 1978, 1984, 1992, 1993, 1998).

19. Most of my theological work has been an effort to weave together what I see as falsely split notions of "being" and "doing," "ontology" and "action," metaphysics and ethics. My reading of Daly is that she is also attempting to address this split.

20. See Tillich 1952.

21. See A. Johnson (1997) and Brown and Bohn (1989) on "patriarchy."

22. I am thinking here of the Cappadocian bishops (and a sister) who, in the fourth century C.E., helped make the evolving Christian image of God a more "relational" *ousia* (could we understand this "common substance" as a matrix or

"womb"?). For the Cappadocians, God was an *ousia* of "persons" (or special forms) rather than, on the one hand, a more indiscriminate unity, or, on the other, a less intrinsically connected federation.

23. Resources on "power" that I have found especially helpful include Ackermann (1996), Harrison (1985), Griscom (1992), hooks (1984, 1990), Lorde (1984), Starhawk (1987), Wink (1992), Williams (1993), Jantzen (1995), and SteinhoffSmith (1998, 1999).

24. As SteinhoffSmith (1998) notices, the major tension between my theological work, especially my recent wrestling with "boundaries," and that of some other feminists, like Fortune (1995), Doehring (1995), and Cooper-White (1995)—whom SteinhoffSmith refers to as "pastoral professionals"— is rooted in our very different understandings of power, mutuality, and love. SteinhoffSmith sees the pastoral professionals, in their efforts to stand with victims of sexual exploitation, to be idealizing power, mutuality, and love. Thus, for example, Fortune suggests that "love does no harm" (1995), to which I would respond, while it may (or may not) be that *love* (God) does no harm, all *lovers* (those who love) do in fact "harm" (hurt, offend, at times betray, etc.) others. Because human (and divine) life is so fraught with ambiguity, complexity, and contradictions, our ethics and politics (how we use whatever power we have) should not simply be grounded in an ideal (such as altruism or, in certain situations, sexual abstinence), but rather reflect the ambiguities, complexities, contingencies, and circumstances in which we actually live, work, and love.

As Christian ethicist Marvin M. Ellison has pointed out in personal conversation, it takes a lot of deeply moral work and struggle, not simple adherence to rules, to live ethically. Do we not owe it to one another—including *especially* those violated by abusive uses of power—to struggle with/in the ambiguities and complexities of our lives and not simply fall in line with—much less create new—orthodoxies, unambiguous definitions, and tight regulations of power, love, sex, etc.? Lebacqz and Barton (1991) seem to me better able than most other authors among the "pastoral professionals" to hold life's complexities, ambiguities, and nuances in their ethical work.

In the realm of these theo-ethical explorations of power, we might try cutting each other a little more slack by assuming that everyone wrestling with these important pastoral, political, and professional matters is doing her/his best and that each of us has much to contribute to an analysis of power—and also much yet to learn from others, including those who believe we're wrong.

25. To the best of my knowledge, the feminist wiccan Starhawk (1987) was the first to name this as "power over." She contrasts this abusive use of power to the experiences of "power within" and "power with." The latter, as I read Starhawk, is a close relative of "mutuality." I may be more inclined than Starhawk to emphasize that "power with" *generates* the internal strength she names as "power within." I would argue, moreover, that any "power within" that is *not* generated

by our mutual connectedness with others (creatures, people, the Spirit) is not "power within" as much as it is, probably, "power over" or perhaps simply an experience of disconnectedness and disempowerment that is passing for internal strength or maybe even integrity. I am not sure Starhawk and I would disagree about this.

26. Everyone wrestling with issues of power in our theological/thealogical, political, psychological, and philosophical work these days risks being misinterpreted, misappropriated, and/or misused by others, whose own understandings are nearly always, of course, at least slightly different. See Foucault (1980) for help in understanding why so many of us get all twisted in knots when we think about power.

27. This seems to me the common root of feminism, liberation theology, and postmodernism—the assumption that whatever has been constructed can be deconstructed.

28. This is one of several points at which I am close kin theologically to the Anglican F. D. Maurice, who understood that, while we can do nothing without God, we are in fact never without God (1853).

29. See Macy (1991) on "dependent co-arising": "[O]ne is not a self-existent being nor are the institutions of society eternally fixed. They are mutable and they mirror our greeds, as does indeed the face of nature itself. Co-arising with our actions, they, like us, can be changed by our actions. As our own dynamic processes can be transformed, so can they. . . . In dependent co-arising, self, society, and world are reciprocally modified by their interaction, as they form relationships and are in turn conditioned by them. The Western idea contrasts with such a view to the extent that it assumes a free association between individuals who remain basically distinct and unaltered by such association" (98–99).

I have been guided toward understanding the deep truths in this teaching by my friends Jim Lassen-Willems and Jan Surrey. And like many contemporary spiritual seekers in the United States and elsewhere, I've been inspired by the life and work of the Vietnamese poet and teacher Thich Nhat Hahn (1976, 1987, 1992, 1995).

30. This, in my judgment, ought to be the basis and aim of all pastoral care and psychotherapy—to enlarge our power in mutual relation. Both or all parties in the counseling or therapy situation should be "enlarged" and changed through the relation. Otherwise it is not a fully trustworthy relational situation for the counselee/client. Our mental health practices in the West are badly in need of deconstruction—and reconstruction—by patients and doctors, clients and counselors, parishioners and pastors, working *together* to envision and help create liberating "professions." What is needed is long term, systemic change, which can happen only insofar as people begin working together now to reform current practices (Greenspan 1983/1993, Heyward 1993, Kitzinger and Perkins 1993, and SteinhoffSmith 1999).

This poses a critical challenge to educators, healers, and religious leaders, including those working largely with the middle class population, who are concerned about the interrelatedness of economic justice, spiritual well-being, and mental health, and also about how we learn to experience ourselves as persons who are being empowered—or more disempowered—in relation to the work of social change and political activism. We ought not be turning the middle classes into a bunch of psychological conformists who are preoccupied with our "inner children." God and the world need us to be "coming out" as much as "going in" and to be learning how to do both at once—moreover, learning how to be healer and healed, strong and vulnerable, simultaneously. We need fewer "professionals" (in the late-twentieth century U.S.A. sense) and more *real presence* among us all.

31. Eighth century Greek theologian John of Damascus used the word *perichoresis* (mutual permeation), which seems to me close to the concept of *coinherence* (mutual inseparability and mutual essence) to describe the intrinsic relatedness of Father, Son, and Spirit.

Drawing upon insights from feminist Christians La Cugna (1991), Johnson (1994), Wilson-Kastner (1989), and the work of Moltmann (1993), Matthew Peter Cadwell, a 1999 graduate of the Episcopal Divinity School, Cambridge, Massachusetts, wrote in his senior thesis: "Drawing upon *perichoresis* and an understanding of relation and communion at the divine level, feminists propose that the divine relations serve as models for human community" (61). Cadwell further notes that, except for Catherine La Cugna, "most of the feminist theologians studied here [Wilson-Kastner and Johnson] do not emphasize the sacraments or life and participation in the Church as a means for sharing in the life of the Trinity" (62).

In his fine historical review of the Trinity's theological development, Cadwell does not attempt to interpret the lack of emphasis on church and sacraments that he finds among Christian feminists. But this fact—that many (probably most) Christian feminist theologians do not emphasize church or sacrament in our theologies—is a significant aspect of trinitarian thought as it is developing among us. Christian feminists, through our critique of the fundamentally *non-mutual* character of patriarchal relationships (including the traditional subordination of Son to Father and of laity, women, children, and other creatures to church fathers, prelates, and clerics), are experiencing and envisioning a much more radical understanding of *perichoresis* than anything we have been taught by the institutional church about the Trinity or the sacraments.

I appreciate Cadwell's thoughtful research and also the thorough work of another student, Katharine D. Kane, on the Trinity. The depth and quality of their interest in a doctrine that often seems obsolete were a source of encouragement to me.

32. Soelle, with Shirley A. Cloyes (1984), presents a wonderfully "trinitarian" Christian theology without ever discussing the doctrine of the Trinity, a doctrine

that does not interest Soelle. When I say Soelle's work is "trinitarian," I mean that she presents a God who is neither synonymous with creation nor set apart from it but rather is radically involved with ("all rolled up in") creation. Soelle writes, "That we are created in the image of God connotes neither the total mystical union between God and humanity nor the total otherness of God. However, any good theology contains a mystical element. It is almost impossible for any theology totally to deny God's empowerment of us. When we understand God as power in relation and ourselves as being empowered, then we are inspired to testify to the goodness of creation" (1984, 45). Soelle continues, "God is not synonymous with omnipotent control; rather, God's power lies in sharing life with others. The admiration God loves is our sense of connectedness with the whole of creation" (52).

Other feminists whose relational theological understandings are especially vibrant include Keller (1986, 1996) and Grey (1990). While neither of these women is writing explicitly about the Trinity, both can provide conceptual resources for those Christians who are looking for some deeper understandings of the relational basis for this Christian doctrine.

For various traditional treatments of the doctrine of the Trinity among earlier modern theologians, see Maurice (1853, esp. 263–301); Baillie (1948, esp. 133–56); Tillich (1951, vol. 1, part 2, section 2; vol. 3, part 4, section 4); and Barth (1956, vol. 1, part 2, esp. 33f; vol. 2, part 1, esp. 203f). Temple, like Maurice and Barth (among the various modern theologians), was careful to present the trinitarian nature of God as implicit in God's ongoing presence and activity throughout the time and space we humans call "history" (1953, 445f).

33. I imagine that this is akin to what Origen and others of the Greek fathers may have had in mind as they discussed (and disputed) the *ousia* of JESUS CHRIST.

34. From the song, "One of Us," by Eric Bazilian, sung by Joan Osborne on her 1995 album *Relish* (New York: Polygram Records).

35. These are examples of the protests voiced during the last thirty years by many Anglicans and Roman Catholics against the ordination of women. For good, brief, commonsense responses to such charges, see Hewitt and Hiatt (1971).

36. More to the point, it is unlikely that such a radically trinitarian faith would have priests!

4. Evil as Betrayal of Mutuality

1. See Pagels (1995) on Satan/Devil and Barstow (1994) on the "witchcraze" as an example of the historical consequences of this kind of projection. In fact, a good case can be made, in my judgment, for much evil being the consequence of these fear-based locations of our own anxieties, fears, and failures somewhere outside ourselves.

2. "Heterosexism is the basic structure of gay/lesbian oppression in this and other societies. Heterosexism is to homophobia what sexism is to misogyny and what racism is to racial bigotry and hatred" (Heyward 1989a, 50).

3. Heyward 1989a.

4. See Brown and Bohn (1989) for a series of essays that make connections between traditional Christian interpretations of sin and evil and the problem of violence, especially the violence done by socially powerful men to those "beneath" them (e.g., women, children, less socially powerful men). See Adams and Fortune (1995) for further attention to the same connections; and Adams (1995) for the development of this theme in relation to animals.

5. See Soelle (1995), who writes, "Perhaps phantasy is a more meaningful and basic word [than obedience] for Christians in this radically changing world" (30). Soelle continues, "Should one consider the death of JESUS from the point of obedience alone, one would overlook the fact that selflessness and a readiness to live sacrificially are possible only when a person has come to himself and has reached the fullest level of personal freedom. Obedience only makes sense when it is expressed by a person who is in harmony with himself. All self-sacrifice, all self-denial, and all suffering which is expressed without this harmony, that is, simply because it has been demanded by others, is senseless and produces nothing. It cannot issue in a resurrection" (57).

6. Maurice 1872 (Lecture 3, 43–63) as quoted in Wondra (1995). Maurice insists that "the external authority of the parent or teacher . . . is useless unless he appeals to that which is within the child, is mischievous unless it is exerted to call that forth." Moreover, he writes, "The external authority must become an internal authority, not co-operating with the forces which are seeking to crush the I in the child but working against those forces, working to deliver the child from their dominion." Maurice continues, "A parent or teacher who [teaches children to dread him as an inflicter of pain] is of all the ministers of a community the one whom it should regard with the greatest abhorrence, seeing that he is bringing up for it, not citizens, but slaves. . . ." Elsewhere (1869, Lecture 2, Part 1, 21–41), Maurice articulates some sense of the patriarchal basis of this misuse of power by those in authority and suggests that "the union of the mother's influence with the fathers *helps* distinguish authority from dominion. . . ."

7. Heyward 1982.

8. See Alcoholics Anonymous (1976) for this description of addiction.

9. McFague 1993.

10. Dillard 1974.

11. Obedient children of authoritarian parents, human or divine, cannot develop courage, because they are pushed into fearful situations and told what to feel and what to do. They are not allowed to experience the transformation of fear through facing and, as they are able, engaging that which frightens them. Courage takes root in such a learning process, and it takes time. An ethics of obedience usually teaches children to avoid, flee from, or destroy whatever they fear

may harm them, especially if it seems strange to them or different in species or culture, custom or behavior, appearance or attitude. Am I saying here that children ought not be taught to fear strangers, flee from people who scare them, and run from danger when they sense they are in it? Certainly *not*. Children must be shown how to stay as safe as possible. I am suggesting that we parents, aunts and uncles, teachers and friends, guardians and older siblings of children have a *spiritual* responsibility to help children *think about* danger and safety—what is dangerous, and why is it dangerous? How can we, children, adults, everyone, help each other stay safe? We need to help children recognize and understand their feelings—especially their feelings of fear, which often are hard for children to accept as okay precisely because we adults seem so ashamed of our own feelings of fear.

Children should be affirmed in feeling whatever they feel. They should be taught to think about what they are feeling. Giving children some license to use their heads is the better part of wisdom and surely the best way to help them learn to live as safely as possible in a world fraught with evil, violence, and danger.

12. The origin of evil will always be, for Christians and other monotheists, a major source of puzzlement and disagreement. This intellectual, as well as spiritual and moral, question has simmered among Christian theologians from the earliest days of the church. There has never been one dominant voice or opinion but rather only an ongoing theological "conversation" from one person, context, or generation to another. Most theologians traditionally have tried to balance a recognition, on the one hand, of the gravity of human sin (and of evil, as either its root or its branches) and, on the other hand, human beings' freedom to choose to do what is right and good. Lohse (1966) suggests that some of the more dualistic and morbid treatments of the origins of sin and evil in human life, like Origen's, were developed under the influence of the Gnostics' radically negative view of the body and all material life.

Of the relation between God and evil, I think Wink (1992) writes with much wisdom: "I have long been struck by the virtual absence of any attempt to explain evil (theodicy) in the New Testament. The early Christians devoted a great deal of energy to discovering the meaning of JESUS' death, but nowhere do they offer a justification of God in the face of an evil world. They do not seem to be puzzled or even perturbed by evil as a theoretical problem. . . . To the question, Why was JESUS crucified, the early church had a ready answer: he was crucified by the Powers because what he said and did threatened their power. The burning question for them was not *why* but *how*: How has God used this evil for good? How has God turned sin into salvation? How has God triumphed over the Powers through the cross?" (314).

Wink is suggesting that the fact of evil—"the Powers"—ought always to be spurring our ethical and pastoral commitments more than simply our philosophical interests. As examples of this practical theo-ethical wrestling with the problem of evil, see Soelle (1975), Heyward (1982), Brock (1988), Smith (1992), Townes (1993, 1999), and Suchocki (1994).

13. See Brock (1988), Brown and Bohn (1989), and Adams and Fortune (1995).

14. Webster's New World Dictionary 1983, 60.

15. These are the forces that Hillary Rodham Clinton had in mind early in 1998 when she remarked that a "vast right-wing conspiracy is trying to destroy my husband." She knew what she was talking about and surely was, and is, aware that this "conspiracy" is trying to destroy her as well.

16. See Williams (1993) for the suggestion that JESUS' "ministry" (and his "quality of life") were the basis of why we remember him. They also provide the foundations for a living, vibrant Christology.

17. See Maurice (1853, 19–29) on "charity," by which he means God's love. "If it is asked what human charity can have to do with the mysteries of the Godhead, the compilers of the Prayer-book would have answered, 'Certainly nothing at all, if human charity is not the image and counterpart of the Divine; if there can be a charity in man which beareth all things, believeth all things, endureth all things, unless it was first in God, unless it be the nature and being of God. If He is Charity, His acts *must* spring from it as ours *should*; Charity will be the key to unlock the secrets of Divinity as well as of Humanity'" (23).

18. Maurice 1853, 281.

19. Ibid., 37.

20. Ibid.

21. See "On Eternal Life and Eternal Death," Maurice 1853, 302–25.

22. Regarding the assumption that the church needs a doctrine of Eternal Death to deter sinners, Maurice wrote, "The doctrine of endless punishment is avowedly put forward as necessary for the reprobates of the world, publicans and harlots, though perhaps religious men might dispense with it. Now, I find in our Lord's discourses, that when He used such words as these, 'Ye serpents, ye generations of vipers, how shall ye escape the damnation of Hell?' He was speaking to religious men, to doctors of the law; but that when he went among publicans and sinners, it was to preach the Gospel of the Kingdom of God. Does not this difference show that our minds are very strangely at variance with His mind? . . . Spiritual pride is the essential nature of the Devil. To be in that, is to be in the deepest hell. Oh! how little are all outward sensual abominations in comparison with this!" (1853, 324).

Regarding the hope for (or fear of) *future* reward (or punishment), he wrote, "The state of eternal life and eternal death is not one we can refer only to the future, or that we can in any wise identify with the future. Every man who knows what it is to have been in a state of sin, knows what it is to have been in a state of death. He cannot connect that death with time; he must say that CHRIST brought him out of the bonds of *eternal* death. Throw that idea into the future and you deprive it of all its reality, of all its power" (323).

A century and a half later, such *transtemporal* experiences and views of good and evil, sin and grace, and bondage and liberation would be voiced by a variety of theologians ranging from existentialists like Tillich (1952) and Driver (1977, 1981), to a radical political mystic like Soelle (1975) to many feminist and womanist Christians, cross-culturally—e.g., Chung (1990), Kwok (1995), Heyward (1993, 1995), and Townes (1997).

23. Maurice 1853, 323.

24. Ibid.

25. Ibid., 40–53.

26. Maurice 1872.

27. This statement of mine should not be interpreted as an assent to either capital or corporal punishment, neither of which I believe is usually, if ever, a right response to violence or wrong-doing. What I mean by the judgment that we often need to exercise in our life together is that, whenever any of us breaks the cord that binds us (and we all do this), we need encouragement to "weep bitterly" with Peter. Such encouragement usually means helping each other realize that our failures to love one another have consequences—such as alienation from the common good, isolation by and from those we have harmed, losses of respect (including self-respect) and perhaps material possessions and/or personal freedom (especially if we have acted violently), and requirements for reparations from those whose lives we have damaged.

28. See Wiesel (1960). In the late 1970s, as I worked on my doctorate at Union Theological Seminary in New York, I was introduced by Professor Robert McAfee Brown to the works of Elie Wiesel. Wiesel's books, especially his autobiographical *Night* and the novels that followed (*Dawn, The Accident, The Town Beyond the Wall, The Gates of the Forest, The Oath*) became primary theological, ethical—and profoundly spiritual— resources for my life and work, especially in relation to the spiritual mystery and moral problem of evil.

29. See Chapter 5 on "nonviolence." Also see Camara (1971) for excellent treatment of how violence leads to more violence. This is, of course, one of the primary moral arguments against capital punishment. See Prejean (1993). See also King (1958, 1963, 1964, 1967, 1968), Gandhi (1951/1961, 1962), Douglass (1991), Wink (1992), Nhat Hahn (1987), and Macy (1991).

30. Wink 1992.

5. The Passion of JESUS: Beyond Moralism

1. Isasi-Díaz 1993.

2. Exemplifying the Religious Right's focus on family values, Campus Crusade for Christ founder Bill Bright and Christian Broadcaster John N. Damoose write, "Christians should be among the first to stand up for traditional family values, for rebuilding parent-child relationships, and for religious education in the home. . . . Yet today millions of Americans have accepted the lie that family

values are outdated. This lie is defended by those who want us to accept the immoral values of modern humanism." In an oblique reference to Hillary Rodham Clinton's book on our shared, social responsibility for the care of children, Bright and Damoose continue, "The idea that 'it takes a village' to raise a child, for example, is a misleading assault on traditional child-rearing. A village of faith and virtue may provide a protective buffer for America's kids, but there is no substitute for a united, caring, supportive, affirming, God-fearing family for raising healthy, well-adjusted children. No village on earth can do the job of mom and dad together. You just cannot improve on God's formula for the family: one man, one woman, for one lifetime. Any other formula leads to broken hearts and broken homes" (1998, 142).

It's been fascinating to observe the extent to which, for leaders of the Religious Right in the 1990s, the Clintons (both Bill and Hillary) have become icons of "modern humanism." There seems to me little question that the impeachment drive was more than anything an assault by the religious and political Right on those who represent family values that are not in keeping with traditional conservative Christian understandings. Whereas to many of us who place ourselves further Left than the Clintons, this President and his spouse have often seemed hopelessly Centrist in their politics, to those on the Right, the Clintons represent feminism, queer liberation, procreative freedom, racial justice, and everything else that seems (at least to the Religious Right) to be antagonistic to the maintenance of the traditional, nuclear, white, middle class Christian family. Recognition of this irony and its political importance is why most feminist and gay/lesbian/bisexual/transgendered groups went on record in strong opposition to the impeachment of this President.

For good, critical analyses of the Religious Right's emphasis on family values, see Lienesch 1993 (esp. Ch. 2 on "Family," 52–93), and Diamond 1995 (esp. Ch. 10, "Undaunted Allies: The Christian Right in the 1980s," 228–56). Diamond, a perceptive social analyst and forecaster, ends her 1995 book with an ominous warning: "Soon after the inauguration of the new [1994] Congress, the Christian Coalition pledged to spend more than one million dollars lobbying for welfare cuts and other legislative proposals in the Republicans' 'Contract with America.' In exchange for Christian Right commitment to Republican economic policies, the party would owe the movement support in backing public school prayer and opposing abortion and gay rights. Despite many obstacles to unity, together the Christian Right and the Republican Party hoped, by 1996, to throw the Democrats out of the White House and to enforce a new era of moral righteousness and economic severity with a vengeance" (312).

For recent queer and feminist theological responses to the Right's theopolitics of the family, see Say and Kowalewski (1998) and Gilson (1999).

3. Heyward 1982.

4. This distorted and damaging image of atonement—the image of a violent, dispassionate God; an obedient son; and the rest of us called to be "sons" of God

(or like the Father, if we have the power)—has been strongly critiqued by Christian feminists and womanists. I discuss it more fully in the last part of this book.

5. Jim came to his body-affirmation through Marxism's attentiveness to the material, physical world. During the next couple of decades, the Christian focus on incarnation would sharpen and strengthen his celebration of body. Through his practice of Buddhism in the 1990s, Jim has been able, most radically and personally, to *experience* both full presence of his own body and a "moreness than" his individual body.

6. Heyward 1984.

7. In fact, I believe that our "spirits" are, for the most part, simply our multiple and infinitely diverse personal "occasions" and experiences of the wonderful creative Spirit of life and liberation. As for spirits that may be evil, I do believe that we meet and are met by them, and that we generate them through our fear of difference and "otherness" and through the hatred and violence that are set in motion by this fear as it grows and spreads among us like toxic waste.

8. See, for example, Rosemary Radford Ruether's assessments of the connections between body-hatred and misogyny (1985, 1992, 1998). Discussing the Platonism already implicit in very early (pre-canonical) Christianity, Ruether describes the work of the Hellenistic Jewish philosopher Philo of Alexandria: "The original Adam, formed according to the image of God, was wholly Spiritual, 'perceptible only to the intellect, incorporeal, neither male nor female, imperishable by nature.' Only secondarily does God form the earthly Adam out of clay, into which God then breathes the divine spirit. This earthly Adam is made up of two parts, the corporeal part that is mortal, and the spirit that is immortal, partaking of the divine Logos, the original Spiritual Adam. This Adam of body and soul was happy and lived an exalted and immortal life as the image of the cosmos, as long as he was single. His downfall was the creation of his wife. With the creation of Eve came sex, 'which is the beginning of iniquities and transgressions, and it is owing to this that men have exchanged their previously immortal and happy existence for one that is mortal and full of misfortune'" (Philo, "On the Creation of the World," in *The Essential Philo*, ed. by Nahum Glatzer [New York: Schocken, 1971], 46, 53; quoted by Ruether 1998).

9. Baillie 1948, 66.

10. I suspect that, often, a creative meeting ground for more and less orthodox Christian theologians is in the realm of *experienced* faith and belief. Theological conversations over the years with such colleagues as Lloyd Patterson and Sarah Coakley have taught me a great deal about the common spiritual ground in which our beliefs are rooted—even when our cognitive understandings of Christian doctrine are at variance and, sometimes, intellectually incompatible.

11. Beverly W. Harrison is currently working with these concepts in her teaching, lectures, and writings in progress.

12. For more on body, see Nelson (1978, 1983, 1992), Harrison (1985), Heyward (1989a), Cooey, Farmer, and Ross (1987), Cooey (1994), Gudorf (1994),

Nelson and Longfellow (1994), Gilson (1995), Ellison (1996), May (1995), Spencer (1996), and Morrison (1998). For connections between erotic power and body, see especially Nelson and Longfellow, Harrison, Heyward, Gilson, Ellison, Spencer, May, and Morrison.

13. Soelle 1967.

14. There are literally thousands of helpful resources on liberation theologies—Latin American, Black [American], Native American, Asian, feminist, womanist, *mujerista*, queer. One of the most useful introductions to Latin American liberation theology written for Christians in the United States is Robert McAfee Brown's *Theology in a New Key* (1978).

15. We usually make "God" in human image through our religious language ("He" and "Father"; less often "She" and "Mother"). We imagine that this anthropomorphizing of deity might strengthen our ability to *experience* God as *personally* accessible not only "in" us but, as importantly, "in" other human beings. However, two millennia of Christian life does not suggest that the making of God in human image (usually of the male) has helped us image what is most sacred in ourselves and others, especially if the "others" have been women, Black and other people of color, poor people, Jews, Moslems, and others without social or political power in the dominant world/churches.

16. I discuss the Truth and Reconciliation Commission as an example of the public and political work of forgiveness in the last part of this book.

17. Camara 1971.

18. See page 86 for poem, "Fear Shrinks Us."

19. See West (1982) and Welch (1985, 1990) for more on "dangerous memory," a term derived from their readings of Foucault.

20. See de le Torre (1982).

21. See Brown and Parker, "For God So Loved the World?" (Brown and Bohn, 1989, 1–30). Brown and Parker end their essay with this powerful reversal of traditional Christian interpretations of Crucifixion and Resurrection: "Resurrection means that death is overcome in those precise instances when human beings choose life, refusing the threat of death. JESUS climbed out of the grave in the Garden of Gethsemane when he refused to abandon his commitment to the truth even though his enemies threatened him with death. On Good Friday, the Resurrected One was Crucified" (28).

22. Kwok 1993, 25.

23. We need to be careful not to grant too high a moral status to "awareness" or "consciousness" lest we contribute to the maintenance of the popular, but fundamentally false, hierarchy of a "moral intelligence" in which those who are "aware" are—or think they can be—"better" than those who are unaware, or who may seem to be less aware or conscious than some others. This is one of the chief moral problems that haunts humankind, in my judgment—our hubris, or false pride, in our human capacity to reflect consciously on matters of right and

wrong, which, we imagine, makes us morally superior to other animals. This is also a serious problem in human life as we often tend to judge as, in some sense, morally inferior those persons of lesser measured-intelligence. While there may be often some important truths in drawing distinctions between the *capacities* of different species and different people to "know" what is what (right, wrong, safe, dangerous, etc.), we Christians (and others too) too often confuse capacity— especially intellectual capacities, such as consciousness—with morality, thereby setting up hierarchies of morality by which we shape customs, laws, and public policy.

24. Might this insight help clarify the traditional christological affirmation of JESUS CHRIST's "fully human" and "fully divine" character (a modern, not classical, term)?

25. See Lorde (1984), hooks (1984, 1990), Cone (1986), West (1993), Frankenburg (1993), and Ignatiev and Garvey (1996).

26. Feminist ethicists, teachers, and co-directors for many years of the Women's Theological Center in Boston, Richardson and Bivens were, to my knowledge, the first people to frame the challenge in this way to white people who are struggling against racism. I've found this image—anti-racist racist—to be a creative teaching-tool precisely because it is so truthful, and so fraught with the tensions embedded in the difficult truth to which it points.

27. The Religious Right's fixation on "America" as God's chosen country is reflected in its antagonism to the development of a more fully mutual relationship between the United States and other nations. Like most other people—in the United States and elsewhere—the Religious Right uses the term "America" as if Canada, Mexico, and all of Latin America weren't American too. It's vital that we in the United States realize and take our place in a more fully global perspective. Can we not be an excellent leader without having to be always best, first, most, and way above everyone else? Moreover, is not our capacity to be an impressive moral leader in the world (which we seldom have been during my lifetime of over 50 years to date!) rooted in our capacity to generate dynamics of mutuality and friendship rather than domination and paternalism throughout the world?

28. This observation is vintage Dorothee Soelle! I have not been able to locate it in her writings, but I am certain it is hers.

29. See Moltmann (1974) and Soelle (1975).

30. It is interesting—and disturbing—to me how few health (mental or medical) and religious professionals are willing at this time even to discuss the debilitating and even deadly effects—emotionally, physically, and spiritually—of the hyper-professionalized ethos being generated by fear. Certainly, we ought to fear violent and abusive relational dynamics. But I submit that the "boundary culture" that has popped up over the last couple of decades is steeped only superficially in our fear of violence and abuse. The professional obsession with "good boundaries" is, more radically, a product of our fear of mutuality—and of the systemic

transformation required by a serious, long-term commitment to mutual empowerment as a primary basis for healing. If we care-givers are really committed to mutuality as a *sacred* root of health and well-being, then let us give up being the "experts" and learn to direct the healing processes *with* those students, parishioners, counsellees, clients, and patients who turn to us for help. And let us re-construct our healing systems on the basis of this commitment. I would ask those Christians who view such a perspective as too idealistic how you yourselves experience and understand the activity of the Spirit that pushes forever against those principalities and powers that I have described in this book as authoritarian, moralistic, and adversarial. See Greenspan (1983/1993), Kitzinger and Perkins (1993), and SteinhoffSmith (1998, 1999).

6. Learning Forgiveness: Way of Compassion

1. Two former students, Carolyn Frank and David Carter, were helpful to me in important ways in thinking about forgiveness.
2. Raymond 1986; Hunt 1991; Daly 1978, 1984, 1998.
3. Heyward 1982, 1984, 1989a, 1993.
4. I am speaking here of people *collectively*. This collectivity is key to understanding atonement as a historical act that is larger than, though inclusive of and affected by, individuals' efforts to make right relation.
5. *Book of Common Prayer* 1979, 370.
6. Baillie 1948, 157–59.
7. Baillie of course, like other white male theologians of his generation, does not acknowledge—or probably even realize—the particularities or limits of his cultural (including his theological) assumptions. This does not strengthen his work, but neither does it invalidate it. It simply is a fact that, when realized, helps the reader recognize the limits of Baillie's theology, as any other.
8. Baillie 1948, 163.
9. Ibid.
10. Ibid., 164.
11. Ibid.
12. Ibid.
13. Ibid.
14. Ibid.
15. *Book of Common Prayer* 1979, 63.
16. Baillie 1948, 163 (emphasis mine).
17. Samuel Shem and Janet Surrey have written a brilliant account (1990) of the founding of Alcoholics Anonymous in 1935 by "Bill W." and "Dr. Bob," in which Shem and Surrey present as radically mutual (relational) the basis of the Founders' experiences of the dynamics that contribute to spiritual, mental, and physical recovery/healing.

18. The "promises" that are often read in AA meetings provide a wonderful summary of the spiritual gifts that come not only with recovery from addiction but also with forgiveness as its giver and recipient. In a very deep way, the capacity to forgive others and ourselves (and to accept that we ourselves are forgiven in and by the Spirit) is a powerful dimension of sobriety and continues, throughout the recovery process (for most of us, a lifetime), to be a basis for sanity, serenity, and gratitude.

Here are the "promises," as set forth in the Big Book of Alcoholics Anonymous: "We are going to know a new freedom and a new happiness. We will not regret the past nor wish to shut the door on it. We will comprehend the word serenity and we will know peace. No matter how far down the scale we have gone, we will see how our experience can benefit others. That feeling of uselessness and self-pity will disappear. We will lose interest in selfish things and gain interest in our fellows. Self-seeking will slip away. Our whole attitude and outlook upon life will change. Fear of people and of economic insecurity will leave us. We will intuitively know how to handle situations which used to baffle us. We will suddenly realize that God is doing for us what we could not do for ourselves" (1976, 83–84).

19. The understanding of atonement as substitutionary (JESUS in our place) and sacrificial (JESUS' life as an offering to "satisfy" God as a payment for our sins) was presented by Anselm, Bishop of Canterbury (d. 1109) in his *Cur Deus Homo?* The concepts and language are those of a harsh and unforgiving feudal system of lords, debts, and payments. One of Anselm's younger contemporaries and critics was Peter Abelard. Arguing against Anselm, Abelard believed that humanity, not God, was blocking the reconciliation process prior to JESUS CHRIST. Thus, for Abelard, it was the *human* JESUS' "*moral example*" to all humankind, rather than God's "satisfaction" through JESUS' death, that becomes the basis of atonement. I believe that the perspective of this book, *Saving Jesus*, radicalizes the Abelardian tradition.

20. See Brown (1967) for a helpful study of the shifts and developments in Augustine's life. As a younger man, prior to his experience of JESUS CHRIST and his conversion, Augustine believed in a more radically dualistic cosmos, in which the world really was in the grip of evil. Ironically, from a more radically relational theological perspective (e.g., Soelle, Brock, Kwok, Chung, Williams, McFague, Suchocki, Driver, Gilson, Heyward), the older and more mature Augustine—whose theology we often interpret as terribly dualistic—was more nuanced and relational than we often realize. This is, of course, because the Christian church, in its patriarchal malestream, has used him to make its dualistic points! In fact, Augustine struggled, like the rest of us, to understand how a good and powerful God relates to evil.

21. Baillie 1948, 173.

22. Abelard 1976.

23. I'm grateful to my colleague at the Episcopal Divinity School, New Testament Professor Joanna Dewey, for her longstanding critical interest in the problematical development of the tradition of "sacrifice" as a way of (mis)understanding JESUS' death. Dewey is currently working on a book on this theme.

24. Baillie 1948, 173.

25. Soelle 1977.

26. See Heyward (1989a), Gilson (1995), Elison (1996), and Spencer (1996) for more on erotic energy as a yearning for God and as our power to make and sustain mutuality.

27. Heyward 1989a; Harrison and Heyward 1989.

28. LeGuin 1975, 256–57.

29. Ibid., 258.

30. Ibid., 259.

31. Whether the Christian Eucharist can be experienced and understood as a thanksgiving for God's real presence among us here and now rather than for God's "holy sacrifice" of Himself (His Son) is a critical pastoral as well as liturgical question for many Christian feminists. How we answer it depends on whether we can loose ourselves and one another from our dreadful patriarchal religious moorings in which "holy sacrifice" requires the letting of blood and giving up of life. Can there be *nonviolent* Eucharist in which we celebrate the giving up of our isolation and self-absorption and in which we give thanks *not* for JESUS' (or anyone's) violent death but rather for his and our own passionate lives together *in God* one day at a time, sisters and brothers in Spirit? The liturgical resources in the final section of this book—especially the first and last ones—reflect several attempts to lift up this kind of theological movement.

32. Two engaging contemporary resources on forgiveness are Battle (1997) and Jones (1995). In the former, a study of Desmond Tutu's *"ubuntu"* (relational) theology, Battle quotes Tutu: "Our people say Ubuntu. Ubuntu is something you say when someone has wronged you. What you long for is not revenge. What you long for is a healing of relationships" (95). Reflecting on this, Battle writes, "Refusal to see related identities is Tutu's definition of sin, the converse of ubuntu" (ibid.). Tutu's theology seems, on the surface, to be much more traditionally Christocentric than what I am proposing. But I think his understanding of "ubuntu" and mine of "mutuality" as the very essence of a radically transcendent and immanent God place us very close together theologically.

Tutu understands forgiveness as the reconciling power of a self-emptying God who meets us—present tense—in JESUS CHRIST, and I would say that forgiveness is the ongoing presence of a God who is constantly reaching toward us—forgiving us—and inviting us to forgive one another. I believe this was manifest in JESUS (past tense) and continues to be shown forth in JESUS' Christic (holy) Spirit—present tense. For both of us, the sacred, redemptive power of forgiveness is the power of God, a mighty relational force that moves us "to see related identities," and to accept ourselves as the sisters and brothers we are in Spirit.

Gregory Jones, in his "theological analysis" of forgiveness (1995), suggests that "When forgiveness is seen in primarily individualistic and private terms, we lose sight of its central role in establishing a way of life—not only with our 'inner' selves but also in our relations with others" (39). This is an echo of the difficulty Baillie had a half century ago (1948) with our modern inclination to psychologize our spiritual malaise. In this thoughtful volume on forgiveness from a Christian perspective, which includes a salient chapter on "loving enemies" (241–78), Jones wrestles with the vitality of accountability and, sometimes, punishment as necessary to the larger social/relational dynamics of forgiveness: "Whenever we undertake the tragic risk of punishment, we cannot abdicate the task of seeing those who have become enemies as human beings who need and deserve our love—a love that holds open the possibility of reconciliation. . . ." (276). Moreover, Jones contends,

> We ought not trivialize the difficulties entailed in learning to love our enemies; even reaching that far on the path of forgiveness and reconciliation, learning to give up desires for vengeance and to wish the other person well, may require considerable struggle. . . . Learning to love our enemies is . . . often a counter-cultural practice. Indeed, in many contemporary contexts, where people are habituated into—and in fact rewarded for—hating their enemies and desiring vengeance, Christians must offer a counter-habituation. It must involve learning the habits and practices necessary to resist the desire for revenge and struggling to have those desires transformed by God's Spirit into desires for love. (277)

33. "'Tis the gift to be simple, 'tis the gift to be free, 'tis the gift to come down where we ought to be, and when we find ourselves in the place just right, 'twill be in the valley of love and delight. When true simplicity is gained to bow and to bend we shan't be ashamed, to turn, turn, will be our delight 'till by turning, turning we come 'round right." Words and music by Joseph Brackett Jr. (1797–1882) in *The Hymnal 1982*.

34. See Battle (1997) for an analysis of Tutu's "ubuntu" theology, for better understanding the theological and political underpinnings of the Commission's work.

35. The poems and prayers that follow in this chapter are from my journal in which, for about ten years, I have wrestled with questions of forgiveness probably more than any other christological theme. This particular poem was published in my book *When Boundaries Betray Us* (1993/repub. 2000).

36. I am grateful to Diane Tingley for this question.

37. Soelle 1995.

38. Naylor 1985.

39. Williams 1993.

40. On nonviolence, see Gandhi (1951/1961, 1962), King (1958, 1963, 1964, 1967, 1968), Douglass (1991), Macy (1991), Miller (1996), Battle (1997), Nhat Hahn (1987, 1995), and Wink (1992, 1998).

41. Physicist David Bohm described "a dialogue" this way: "In a dialogue . . . nobody is trying to win. Everybody wins if anybody wins. There is a different sort of spirit to it [different from "discussion" or "debate," for example]. In a dialogue, there is no attempt to gain points, or to make your particular view prevail. Rather, whenever any mistake is discovered on the part of anybody, everybody gains. It's a situation called win-win, whereas the other game is win-lose—if I win, you lose. But a dialogue is something more of a common participation, in which we are not playing a game against each other but *with* each other. In a dialogue, everybody wins" (1987, 2).

This is very much my understanding of the dynamic of mutual relation. Like M. L. King, Thich Nhat Hahn, and other peacemakers, Bohm understood that this "dialoguing"—which is the ongoing basis of nonviolence—is difficult to generate and sustain in the dominant social order (East or West, North or South). In the ethos of advanced patriarchal capitalism, such dialoguing is always counter-cultural and, therefore, will be trivialized by the powers that be (within us as well as around us). In order to actually live this way, I am more and more persuaded that we have to build community wherever we are and that we can only do this on the basis of faith in the liberating power of mutual relation. I believe that such faith can only be cultivated together.

The Twelve-Step program of Alcoholics Anonymous is, in my experience, one arena in which this kind of counter-cultural "dialoguing" is shared and sustained. It is a grassroots, populist spiritual movement with radical political implications from which there is much to be learned. In it, I believe, are seeds of hope and strength for the world. It has certainly been a forum and a movement in which I personally have learned a great deal about compassion, nonviolence, human beings, and our differences (including our various experiences—and non-experiences—of a "Higher Power").

42. As my good friend and mentor Tom F. Driver taught me many years ago, paradox is not contradiction, in which different experiences or views actually work at cross-purposes. Here I am discussing forgiveness as a compassionate and nonviolent way of being in the world in which paradoxically we sometimes are coming into joy through sorrow, and into serenity through loneliness. It is a way of life in which we do not experience these feelings and states of being as contradictory but rather as belonging together.

43. John of the Cross 1990. In a racist social order such as ours, using the word "dark" as a synonym for "bad" or "evil" is problematic and just plain racist in my opinion. As a metaphor, however, for something that is difficult, not bad, "dark" can convey depth rather than shallowness; real substance rather than the artificial

"brightness" and "lightness" of one-dimensional experience. This is how I interpret such a metaphor as "the dark night of the soul."

Epilogue

1. Bishop Robert L. DeWitt, former Bishop of Pennsylvania, editor of *The Witness*, and one of the Episcopal bishops who in 1974 ordained the first women priests in the Episcopal church, prior to the church's authorization of women's ordination, often signs his letters to those he ordained (and others), "Keep your courage." Coming from a man who has done exactly that, this counsel has always meant a great deal to me and to many.

Liturgical Resources

1. Written for a litany commemorating International Women's Year, Lafayette Park, Washington, D.C., spring 1978, and published in *Our Passion for Justice: Images of Power, Sexuality, and Liberation* (New York: Pilgrim, 1984), 49–51.
2. Adapted from prayer written for services at Episcopal Divinity School, Cambridge, Massachusetts, in 1980 and published in *Our Passion for Justice: Images of Power, Sexuality, and Liberation* (New York: Pilgrim, 1984), 148–50.
3. Written for services at Episcopal Divinity School (unpublished).
4. Published in *Celebrating Women*, eds. Janet Morley and Hannah Ward, "Women in Theology" and Movement for the Ordination of Women (London: Holy Trinity House, 1986), 39.
5. "The Great Thanksgiving: A Rite Based on the Song of Mary," in *Equal Rites: Lesbian and Gay Worship, Ceremonies, and Celebrations*, ed. Kittridge Cherry and Zalmon Sherwood (Louisville: Westminster John Knox, 1995), 113–15.
6. Written in honor of Beverly Wildung Harrison for a Celebration at Union Theological Seminary, March 25, 1999, drawing from and inspired by her essays in *Making the Connections: Essays in Feminist Social Ethics*, ed. Carol S. Robb (Boston: Beacon), 1985.
7. The word *god* is used here as a verb.

Selected Resources

On the Christian Right in the U.S.

Bawer, Bruce. 1997. *Stealing Jesus: How fundamentalism betrays Christianity*. New York: Crown.

Berlet, Chip (and Political Research Associates), eds. 1995. *Eyes right! Challenging the right wing backlash*. Boston: South End.

Bright, Bill and John N. Damoose. 1998. *Red sky in the morning: How you can help prevent America's gathering storms*. Orlando: New Life.

Clapp, Rodney. 1993. *Families at the crossroads: Beyond traditional and modern options*. Downers Grove, Ill.: InterVarsity.

Diamond, Sara. 1995. *Roads to dominion: Right-wing movements and political power in the United States*. New York: Guilford.

Forbes, Steve. 1998. *The moral basis of a free society*. Washington, D.C.: Regenery.

Gilson, Anne Bathurst. 1999. *The battle for America's families: A feminist response to the religious right*. Cleveland: Pilgrim.

Lapin, Daniel. 1999. *America's real war: An Orthodox Rabbi insists that Judeo-Christian values are vital for our nation's health*. Mercer Island, Wash.: Cascadia.

Lienesch, Michael. 1993. *Redeeming America: Piety and politics in the new Christian right*. Chapel Hill: University of North Carolina Press.

Marsden, George M. 1991. *Understanding fundamentalism and evangelicalism*. Grand Rapids: Eerdmans.

Marty, Martin E. and R. Scott Appleby, eds. 1991. *Fundamentalisms observed*. The Fundamentalism Project, vol. 1. Chicago: University of Chicago Press.

———. 1993. *Fundamentalisms and society: Reclaiming the sciences, the family, and education*. The Fundamentalism Project, vol. 2. Chicago: University of Chicago Press.

———. 1993. *Fundamentalisms and the state: Remaking polities, economies, and militance*. The Fundamentalism Project, vol. 3. Chicago: University of Chicago Press.

————. 1994. *Accounting for fundamentalisms: The dynamic character of movements*. The Fundamentalism Project, vol. 4. Chicago: University of Chicago Press.

————. 1995. *Fundamentalisms comprehended*. The Fundamentalism Project, vol. 5. Chicago: University of Chicago Press.

Nassif, Tony. 1996. *Jesus, politics, and the church: The mind of Christ on Christians in politics*. Mukilteo, Wash.: WinePress.

Peretti, Frank E. 1986. *This present darkness*. Wheaton, Ill.: Crossway.

————. 1992. *Prophet*. Wheaton, Ill.: Crossway.

Ritter, Kathleen and Craig O'Neill. 1996. *Righteous religion: Unmasking the illusions of fundamentalism and authoritarian Catholicism*. New York: Haworth.

Say, Elizabeth A. and Mark R. Kowalewski. 1998. *Gays, lesbians, and family values*. Cleveland: Pilgrim.

Watson, Justin. 1997. *The Christian Coalition: Dreams of restoration, demands for recognition*. New York: St. Martin's.

Other Resources, Cited or Selected

Abelard, Peter. 1976. *Sic et non: A critical edition*. Edited by Blanche B. Boyer and Richard McKeon. Chicago: University of Chicago Press.

Ackerman, Denise. 1985. Liberation and practical theology: A feminist perspective on ministry. *Journal of Theology for Southern Africa*, no. 52:30–41.

Adams, Carol J. 1995. *Neither man nor beast: Feminism and the defense of animals*. New York: Continuum.

Adams, Carol J. and Marie M. Fortune, eds. 1995. *Violence against women and children: A theological sourcebook in the Christian tradition*. New York: Continuum.

Alcoholics Anonymous. 3d ed. of the Big Book. 1976. New York: AA World Services.

Altizer, Thomas J. J. 1966. *The gospel of Christian atheism*. Philadelphia: Westminster.

Altizer, Thomas J. J. and William Hamilton. 1966. *Radical theology and the death of God*. Indianapolis: Bobbs-Merrill.

The Amanecida Collective. 1986. *Revolutionary forgiveness: Feminist reflections on Nicaragua*. Maryknoll, N.Y.: Orbis.

Anselm. 1962. *Cur Deus Homo?* In *Saint Anslem: Basic writings*, translated by S. W. Deane. La Salle, Ill.: Open Court.

Anzaldúa, Gloria. 1987. *Borderlands/la frontera: The new mestiza*. San Francisco: Aunt Lute.

Augustine. 1991. *Confessions*. Translated with introduction and notes by Henry Chadwick. Oxford: Oxford University Press.

Baillie, D. M. 1948. *God was in Christ: An essay on incarnation and atonement*. New York: Scribner's.

Barstow, Anne L. 1994. *Witchcraze: A new history of the European witch-hunts—Our legacy of violence against women*. San Francisco: Harper San Francisco.

Barth, Karl. 1956. *Church dogmatics*. Edinburgh: T. & T. Clark.

Battle, Michael. 1997. *Reconciliation: The ubuntu theology of Desmond Tutu*. Cleveland: Pilgrim.

Bazilian, Eric. 1995. *One of us*. Performed by Joan Osborne on *Relish*. New York: Polygram Records.

Bergmann, Emilie L. and Paul Julian Smith, eds. 1995. *¿Entiendes? Queer readings, Hispanic writings*. Durham and London: Duke University Press.

Bettenhausen, Elizabeth. 1996. Evil. In *Dictionary of feminist theologies*, edited by Letty M. Russell and J. Shannon Clarkson. Louisville: Westminster John Knox.

Bohm, David. 1990. *On dialogue*. Ojai, Calif.: David Bohm Seminars.

Bohm, David and David Peat. 1987. *Science, order, and creativity*. New York: Bantam.

Bonhoeffer, Dietrich. 1972. *Letters and papers from prison*. Greatly enlarged edition edited by Eberhard Bethge. New York: Collier.

The Book of Common Prayer and administration of the sacraments and other rites and ceremonies of the church: According to the use of the Episcopal Church. 1979. New York: Church Hymnal Corporation.

Borg, Marcus. 1994. *Meeting Jesus again for the first time*. San Francisco: Harper San Francisco.

Bornstein, Kate. 1994. *Gender outlaw: On men, women, and the rest of us*. New York: Vintage.

Brock, Rita Nakashima. 1988. *Journeys by heart: A christology of erotic power*. New York: Crossroad.

Brock, Rita Nakashima and Susan Brooks Thistlethwaite. 1996. *Casting stones: Prostitution and liberation in Asia and the United States*. Minneapolis: Fortress.

Brown, Joanne Carlson and Carole R. Bohn, eds. 1989. *Christianity, patriarchy, and abuse: A feminist critique*. Cleveland: Pilgrim.

Brown, Peter. 1967. *Augustine of Hippo: A biography*. Berkeley: University of California Press.

Brown, Robert McAfee. 1978. *Theology in a new key: Responding to liberation*. Philadelphia: Westminster.

Brown Douglas, Kelly. 1994. *The black Christ*. Maryknoll, N.Y.: Orbis.

Buber, Martin. 1958. *I and thou*. New York: Scribner's.

Cadwell, Matthew Peter. 1999. "God in relation: The Holy Trinity in biblical, historical, and contemporary perspectives." Unpublished thesis. Cambridge, Mass.: Episcopal Divinity School.

Camara, Helder. 1971. *Spiral of violence*. Translated by Della Couling. London: Sheed and Ward.

Cannon, Katie Geneva. 1988. *Black womanist ethics*. Atlanta: Scholars.

Chapple, Christopher Key. 1993. *Nonviolence to animals, earth, and self in Asian traditions*. Albany: State University of New York.

Cherry, Kittredge and Zalmon Sherwood, eds. 1995. *Equal rites*. Louisville: Westminster/John Knox.

Chopp, Rebecca. 1989. *The power to speak: Feminism, language, God*. New York: Crossroad.

Chopp, Rebecca and Mark Taylor, eds. 1994. *Reconstructing Christian theology*. Minneapolis: Fortress.

Christ, Carol P. and Judith Plaskow, eds. 1979. *Womanspirit rising: A feminist reader in religion*. San Francisco: Harper and Row.

Chung Hyun Kyung. 1990. *Stuggle to be the sun again*. Maryknoll, N.Y.: Orbis.

Coakley, Sarah. 1998. "'Persons' in the 'social' doctrine of the Trinity: Gregory of Nyssa and current analytic discussion." Unpublished ms. Lecture, Harvard Divinity School.

Cobb, John B. 1965. *A Christian natural theology, based on the thought of Alfred North Whitehead*. Philadelphia: Westminster.

——. 1972. *Is it too late?: A theology of ecology*. Beverly Hills: Bruce.

——. 1975. *Christ in a pluralistic age*. Philadelphia: Westminster.

————. 1976. *Process theology: An introductory exposition*. Philadelphia: Westminster.

Comstock, Gary and Susan E. Henking, eds. 1997. *Que(e)rying religion: A critical anthology*. New York: Continuum.

Cone, James H. 1986. *A black theology of liberation*. 2d ed. Maryknoll, N.Y.: Orbis.

Cooey, Paula. 1994. *Religious imagination and the body: A feminist analysis*. Oxford: Oxford University.

Cooey, Paula, S. A. Farmer, and M. E. Ross, eds. 1987. *Embodied love: Sensuality and relationship as feminist values*. San Francisco: Harper and Row.

Cooper-White, Pamela. 1995. *The cry of Tamar: Violence against women and the church's response*. Minneapolis: Fortress.

The Cornwall Collective. 1980. *Your daughters shall prophesy: Feminist alternatives in theological education*. New York: Pilgrim.

Crossan, John Dominic. 1994. *Jesus: A revolutionary biography*. San Francisco: Harper San Francisco.

Daly, Mary. 1968. *The church and the second sex*. Reissued with Autobiographical Preface to the 1975 Edition and Feminist Postchristian Introduction, 1975; Reissued with New Archaic Afterwords, 1985. Boston: Beacon.

————. 1973. *Beyond God the father: Toward a philosophy of women's liberation*. Reissued with Original Reintroduction by the Author, 1985. Boston: Beacon.

————. 1978. *Gyn/Ecology: The metaethics of radical feminism*. Reissued with New Intergalactic Introduction by the Author, 1990. Boston: Beacon.

————. 1984. *Pure lust: Elemental feminist philosophy*. London: Women's.

————. 1992. *Outercourse: The be-dazzling voyage*. London: Women's.

————. 1993. *Webster's first new intergalactic wickedary of the English language*. Conjured in Cahoots with Jane Caputi. London: Women's.

————. 1998. *Quintessence ... Realizing the archaic future: A radical elemental feminist manifesto*. 2048 BE (Biophilic Era) Edition. Boston: Beacon.

de la Torre, Edicio. A message from the Philippino struggle. In *Theology in the Americas, Detroit II Conference Papers*. Edited by Cornel West, Caridad Guidote, and Margaret Coakley. Maryknoll, N.Y.: Orbis, 44–50.

Dillard, Annie. 1974. *Pilgrim at Tinker Creek*. New York: Harper's Magazine.

Doehring, Carrie. 1995. *Taking care: Monitoring power dynamics and relational boundaries in pastoral care and counseling*. Nashville: Abingdon.

Douglass, James W. 1991. *The nonviolent coming of God*. Maryknoll, N.Y.: Orbis.

Driver, Tom F. 1977. *Patterns of grace: Human experience as word of God*. New York: Harper and Row.

———. 1981. *Christ in a changing world: Toward an ethical christology*. New York: Crossroad.

Ellison, Marvin M. 1996. *Erotic justice: A liberating ethic of sexuality*. Louisville: Westminster John Knox.

Fabella, Virginia and Park Sun Ai Lee, eds. 1989. *We dare to dream: Doing theology as Asian women*. Maryknoll, N.Y.: Orbis.

Feinberg, Leslie. 1996. *Transgender warriors: Making history from Joan of Arc to Dennis Rodman*. Boston: Beacon.

Fortune, Marie M. 1983. *Sexual violence: The unmentionable sin*. New York: Pilgrim.

———. 1995. *Love does no harm: Sexual ethics for the rest of us*. New York: Continuum.

Foucault, Michel. 1980. *Power/Knowledge: Selected interviews and other writings, 1972–1977*. New York: Pantheon.

Fox, Michael W. 1996. *The boundless circle: Caring for creatures and creation*. Wheaton, Ill.: Quest.

Frankenberg, Ruth. 1993. *White women, race matters: The social construction of whiteness*. Minneapolis: University of Minnesota Press.

Fulkerson, Mary M. 1994. *Changing the subject: Women's discourses and feminist theology*. Minneapolis: Fortress.

Gandhi, Mahatma. 1961. *Non-violent resistance (Satyagraha)*. New York: Schocken.

———. 1962. *The essential Gandhi, an anthology*. Edited by Louis Fischer. New York: Random House.

The General Assembly Special Committee on Human Sexuality, Presbyterian Church USA. 1991. *Keeping body and soul together: Sexuality, spirituality, and social justice.* Louisville: PCUSA.

Gilligan, Carol, Annie G. Rogers, and Deborah L. Tolman, eds. 1991. *Women, girls and psychotherapy.* New York: Haworth.

Gilson, Anne Bathurst. 1995. *Eros breaking free: Interpreting sexual theoethics.* Cleveland: Pilgrim.

Goss, Robert. 1993. *Jesus acted up: A gay and lesbian manifesto.* San Francisco: HarperSanFrancisco.

Grant, Jacquelyn. 1992. *White women's Christ and black women's Jesus: Feminist christology and womanist response.* Atlanta: Scholars.

Greenspan, Miriam. 1993. *A new approach to women and therapy.* New York: McGraw-Hill, 1983. Reprint, Blue Ridge Summit, Penn.: TAB Books; Bradenton, Fla.: Human Services Institute.

Grey, Mary. 1990. *Feminism, redemption, and the Christian tradition.* Mystic, Conn.: Twenty-Third.

Griffin, David Ray. 1973. *A process christology.* Philadelphia: Westminster.

Griscom, Joan L. 1992. Women and power: Definition, dualism, and difference. *Psychology of Women Quarterly* 16:389–414.

Gutiérrez, Gustavo. 1973. *A theology of liberation: History, politics, and salvation.* Translated and edited by Sister Caridad Inda and John Eagleson. Maryknoll, N.Y.: Orbis.

Harrison, Beverly Wildung. 1985. *Making the connections: Essays in feminist social ethics.* Edited by Carol S. Robb. Boston: Beacon.

Harrison, Beverly W. and Carter Heyward. 1989. Pain and pleasure: Avoiding the confusion of Christian tradition in feminist theory. In *Christianity, patriarchy, and abuse: A feminist critique*, edited by Joanne Carlson Brown and Carole R. Bohn. Cleveland: Pilgrim. 148–173.

Hewitt, Emily C. and Suzanne R. Hiatt. 1973. *Women priests: Yes or no?* New York: Seabury.

Heyward, Carter. 1976. *A priest forever.* Reissued for the 25th Anniversary of Philadelphia Ordination, with New Introduction, 1999. Cleveland: Pilgrim.

————. 1982. *The redemption of God: A theology of mutual relation.* Lanham, Md.: University Press of America.

———. 1984. *Our passion for justice: Images of power, sexuality, and liberation*. New York: Pilgrim.

———. 1989a. *Touching our strength: The erotic as power and the love of God*. San Francisco: Harper and Row.

———. 1989b. *Speaking of Christ: A lesbian feminist voice*. Edited by Ellen C. Davis. Cleveland: Pilgrim.

———. 1993. *When boundaries betray us: Beyond illusions of what is ethical in therapy and life*. San Francisco: Harper Collins. To be republished with Introduction by Roy SteinhoffSmith. Cleveland: Pilgrim, 2000.

———. 1995. *Staying power: Images of gender, justice, and compassion*. Cleveland: Pilgrim.

hooks, bell. 1984. *Feminist theory: From margin to center*. Boston: South End.

———. 1990. *Yearning: Race, gender, and cultural politics*. Boston: South End.

The Hymnal 1982. 1982. New York: The Church Hymnal Corporation.

Ignatiev, Noel and John Garvey, eds. 1996. *Race traitor*. New York: Routledge.

Isasi-Díaz, Ada María. 1993. *En la lucha: Elaborating a mujerista theology*. Minneapolis: Fortress.

Isasi-Díaz, Ada María and Yoland Tarango. 1988. *Hispanic women: Prophetic voice in the church: Toward a Hispanic women's liberation theology*. Minneapolis: Fortress. Reprinted 1993.

Isherwood, Lisa and McEwan, Dorothea, eds. 1996. *An A to Z of feminist theology*. Sheffield, England: Sheffield Academic Press.

Jantzen, Grace. 1995. *Power, gender, and Christian mysticism*. Cambridge: Cambridge University Press.

John of the Cross. 1990. *Dark night of the soul*. Translated, edited, and with an introduction by E. Allison Peers from the critical edition of Silverio de Santa Teresa. New York: Image Books/Doubleday.

Johnson, Allan B. 1997. *The gender knot: Unraveling our patriarchal legacy*. Philadelphia: Temple University.

Johnson, Elizabeth A. 1992. *Consider Jesus: Waves of renewal in christology*. New York: Crossroad.

————. 1994. *She who is: The mystery of God in feminist theological discourse*. New York: Crossroad.

Johnson, James Weldon. 1927. *God's trombones: Seven negro sermons in verse*. New York: Viking.

Jones, Gregory L. 1995. *Embodying forgiveness: A theological analysis*. Grand Rapids: Eerdmans.

Jordan, Judith V., Alexandra Kaplan, Jean Baker Miller, Irene P. Stiver, and Janet L. Surrey. 1991. *Women's growth in connection: Writings from the Stone Center*. New York: Guilford.

Kaye/Kantrowitz, Melanie. 1992. *The issue is power: Essays on women, Jews, violence, and resistance*. San Francisco: Aunt Lute.

Keller, Catherine. 1986. *From a broken web: Separation, sexism, and self*. Boston: Beacon.

————. 1996. *Apocalypse now and then: A feminist guide to the end of the world*. Boston: Beacon.

King, Martin Luther, Jr. 1958. *Stride toward freedom: The Montgomery story*. New York: Harper.

————. 1963. *Strength to love*. New York: Harper and Row.

————. 1964. *Why we can't wait*. New York: Harper and Row.

————. 1967. *Conscience for change*. Toronto: Canadian Broadcasting Co.

————. 1968. *The measure of a man*. Philadelphia: Pilgrim.

————. 1986. *A testament of hope: The essential writings of Martin Luther King, Jr.* Edited by James Melvin Washington. San Francisco: Harper.

Kitzinger, Celia and Rachel Perkins. 1993. *Changing our minds: Lesbian feminism and psychology*. New York: New York University Press.

Kwok Pui-lan. 1993. Chinese non-Christian perceptions of Christ. *Concilium*, no. 2.

————. 1995. *Discovering the Bible in the non-biblical world*. Maryknoll, N.Y.: Orbis.

La Cugna, Catherine Mowry. 1991. *God for us: The Trinity and Christian life*. San Francisco: Harper.

Lebacqz, Karen and Ronald G. Barton. 1991. *Sex in the parish*. Louisville: Westminster John Knox.

LeGuin, Ursula. 1975. The ones who walk away from Omelas. In *The wind's twelve quarters*. New York: Harper and Row.

Leunig, Michael. 1991. *The prayer tree*. North Blackburn, Vic., Aus.: Collins Dove.

Lohse, Bernhard. 1966. *A short history of Christian doctrine from the first century to the present*. Translated by F. Ernest Stoeffler. Philadelphia: Fortress.

Lorde, Audre. 1984. *Sister outsider*. Trumansburg: Crossing.

Macy, Joanna. 1991. *World as lover, world as self*. Berkeley: Parallax.

Maurice, Frederick Denison. [1853] 1957. *Theological essays*. London: James Clark and Co.

————. [1869] 1886. *Social morality: Twenty-one lectures delivered in the University of Cambridge*. London: Macmillan and Co.

————. 1872. *The conscience*. 2d ed. London: Macmillan and Co.

————. 1995. *Reconstructing Christian ethics: Selected writings of F. D. Maurice*. Edited by Ellen K. Wondra. Louisville: Westminster John Knox.

May, Melanie. 1995. *A body knows: A theopoetics of death and resurrection*. New York: Continuum.

McFague, Sallie. 1993. *The body of God: An ecological theology*. Minneapolis: Fortress.

————. 1997. *Super, natural Christians: How we should love nature*. Minneapolis: Fortress.

McFerrin, Bobby. *The twenty-third psalm*. Performed by Bobby McFerrin. EMI-USA CDP-7-92048-2. Compact disc.

McNeill, John. 1976. *The church and the homosexual*. Kansas City: Sheed, Andrews, and McMeel.

————. 1995. *Freedom, glorious freedom: The spiritual journey to the fullness of life for gays, lesbians, and everybody else*. Boston: Beacon.

Miller, Rhea. 1996. *Cloudhand, clenched fist: Chaos, crisis, and the emergence of community*. San Diego: Lura Media.

Mollenkott, Virginia Ramey. 1987. *Godding: Human responsibility and the Bible*. New York: Crossroad.

————. 1992. *Sensuous spirituality: Out from fundamentalism*. New York: Crossroad.

Moltmann, Jürgen. 1974. *The crucified God: The cross of Christ as the foundation and criticism of Christian theology*. New York: Harper and Row.

————. 1993. *Trinity and the kingdom: The doctrine of God*. Minneapolis: Fortress.

Morrison, Melanie S. 1998. *The politics of sin: Practical theological issues in lesbian feminist perspective*. Netherlands: Rijksuniversiteit Groningen.

The Mudflower Collective. 1985. *God's fierce whimsy: Christian feminism and theological education*. New York: Pilgrim.

Naylor, Gloria. 1985. *Linden Hills*. New York: Ticknor and Fields.

Nelson, James B. 1978. *Embodiment: An approach to sexuality and Christian theology*. Minneapolis: Augsburg.

————. 1983. *Between two gardens: Reflections on sexuality and religious experience*. New York: Pilgrim.

————. 1992. *Body theology*. Louisville: Westminster/John Knox.

Nhat Hahn, Thich. 1976. *The miracle of mindfulness: A manual of meditation*. Boston: Beacon.

————. 1987. *Being peace*. Berkeley: Parallax.

————. 1992. *Touching peace: Practicing the art of mindful living*. Berkeley: Parallax.

————. 1995. *Living Buddha, living Christ*. New York: Riverhead.

Niebuhr, H. Richard. 1951. *Christ and Culture*. New York: Harper and Row.

Norris, Richard A., ed. 1980. *The christological controversy*. Philadelphia: Fortress.

Pagels, Elaine H. 1995. *The origin of Satan*. New York: Random House.

Phelan, Shane. 1989. *Identity politics: Lesbian feminism and the limits of community*. Philadelphia: Temple University Press.

Philo of Alexandria. 1971. *The essential Philo*. Edited by Nahum Glatzer. New York: Schocken.

Plaskow, Judith. 1990. *Standing again at Sinai: Judaism from a feminist perspective*. San Francisco: Harper and Row.

Plaskow, Judith and Carol P. Christ, eds. 1989. *Weaving the visions: New patterns in feminist spirituality*. San Francisco: Harper and Row.

Pratt, Minnie Bruce. 1995. *S/He*. Ithaca, N.Y.: Firebrand.

Prejean, Helen. 1994. *Dead man walking: An eyewitness account of the death penalty in the United States*. New York: Vintage.

Rasmussen, Larry L. 1996. *Earth community, earth ethics*. Maryknoll, N.Y.: Orbis.

Raymond, Janice G. 1986. *A passion for friends: Toward a philosophy of female affection*. Boston: Beacon.

Ruether, Rosemary Radford. 1979. *Faith and fratricide: The theological roots of anti-semitism*. New York: Seabury.

———. 1985. *Sexism and God-talk: Toward a feminist theology*. Boston: Beacon. Reprinted 1993.

———. 1992. *Gaia and God: An ecofeminist theology of earth healing*. San Francisco: HarperSanFrancisco.

———. 1998. *Women and redemption: A theological history*. Minneapolis: Fortress.

Russell, Letty M. and J. Shannon Clarkson, eds. 1996. *Dictionary of feminist theologies*. Louisville: Westminster John Knox.

Sands, Kathleen M. 1994. *Escape from paradise: Evil and tragedy in feminist theology*. Minneapolis: Fortress.

Schillebeeckx, Edward. 1979. *Jesus: An experiment in christology*. New York: Seabury.

———. 1980. *Christ: The experience of Jesus as Lord*. New York: Seabury.

Schottroff, Luise. 1995. *Lydia's impatient sisters: A feminist social history of early Christianity*. Louisville: Westminster John Knox.

Schüssler Fiorenza, Elisabeth. 1993. *Discipleship of equals: A critical feminist ekklesialogy of liberation*. New York: Crossroad.

———. 1994. *Jesus: Miriam's child, Sophia's prophet*. New York: Continuum.

Shem, Samuel and Janet Surrey. 1990. *Bill W. and Dr. Bob*. New York: Samuel French.

Sinfield, Alan. 1994. *Cultural politics—queer reading*. Philadelphia: University of Pennsylvania Press.

Skerrett, K. Roberts. 1996. When no means yes: The passion of Carter Heyward. *Journal of Feminist Studies in Religion* 12:1, 71–92.

Smith, Christine M. 1992. *Preaching as weeping, confession, and resistance: Radical responses to radical evil*. Louisville: Westminster John Knox.

Soelle, Dorothee. 1967. *Christ the representative: An essay in theology after "The death of God."* Philadelphia: Fortress.

———. 1975. *Suffering*. Philadelphia: Fortress.

———. 1977. *Revolutionary patience*. Maryknoll, N.Y.: Orbis.

———. 1995. *Creative disobedience*. Cleveland: Pilgrim.

Soelle, Dorothee and Shirley A. Cloyes. 1984. *To work and to love: A theology of creation*. Philadelphia: Fortress.

Spencer, Daniel T. 1996. *Gay and Gaia: Ethics, ecology, and the erotic.* Cleveland: Pilgrim.

Spong, John S. 1988. *Living in sin? A bishop rethinks human sexuality.* San Francisco: Harper and Row.

Starhawk. 1979. *The spiral dance: A rebirth of the ancient religion of the great goddess.* San Francisco: Harper and Row.

————. 1982. *Dreaming the dark: Magic, sex, and politics.* Boston: Beacon.

————. 1987. *Truth or dare: Encounters with power, authority, and mystery.* San Francisco: Harper and Row.

SteinhoffSmith, Roy. 1998. The boundary wars mystery. *Religious Studies Review* 24, no. 2:131–42.

————. 1999. *The mutuality of care.* St. Louis: Chalice.

Suchocki, Marjorie. 1982. *God-Christ-Church: A practical guide to process theology.* Revised edition 1989. New York: Crossroad.

————. 1994. *The fall to violence: Original sin in relational theology.* New York: Continuum.

Tanner, Kathryn. 1992. *The politics of God: Christian theories and social justice.* Minneapolis: Fortress.

————. 1997. *Theories of culture: A new agenda for theology.* Minneapolis: Fortress.

Tatum, W. Barnes. 1997. *Jesus at the movies: A guide to the first hundred years.* Santa Rosa, Calif.: Polebridge.

Temple, William. 1953. *Nature, man, and God.* London: Macmillan & Co.

Thistlethwaite, Susan Brooks. 1983. *Metaphors for the contemporary church.* New York: Pilgrim.

————. 1989. *Sex, race, and God—Christian feminism in black and white.* New York: Crossroad.

Thistlethwaite, Susan Brooks and Mary Potter Engel, eds. 1990. *Lift every voice: Constructing Christian theology from the underside.* Reissued in 1998. San Francisco: Harper and Row.

Thompsett, Fredrica Harris. 1993. *Courageous incarnation: In children, aging, work, and intimacy.* Cambridge, Mass.: Cowley.

Tillich, Paul. 1951–1963. *Systematic theology.* 3 vols. Chicago: University of Chicago Press.

————. 1952. *The courage to be.* New Haven: Yale University.

Townes, Emilie M. 1999. *Breaking the fine rain of death:African American health issues and a womanist ethic of care*. New York: Continuum.

Townes, Emilie M., ed. 1993. *A troubling in my soul:Womanist perspectives on evil and suffering*. Maryknoll, N.Y.: Orbis.

———. 1997. *Embracing the spirit:Womanist perspectives on hope, salvation, and transformation*. Maryknoll, N.Y.: Orbis.

Trible, Phyllis. 1984. *Texts of terror: Literary-feminist readings of biblical narratives*. Philadelphia: Fortress.

Van Buren, Paul Matthews. 1963. *The secular meaning of the gospel, based on an analysis of its language*. New York: Macmillan.

Vincent of Lerins. 1890. The Commonitory. In *Nicene and Post-Nicene fathers of the Christian Church*. 2d ser., vol. 11. Edited by Philip Schaff and Henry Wace. New York: Christian Literature.

Warner, Michael, ed. 1993. *Fear of a queer planet:Queer politics and social theory*. Minneapolis: University of Minnesota.

Webster's New World Dictionary. 1983. New York: Warner.

Weeks, Jeffrey. 1985. *Sexuality and its discontents: Meanings, myths, and modern sexualities*. London and Boston: Routledge and Kegan Paul.

———. 1991. *Against nature: Essays on history, sexuality, and identity*. London: Rivers Oram.

———. 1995. *Invented moralities: Sexual values in an age of uncertainty*. New York: Columbia University.

Welch, Sharon D. 1985. *Communities of solidarity and resistance:A feminist theology of liberation*. Maryknoll, N.Y.: Orbis.

———. 1990. *A feminist ethic of risk*. Minneapolis: Fortress.

West, Cornel. 1982. *Prophesy deliverance!:An Afro-American revolutionary Christianity*. Philadelphia: Westminster.

———. 1993. *Race matters*. Boston: Beacon.

Wetherwilt, Ann Kirkus. 1994. *That they may be many:Voices of women, echoes of God*. New York: Continuum.

Wiesel, Elie. 1960. *Night*. New York: Hill and Wang.

———. 1964. *The town beyond the wall*. New York: Holt, Rinehart, and Winston.

———. 1966. *The gates of the forest*. New York: Schocken.

———. 1972. *Night, Dawn,The Accident:Three tales by Elie Wiesel*. New York: Hill and Wang.

————. 1973. *The oath*. New York: Random House.

Williams, Charles. [1949] 1973. *Descent into hell*. Grand Rapids: Eerdmans.

Willams, Delores S. 1993. *Sisters in the wilderness: The challenge of womanist God-talk*. Maryknoll, N.Y.: Orbis.

Wilson-Kastner, Patricia. 1983. *Faith, feminism, and the Christ*. Philadelphia: Fortress.

Wink, Walter. 1984. *Naming the powers: The language of power in the New Testament*. Minneapolis: Fortress.

————. 1986. *Unmasking the powers: The invisible forces that determine human existence*. Minneapolis: Fortress.

————. 1992. *Engaging the powers: discernment and resistance in a world of domination*. Minneapolis: Fortress.

————. 1998. *The powers that be: Theology for a new millennium*. New York: Doubleday.

Acknowledgments

I am delighted by Betty LaDuke's offering of her splendid, evocative painting, "Guatemala: Procession," to be the cover of the book.

My thanks to the faculty and students of the Episcopal Divinity School in Cambridge, Massachusetts, for so many years my co-learners. Without the students in my Christology classes over the years, as well as wonderfully supportive colleagues, this book could not have come into being. When I began to review faces and names of those students who have had an impact on my christological work, I was over-whelmed and awed, by how many of you there have been and how deeply moved I have been by your christological wrestling. A few teaching assistants, doctoral students, and senior advisees working specifically on Christology contributed more than perhaps you know to how I experience and think about JESUS. Special thanks to you—Ann Wetherilt, Pat Hawkins, Sharon Lewis, Cyndi Morse, Hea Sun Kim, Norene Carter, Ali Wurm, Barbara Plimpton, Michele Torres, and Marlene Walker.

Heartiest thanks to Alice Dodds and Jeffrey Mills for their good secretarial help over the years, and to Pat Hawkins, sister theologian and friend, for her patience and skill in researching and word process-ing this project.

I am grateful for the editorial sensibilities and friendship of Michael West at Fortress Press, who knew when to step in and when to let go, the mark of a wise editor. Beth Wright and others at Fortress were also most helpful in the final stages of production.

A number of theological colleagues have been especially important to the development of my christological thinking over the last twenty-five years—I think most of all of Tom F. Driver, and also Dorothee Soelle, Beverly W. Harrison, Delores S. Williams, Norene Carter, Ann K. Wetherilt, Jim Lassen-Willems, Robin Gorsline, Anne Bathurst Gilson, Barbara Lundblad, Sydney Caitlin Howell, Kwok Pui-lan,

Donald F. Winslow, Melanie Morrison, Robert McAfee Brown, Christopher Morse, Shelley Finson, and Mary Solberg. You have been my teachers, co-learners, and partners in the desire to teach something real and alive and liberating about JESUS CHRIST wherever life has been decimated, which in this world is just about everywhere.

No words from me about JESUS and why all of this matters could have been spoken in quite this way without my experiences in two writing groups in the early to mid 1980s: the MudFlower Collective, which wrote *God's Fierce Whimsy: Christian Feminism and Theological Education* (New York: Pilgrim, 1985), and the Amanecida Collective, which traveled to Nicaragua and wrote about it theologically in *Revolutionary Forgiveness: Feminist Reflections in Nicaragua* (Maryknoll, N.Y.: Orbis, 1987). Thanks forever to the women (and one man) in these Collectives—to Katie Cannon, Beverly Harrison, Ada María Isasi-Díaz, Mary Pellauer, Nancy Richardson, and Delores Williams (from MudFlower); and to Anne Gilson, Laura Biddle, Flo Gelo, Susan Harlow, Elaine Koenig, Virginia Lund, Kirsten Lundblad, Pat Michaels, Laurie Rofinot, Margarita Suarez, Jane van Zandt, and Carol Vogler (from Amanecida). *¡Adelante!*

In recent years, some very special friends have helped me touch the core of what I have wanted to say about JESUS in particular—and then say it—Angela, c.c., Angela Moloney, Peggy Hanley-Hackenbruck, Megan Crouse, Chris Morton, Mari Castellanos, Barbara Plimpton, Lucy Tatman, Reinhild Traitler, Drew Hanlon, Roger Smith, Mari Irvin, Patricia Brennan, Susan Adams, and Janie Spahr. Each of you has been a resource of courage for me in this project, more than you know.

To Bonnie Engelhardt, whose strong sisterly support and counsel over the years has continued to be a steadfast resource of confidence to speak boldly, my thanks and love. Similarly, my friendships with Steve Bergman, Miriam Greenspan, Demaris Wehr, Alison Cheek, Sue Hiatt, Bob DeWitt, Marvin Ellison, Irene Monroe, Jennifer Rouse, Gerrie Kiley, Ann Franklin, Elly Andújar, Peg Huff, Jim Harrison, David Conolly, Selisse Berry, Chris Blackburn, and Darlene Nicgorski have helped keep me in touch with what matters.

Appreciation also to many other folks in various places for whom these christological questions have been pressing—from Atlanta to

Seattle to Dallas to Boston; from Holden Village to Kirkridge to the Graduate Theological Union to Warren Wilson College; from the Cathedral of Hope, the National Cathedral, Emmanuel Church in Boston, and St. Luke's in Montclair, New Jersey, to CLOUT in Madison, Wisconsin; from Zurich to Sydney to Managua to Toronto. Thank you, friends near and far, for sharing your insights and passion, a constant wellspring of energy and hope for me in this work.

My gratitude also to Friends of Bill everywhere for walking the walk, which is really what this book is about, and to my beloved companion and soulmate, Jan Surrey, for walking with me—in life. A feminist Buddhist Jew and relational psychologist, you, as much as anyone, have helped this christological vision take shape.

As the book was going to press in the early spring of 1999, my small seminar in relational theology read parts of it and gave me some immensely critical, valuable feedback. Hearty thanks to each of you— Kathy Kane, Chris Medeiros, Pam Parker, Sara Patek, Diane Tingley, Reinhild Traitler, John Vail, and Rose Wu.

Special appreciation to Beverly W. Harrison and Joanna Dewey for helping me think about how to speak of JESUS with both intellectual integrity and spiritual passion.

I'm always grateful to my family of origin, in particular my mother, Mary Ann Heyward, my brother, Robbie Heyward, my sister, Ann Heyward, and my irrepressible niece and nephew, Isabel and Rob Drinkwater, and to my in-laws, Robert Dulin, Ramsey Dulin, and Betsy Alexander, for their love and support through all manner and means of disagreements and controversies including, I am sure, those we may yet entertain about JESUS.

Thanks beyond these words to Sue Sasser, whose presence, sweet wit, and wisdom makes so much difference, and to Bev Harrison, who, more than any, helps me tap faith in our Sacred Power. Both of you, loving companions, were indispensable helpmates in the last stages of this production with your critical, constructive readings of the text. And to Sue, thanks for helping me find my way through cyberspace and get this project in, almost on time.

Finally, to all the critters of many kinds who go with us, I say, you're part of this, however you figure it. Without you I couldn't have come to believe these things in quite this way.

Index

nationalism, Religious
Right's embrace of,
14–15, 220n16
national self-absorp-
tion, 14
nonviolence
compassion and,
192–99, 244n41
as response to evil,
112–14, 235n29

obedience
ambiguity *vs.*, 102–6
questions of evil and,
11, 79–82,
87–88, 232n5
Oduyoye, Mercy
Amba, xiii
Oh Dong Kyun, 33–34
ontology, Christianity
and, 216n5
Operation Rescue, 140
Origen, 231n33
orthodox Christianity,
theocracy and, 15–16
ousia (essence) of incarnation, 149–59

Parks, Rosa, 139
passion
body knowledge as
source of,
123–27
boundary breaking
and, 137–41
characteristics of,
120–23
faith as resource for,
141–44
fear of, 130–31
holographic proper-
ties of, 146–49

justice-love and,
131–33
limits of, 144–46
ousia (essence) of
incarnation and,
149–59
solidarity through,
133–36
vision and, 127–31
pastoral professionals,
power of, 228n24
patriarchy
blood sacrifice and
logic of, 176–78
body images and,
150–59
in Christianity,
60–64, 217n5,
219n11, 226n10,
227n18, xiii
concepts of evil and,
79–82, 90
family values and,
118–20
relational power of
God and, 64–65
self-absorption of, 14
Patterson, Lloyd,
237n10
Peretti, Frank, 17–18
perfection, concept of,
222n29
perichoresis concept,
230n31
personal interaction,
social change and,
36–46
Peter's denial, as
metaphor for evil,
95–101
"phantasy" concept, 47,
49

imagination and, 189
politics, self-knowledge
and, 40–46
Pollitt, Katha, 46
postmodernism, Chris-
tology and, 49–54,
225n10, 229n27
poverty, liberation the-
ology regarding,
224n4
power structure
evil in relation to,
95–101
liberation theology
analysis of,
133–36
in mutual relation,
55–56, 65–76,
228n23n26
passion as solidarity
against, 133–36
racism and sexism in
Christianity and,
13–15, 217n5,
220n15
prayer
forgiveness and,
188–89
importance of, 7
process theology,
mutuality and,
226n15
psychotherapy, mutual
relation and, 229n30

Quayle, Dan, 220n16
queer-bashing, upsurge
of, 17
queer people (gay/les-
bian/bisexual/trans-
gendered people and
allies), xii

About the author

Carter Heyward is a pioneering feminist theologian and a leading feminist voice in world Christianity. Among the first women ordained in the
U.S. Episcopal Church, she has taught for twenty-five years at Episcopal
Divinity School in Cambridge, Massachusetts, where she is the Howard
Chandler Robbins Professor of Theology. Since *The Redemption of God*
(1981) her works have explored issues of power, sexuality, and social and
gender justice in relation to salvation; among them are *Our Passion for Justice* (1984), *Speaking of Christ* (1989), *Touching Our Strength* (1989), *When
Boundaries Betray Us* (1993), and *Staying Power* (1995).

CPSIA information can be obtained
at www.ICGtesting.com
Printed in the USA
BVHW030310300620
582349BV00014B/12